Overreach

MICHAEL MacDONALD

Overreach

Delusions of Regime Change in Iraq

Harvard University Press

Cambridge, Massachusetts

London, England   2014

First printing

Library of Congress Cataloging-in-Publication Data

MacDonald, Michael, 1952–
    Overreach : delusions of regime change in Iraq / Michael MacDonald.
        pages cm.
    Includes bibliographical references and index.
    ISBN 978-0-674-72910-0 (hardcover : alk. paper)
    1. Iraq War, 2003–2011—Causes.   2. Iraq War, 2003–2011—Decision making.
3. Iraq War, 2003–2011—Political aspects.   4. United States—Politics and
government—1989–   5. United States—Foreign relations—21st century.
I. Title.   II. Title: Delusions of regime change in Iraq.
    DS79.757.M55 2014
    956.7044'3—dc23   2014007979

To Mary Alvord MacDonald

Contents

Overreach

Introduction

America's vital interests and our deepest beliefs are
now one.

George W. Bush

From 2003 to 2011 the United States fought a major war in Iraq at
the price of nearly 4,500 dead and over 32,000 wounded. The war
pushed aside other, more important, priorities and, according to
estimates, will total around $3 trillion once all expenses are tallied.
Yet after eight years, more than twice the time it spent fighting in
World War II, the United States withdrew from Iraq to sighs of relief, not parades of triumph. The war did remove Saddam Hussein
from power. But it did not eliminate his weapons of mass destruction (WMDs), because he had none, or end his ties to Al Qaeda, because he had none of those either. These failures, however, were of
secondary importance because the war was not motivated by the
specters of Saddam's putative WMDs or Al Qaeda's alleged influence. Its purpose was to enact regime change in Iraq, and the United
States did not succeed on its primary score. The goal, as policy-
makers stated, was to remove Saddam from power and then to convert Iraq into a liberal capitalist democracy and a member in good
standing of the global community.

This book addresses three fundamental issues about why American policy-makers chose the war and why the war failed to achieve

their goals. First, it explores the war's objectives. Although senior American officials declared repeatedly that they meant to enact regime change in Iraq, they did not resolve what regime change meant in theory or in practice before they launched the war. But by reviewing what policy-makers actually said about and expected of regime change, by observing the actions they took in Iraq, and by analyzing the arguments hawks outside the government made in favor of regime change, several distinguishable meanings of regime change can be exhumed. It was a bad omen, perhaps, that differences among the several notions of regime change not only were substantial but passed unnoticed as the war was being contemplated in the late 1990s and 2000s.

The Central Intelligence Agency (CIA), the National Security Council (NSC), the Department of Defense (DoD), and senior military officers promulgated one influential definition. Wary of highfalutin talk, regime change for national security bureaucracies meant getting rid of Saddam, disarming Iraq, and, they imagined, exiting Iraq quickly. The version was disseminated widely, was adopted by civilian elites in Washington even though it was inconsistent with their more expansive conceptions of liberalizing and marketizing Iraq, and was pursued by those charged with fighting the war and implementing the occupation. Yet this bare-boned definition, although issued by bureaucracies that epitomize hard-nosed realism, was thoroughly unrealistic. The United States initiated a full-fledged and expensive war in Iraq over the objections of key European allies precisely for the purpose of leaving footprints in Iraq. The United States meant to achieve lasting gains. The national security bureaucracies might have told themselves they wanted a snappy, in-and-out operation with no complications, but they also meant to promote national interests. They wanted to install a friendly government and consolidate American influence in Iraq and the Middle East, to improve America's geopolitical position and secure oil supplies, to help Israel and Saudi Arabia, and, perhaps, to position the

United States to attack Iran. Whatever the national security bureaucracies thought they intended, then, the point was *not* to withdraw politically after winning the war militarily. Their larger objectives required them to stay in Iraq.

Civilian elites agreed with their national security counterparts on the importance of increasing American power, but they took for granted additionally that American national interests entail spreading capitalism. For civilians the point of regime change was to promote globalization, liberalization, and modernization in Iraq. They expected the new regime to respect property rights, free markets from Saddam's stranglehold, and bring the blessings of the global economy to Iraq. Nourished by a growing economy, Iraq was to demonstrate to Muslims throughout the Middle East the benefits of freedom, rights, and markets. Instead of standing as an island amid a sea of angry Muslims, liberated Iraq was to become the exemplar of liberal capitalism that its neighbors would emulate.

These hopes were dashed. A decade after deposing Saddam, Iraq still lacks the basic liberal institutions of rule of law, effective constitutional government, and credible markets. Its economy remains dominated by the state, and the state is riddled with corruption and controlled by Shiʻi parties that are openly sectarian. The Shiʻi government excludes the Sunni minority from meaningful political influence, sustains Kurdish separatism, and presents sectarian hegemony as democracy (presuming that civil war does not resume and anti-Shiʻa jihad does not erupt). Regime change, in other words, succeeded in removing Saddam from power, but it failed to achieve its positive objectives. Instead of ushering in a regime of liberal rights, regime change delivered hegemony to Shiʻas and, embarrassingly, worsened America's geopolitical position in the region. It did, however, suit Iran's purposes admirably.

Second, the book examines why the United States opted for war against Iraq. Granting that the United States wanted regime change in Iraq, what possessed a generation of leaders to decide that war against Iraq was not only a good idea but a compelling one? Just because the war turned out badly for the United States obviously does not prove that it was a bad idea, but it does shift the burden of proof to hawks. The incentives of national security and neoliberal marketization might have been tempting, but the disincentives were stronger. War is costly, risky, and unpredictable, and electing war against Saddam made sense only on the assumptions that the United States would win, that the desserts of victory would justify the real costs and the opportunity costs of fighting a war in the midst of a region that was notoriously hostile to both American power and the liberal order, and that the new regime, which would accord with American interests and values, was achievable politically. The war, in other words, rested on profoundly ambitious assumptions about victory, the value of the stakes, and the prospects for transforming Iraq. Yet American leaders—and this is the pivotal point—scarcely registered the aggressiveness of their ambitions. If the United States was going to choose war in Iraq from all the possibilities that were open to the world's sole superpower and the leading sponsor of neoliberalism, American leaders had to calculate that the rewards for going to war, after the costs were subtracted, were more enticing than alternate uses of American lives, money, and leadership. It is not obvious why they made that calculation.

The Bush administration is accused of using high-minded claptrap about freedom, democracy, and markets to sell the war, but the accusation gets the decision exactly wrong. The key to explaining the choice for regime change is that the Bush administration, and most American political and foreign policy elites too, subscribed to the shibboleths, euphemisms, and platitudes. They believed their fictions. The United States went to war because they saw liberalism as the answer to Iraq's problems and because they expected that most Iraqis would understand that liberal values, which would fit naturally in Iraq, would emancipate them. If, however, these expectations turned out to be overly optimistic, then the United States was breaking the old order without a viable substitute at hand.

Third, this book analyzes why the United States failed to enact its liberal visions of regime change in Iraq, and suggests that its undoing arose from a solipsistic rendering of American exceptionalism. Not realizing the radicalism of trying to liberalize, capitalize, and modernize Iraq, American leaders thought they either were implanting, nurturing, or clearing way for the liberal order —the confusion about the verbs reflects significant confusion about the project— because of two conceits at the heart of American foreign policy. For one, American elites for purposes of policy, and not just for reasons of propaganda, hold that American power interests are entwined with liberal values, and that America's most important national interests feature rights, prosperity, and progress, and not just weapons and military bases. Consequently, American policy is predicated on the assumption that its power would be liberating. Having identified American power interests with American values, American leaders next assume that their liberal values apply universally. When American politicians make these claims, they sound like platitudes, but they performed the actual function of downplaying risks in Iraq. These two axioms aligned American interests with the preferences of Iraqis, assumed away the prospect of serious resistance to American power, and insinuated that the liberal values already were present in Iraq incipiently. American ideology, in other words, minimized the challenge of regime change. Instead of transforming an alien society, the United States was releasing liberal values that, because they are universal, belonged in Iraq.

The great mystery of the war is why, after defeating Saddam, the United States immediately vitiated the authority and power of what remained of Iraq's state by disbanding its army and purging Ba'ath Party members from state employment. The decision came to be panned for causing all manner of problems in Iraq, and especially for fueling the Sunni insurgency. But what the critics overlook is what the decision reveals about those who made it. The civilians who issued the decrees—over the opposition of the national security bureaucracies—proceeded as if the *terms* of civil order were self-evident and as if the *substance* of civic order would become self-sustaining once the debris of the old order was cleared away and markets were instituted. The United States might face transitional problems, but the end was uncontroversial and attainable. That is, the United States deliberately opened the Pandora's box of statelessness by disbanding Iraq's army and de-Ba'athifying its state administration and yet, astonishingly, did not expect mayhem to escape. What explains the beliefs that liberal order would materialize and that the occupation would encounter minimal resistance in spite of a crippled state also explains the prior decision to go to war in Iraq. American policy-makers first chose war, next broke the Iraqi state's monopolies on violence and administration, and then decreed, without having the means to implement, the institutions of the neoliberal economy because they assumed that liberal values are natural in origin, universal in scope, and ordering in effect.

The United States broke Iraq's old state, and the ensuing civil war produced the semi-sovereign and semi-legitimate regime that Shi'i political parties now control. None of this should have been unexpected. If state power is broken, neoliberal reforms fail and order collapses; if order collapses, civil war follows; and if civil wars are fought, the biggest community usually wins, especially if it also controls what remains of the state by virtue of (American-sponsored) elections that empower it. Yet the predictable outcome of American designs waylaid American political and foreign policy elites, and not just President Bush. Having conceived of American power as liberal and liberal values as universal goods, the regime-changing elites who wanted the war ended up failing the geopolitical and neoliberal interests that animated them in the first place. Originally, American elites called for regime change to advance national power and neoliberal globalization in Iraq. But their delusions of universality blotted out the risks their naiveté posed to their material interests. The United States launched the war and lost the war because its leaders believe their vision of American exceptionalism is universal.

1

Why Elect a Self-Defeating War?

Our nation is still somewhat sad, but we're angry.
There's a certain level of blood lust, but we won't let it
drive our reaction. . . . We're steady, clear-eyed and
patient, but pretty soon we'll have to start displaying
scalps.

George W. Bush

There is a joke economists tell. A physicist, a chemist, and an economist are stranded on a deserted island. They have no food, except for a can of beans. Arguing about how to open it, the physicist suggests climbing up a tree, and then dropping the can onto sharp rocks in the hope of puncturing the top. That does not work. Next, the chemist proposes spreading sand on the top of the can, positioning his eyeglasses just so, and then creating a chemical reaction that will allow him to peel off the top. That does not work either. Finally, the economist offers the solution: "Assume a can opener!"

The path to war in Iraq was rife with assumptions, but they were different from the one the economist made. Economists are aware they make assumptions. They know that markets are conceptual constructs; that is the point of the punch line. The critical assumptions that lured the United States into war in Iraq, by contrast, operated unconsciously. Policy-makers did not recognize what they were assuming. In keeping with the dual character of American foreign policy, they aimed both to increase national power through

military means and to install the institutional framework for neoliberal capitalism in the area of the world that had proved most
resistant to it.[1] Yet policy-makers failed to register what seemed to
be the obvious costs and risks posed by the war. They assumed they
could get what they wanted—that they could remake Iraq to their
specifications, bask in accolades from Iraqis, and get out free and
easy. They were wrong. In addition to the casualties and budgetary
costs, the United States also lost prestige; upset regional stability
in the oil patch; set aside more important foreign policy priorities,
such as responding to China's growing power; and lost credibility
with both the international community and the American public—
all to fight a war whose risks were plain and whose gains were suspect from the outset.[2]

If the United States was bent on introducing democracy to Iraq,
as it claimed, why did regime-changing hawks not appreciate that
the obvious beneficiary of enfranchising Iraq's large Shi'i majority
would be Iran? How could American policy-makers have been
oblivious to the clear geopolitical import of their acts? Certainly, they
did not intend to improve the strategic position of their most formidable enemy in the region (and a charter member of the "axis of
evil"). Why, instead of weighing political realities like they were supposed to do, did policy-makers think their dreams of markets, democracies, and liberal values in Iraq were achievable? What beguiled
elites into assuming that American national interests and neoliberal
economic commitments were congruent with the aspirations of
Iraqis? The answers to these questions are contested, with five theses circulating more or less coherently in official circles, informed
commentary, and public opinion.

The first thesis explains the war through the personality of President George W. Bush. Commonly accepted by elite and public opinion alike, the thesis points out that Bush made the decision to go
to war. He also planted the question atop Washington's political
agenda and raised it into a central issue in the 2002 congressional

election, and he did this of his own volition. Bush was responding neither to a dire threat nor to pressure pushing him against his will (as might be imagined happening to his predecessor, Bill Clinton, or his successor, Barack Obama). The war was intensely personal for Bush; he confided, "I have never felt more comfortable in my life."[3] Bush personally dominated the war party, publicized its cause, stirred it up, and gave it presidential leadership. On September 12, 2001, before much of anything was clear about the previous day's attacks, Bush already was applying pressure to attack Iraq. He "grabbed" Richard Clarke, the White House specialist on terrorism, and instructed him and his associates: "See if Saddam did this. See if he's linked in any way." Bush received the news that Al Qaeda staged the attacks "incredulously." Undeterred, Bush "testily" ordered his counterterrorism office, "Look into Iraq, Saddam."[4] The next day, Bush responded to the prompting of Secretary of Defense Donald Rumsfeld by declaring that military action in Iraq "would bring about a new government."[5]

Some ascribe Bush's preoccupation with Saddam to his relationship with his father.[6] Maybe the son was completing his father's victory in Gulf War I, which Bush I had ended even though Saddam Hussein still clung to power. Maybe the son was seeking revenge, Texas style, on Saddam for disrespecting the United States and (allegedly) sending an assassination team to Kuwait on a mission to kill the senior Bush.[7] Or, as those inclined to oedipal explanations speculate, maybe Bush II was trying to show up and surpass his father. The father and son are said to have a complicated relationship. Speaking of his father, the son did say, "You know, he is the wrong father to appeal to in terms of strength. There is a higher father that I appeal to."[8] Or maybe Bush II was conflicted, torn between competing desires to honor and supplant his father.

Bush's personality does suggest a predisposition to go to war. He obsessively declared that he was a "war" president and his staff frequently compared him to Winston Churchill, which suggests he saw the war as an opportunity for self-aggrandizement. But a president's biography alone cannot explain the national decision to go to war. Institutions, ideologies, interests, elites, and international circumstances must have their say too. If, for example, the decision began and ended with Bush, then it follows that it would not have been taken if Bush had not been president in the aftermath of 9/11. And, in fact, Al Gore, who essentially tied Bush in the 2000 presidential election, spelled out his opposition during the debate in the autumn of 2002 about going to war. But contrary to the sense of the thesis, Gore was ridiculed for his efforts.[9]

If perchance Bush had left office before he launched the invasion in March 2003, Vice President Richard Cheney would have been making the decision. In view of his record of unwavering advocacy for the war, his role in exaggerating the threat Saddam posed, and his unseen but suspected guidance of the decision-making process, it seems unlikely that Cheney's decision would have been different from Bush's. Moreover, if the Supreme Court had declared Gore the winner in 2000 but for some reason he had left office, Senator Joseph Lieberman, the foremost hawk in the Democratic Party, would have been deciding. And if Bush had not acquired the Republican nomination in 2000, it probably would have gone to Senator John McCain, who during the Republican primaries was more hawkish on the question of Iraq than Bush (and who later supported the war passionately). In other words, lots of hawks could have been in the position to make the decision about going to war with Iraq, which makes blaming Bush individually or attributing decisions of state to father issues suspect. Were Cheney, McCain, and Lieberman working out family relationships too?[10]

There is a second problem with assigning sole responsibility for the war to Bush II. If he was acting for personal reasons, he should have encountered active opposition, or at least serious foot-dragging, from political and foreign policy elites. They should have warned him and the country of the folly of risking much for a war whose benefits were uncertain. But that dog did not bark. Elites facilitated Bush. They argued aplenty about *how* to go to war. Democrats, British Prime Minister Tony Blair, and Secretary of State Colin Powell pressed the White House to win approval from the US Senate and to seek approval from the United Nations Security Council before invading Iraq. But these arguments about means assumed agreement on ends. They were disagreements about how to get the war that they stipulated should be fought. In fact, endorsing the war became emblematic of elite status. Leslie Gelb, a hawk and a paragon of the foreign policy establishment, admitted that he backed the war in part to "retain political and professional credibility."[11]

The thesis that concentrates on Bush for taking the United States to war, then, absolves elites both for the role they did play in making the war and for the role they did not play by not asking troubling questions. Not suspecting the war's radicalism, elites never examined what "regime change" actually meant or what the United States really meant to do in Iraq. Either elites did not see that regime change meant breaking the integrity of the Iraqi state, or they did not understand that breaking the state's integrity meant breaking political order, or they did not care that they were breaking political order. The economist in the joke recognized that he was assuming the can opener. But America's pragmatic political and foreign policy elites were assuming, without recognizing that they were assuming, that political order would prevail even though the very purpose of the war was to break state power in Iraq. They assumed the can opener of political order.

The Background

After scurrying from Kuwait in 1991, Saddam bided time before he tested American resolve, at first tentatively and then more brazenly. Saddam toyed with developing illegal weapons programs before he dismantled them secretly; played cat-and-mouse games over the no-fly zone that the United States and United Kingdom enforced over 40 percent of Iraq; encroached into Kurdish regions of Iraq, which he did not control, by cutting a deal with one of the two main Kurdish party-militias; and sniffed out the coups d'état that the CIA sponsored, tortured the conspirators, and even had his torturers telephone CIA officials so that the Americans could hear the cries of pain. Saddam also survived sanctions.

The UN Security Council had responded to Saddam's invasion of Kuwait in August 1990 by imposing economic sanctions on Iraq, and they were enforced until he was deposed. Economically devastating, sanctions combined with the damage caused by Gulf War I to ruin, in the words of Joy Gordon, "nearly all of Iraq's infrastructure, industrial capacity, agriculture, telecommunications, and critical public services, particularly electricity and water treatment. For the next twelve years [until the 2003 invasion] the sanctions would prevent Iraq from restoring any of these to the level Iraq had achieved in the 1980s and would devastate the health, education, and basic well-being of almost the entire Iraqi population."[12] "[I]t was the consistent policy of all three U.S. administrations, from 1990 to 2003, to inflict the most extreme economic damage possible on Iraq." The human toll was vast. About 500,000 Iraqi children under the age of five are estimated to have died as a result. By way of comparison, Human Rights Watch estimated that Saddam killed about half that number during his reign.[13]

Bush I defeated Saddam, enforced the sanctions, sold arms to Saddam's enemies and America's friends, and adopted a strategy of containment. Ultimately, however, Bush I acquiesced to the reality that Saddam served the paramount function of upholding the regional status quo. Besides, Bush I was defeated for reelection before he had to devise a lasting strategy for coping with Saddam. The incoming Clinton administration soon tired of Saddam's shenanigans and made clear that it wanted to remove him from power. National Security Advisor Sandy Berger called for a "new government";[14] Secretary of State Madeleine Albright advocated introducing smart sanctions and removing Saddam (with the incidental effect of depriving Saddam of any incentive to moderate his conduct, given that the Clinton administration was committed to deposing him anyway);[15] and senior figures toyed with ideas for provoking war. General Hugh Shelton, the chairman of the Joint Chiefs of Staff under Clinton, recalls a request made by an unnamed Clinton cabinet secretary to arrange for Iraq to shoot down an American U-2 and its crew, thus providing the "precipitous event" that "we really need in order to go in and take out Saddam."[16] Although the idea fell flat, the Clinton administration did bomb Baghdad for violating the terms of Saddam's 1991 surrender and did proclaim the objective of regime change.

But Clinton did not really want war. Like Bush I, he hoped Saddam's security apparatuses would stage a coup, and in the meantime he sustained his predecessor's policy of containment plus sanctions. Containment meant continuing arms sales to neighbors like Saudi Arabia and Kuwait, buttressing King Hussein in Jordan, and vowing to retaliate in the event Saddam launched another attack on his neighbors. Sanctions meant obstructing Iraq from exporting the oil and importing the goods that sustained its semimodern economy, with the effects of impoverishing much of the population and crippling the erstwhile middle classes that were rooted in the formal economy.[17] Per capita income, according to Daniel Byman, fell "to less than one-fifth of the level Iraq achieved in the 1980s."[18] Iraq's health care had been excellent by Arab standards in the 1970s; by the time of Gulf War II, it had collapsed. Yet to the great frustration of American policy-makers, the economic crisis spared Saddam. In fact, by weakening modern, more liberal elements in Iraq, by furnishing an obvious scapegoat for the suffering of the Iraqi people, and by inviting Iraq's rulers to ration or withhold food according to their interests, sanctions inadvertently consolidated Saddam's hold on power.[19] Friends ate; enemies scavenged.

In addition to upholding the combination of containment plus sanctions that it inherited from Bush I, the Clinton administration innovated a policy of its own for dealing with Iraq (and Iran). Bitter enemies, Iraq and Iran had fought an eight-year, one-million-dead war to a stalemate in the 1980s. Even when the war ended in 1988, each retained more reason to fear the other than to fear the United States (or Israel). Iraq worried about Iran's thrice-larger population, Iran's appeals to Iraq's Shi'i majority, and Iran's armies to the east and its alliance with Syria to the west. Iran remembered Iraq's invasion in 1980 and suspected the Saudis might fund Saddam as the Sunni spear against Shi'i theocracy. Employing standard diplomatic practices, Reagan and Bush I took advantage of the opportunity. With Iraq and Iran preoccupied with each other, the United States would let them balance out and keep itself free to do as it pleased.

"Dual containment" broke the pattern.[20] As devised by Martin Indyk, the idea was that the United States could escape dependence on Iran to thwart Iraq, and vice versa, by doing both jobs itself. Instead of relying on one enemy to counter the other, the United States would blunt each directly. While not meaning to go to war with either Iraq or Iran, the Clinton administration, in the words of F. Gregory Gause, was moving toward "an increasingly direct American strategic role in the gulf."[21] Nevertheless, the most aggressive hawks were unimpressed. Claiming that sanctions and containment were ineffectual, that Saddam was incorrigible in his quest for nuclear weapons, and that American policy resembled Neville Chamberlain's appeasement of Hitler, neoconservatives found a ready audience in Congress. In 1998 the Iraqi Liberation Act (ILA) passed the House of Representatives by a vote of 360 to 38 and the Senate by unanimous consent, drew overwhelming support from both parties, and was signed by Clinton. The ILA reiterated that Saddam could not be allowed to acquire WMDs, committed the United States to assisting Iraq's "democratic opposition," and put both the legislative and executive branches of the US government on record in favor of regime change. But Clinton, as was his wont, pulled the string. Recognizing that the democratic opposition was disorganized and that aiding them would yield few real benefits, his administration withheld most of the funds the ILA authorized.[22]

Clinton declared that regime change in Iraq was both a moral and a security imperative, that Saddam was dangerous, illiberal, and morally reprehensible. Then he finessed the conclusion. After affirming the case for war, Clinton turned to more urgent foreign policy priorities, including the fallout from the East Asia financial crisis of 1997, enlargement of NATO, globalization, and Israeli-Palestinian negotiations. Hawks complained about Clinton's irresolution, but they pocketed substantial gains. Building momentum for the future, Clinton had blessed regime change with bipartisan assent and had positioned hawks to denounce as betraying America's solemn commitments any measures that did not achieve regime change. Regime change was unrealized, but it also was inscribed as official policy.

The Bush II administration prepared to escalate as soon as it assumed office in 2001. Bush instructed Powell to develop effective sanctions and Rumsfeld to "examine our military options." Tellingly, the first two National Security Council meetings, instead of reviewing the international situation and outlining the principles that would guide the incoming administration, were devoted to the question of Iraq.[23] But the new administration's efforts amounted to little. Public opinion was uninterested in war, and the administration, which was led by practical figures with extensive experience in Washington, appreciated that war with Iraq was not in the cards any time soon. Turning to more promising priorities, Bush concentrated on cutting taxes, deregulating business, consolidating a governing majority, increasing military spending, and staffing the government.

Before 9/11, then, Congress, the Clinton administration, and political elites had conceded the political and rhetorical high ground to hawks, denounced Saddam as unacceptable, and explored options against Iraq. Yet public opinion remained unenthusiastic. Then the 9/11 attacks shuffled the deck. When Bush, acting on his predispositions, decided to exploit the opportunity to attack Iraq, public opinion was supportive but qualified, and both parties, both political branches of the federal government, and both political and foreign policy elites already had avowed regime change in Iraq as the objective of American policy. The means remained unspecified, but the end implied them. Bush raised regime change to a supreme priority, and therefore he is an essential part of explaining why the United States went to war. But he is not a sufficient explanation.

The Republican, Oil, and Israeli Theses

The junior partner to the Bush thesis is the Republican Party thesis. Less a scholarly proposition than a sense that circulates through various liberal media, the second thesis begins with the observations that Republicans controlled the executive, the House, and almost the Senate, and that they exploited the prospect of war to electoral advantage in 2002 and 2004.[24] Connecting these points, the thesis reasons that Republicans wanted the war because they wanted to charge Democrats with vacillating on terrorism. In effect, the thesis accuses Republicans of subordinating national interests to partisan advantage.

Republicans backed the war foursquare. It was advocated, sold, and launched by a Republican president, who relished his self-image as a "war president." It was carried through Congress by overwhelmingly Republican majorities. Senate Republicans voted for authorization by a margin of 48 to 1 and House Republicans by 215 to 6. Republicans gained seats in the 2002 elections, which was only the third time since Reconstruction that the president's party won midterm congressional elections. Although the memory of 9/11 weighed more heavily than Iraq in the minds of many voters, congressional elections in 2002 and congressional and presidential elections in 2004 did vindicate the belief that talk of war, national security, and Iraq helped Republicans.

Nevertheless, attributing the war to Republican electoral ambitions fails for three reasons. First, the bulk of the Republican foreign policy establishment endorsed the war. Several retired figures did oppose it, including the two-time national security advisor Brent Scowcroft, former secretary of state Lawrence Eagleburger, President Gerald Ford (quietly), and, reputedly, Bush I himself. But most retired Republican statesmen urged the war forcefully and publicly, including former secretaries of state Henry Kissinger, George Shultz, and James Baker. That is, Republicans with the least political ambition favored the war, presumably because they thought it served their conception of the national interest.

The second problem with attributing the war to Republican ambitions is that Democratic elites approved the war too. As Bill Keller, the editor of the *New York Times,* wrote during the interval between the congressional vote authorizing the war and the onset of hostilities,

> The president will take us to war with support—often, I admit, equivocal and patronizing in tone—from quite a few members of the East Coast liberal media cabal. The I-Can't-Believe-I'm-a-Hawk Club includes op-ed regulars at this newspaper and *The Washington Post,* the editors of *The New Yorker, The New Republic* and *Slate,* columnists in *Time* and *Newsweek.* . . . The president also has enough prominent Democrats with him—some from conviction, some from the opposite—to make this endeavor credibly bipartisan. Four of the six declared Democratic presidential hopefuls support war, with reservations.[25]

The partisan explanation of the war falters because those Democrats who were least susceptible to electoral pressure—including retired foreign policy figures and former president Clinton along with Keller's liberal elites inside and outside the media—were unlikely to back a war that was inspired by the pursuit of Republican advantage. Moreover, senior Democrats supported the war more emphatically than junior Democrats did. Richard Holbrooke, a mainstay of Clinton's foreign policy circle, described Saddam as the most dangerous man in the world.[26]

The third problem with reducing the war to Republican electoral calculations is that it overlooks the significance of the liberal hero of the time, Tony Blair. A "third way" neoliberal with a pronounced moral streak, British Prime Minister Blair was Clinton's closest foreign associate, and against the bitter opposition of his base, he backed the war passionately. Blair's isolation in the Cabinet, the Labour Party, and "large parts of media and public opinion," he later wrote, "was colossal."[27] That is, the foreign leader whose foreign policy commitments most resembled those of the Democratic establishment championed the war, and he pushed for it in spite of political interests that pulled him in the opposite direction. Why, then, rule out the possibility that kindred Democrats likewise favored war not because they were craven but because they agreed with it? And if Democrats could agree with the war, why not Republicans too?

Republicans did demand the war and did exploit it politically. But it is another step entirely to infer that they wanted the war so that they could exploit it electorally. Subsequent behavior does not prove prior motivation. Republicans called for the war because of the interests it served, because it accorded with their understanding of America's role in the world, and because, specifically, Republican politicians and foreign policy elites were committed to projecting American military strength in the Middle East. The political dividends were icing on the cake. Besides, Republican electoral interests did not require actual war, only an occasion to expose Democratic timidity. The mere threat of war would have done the trick, at least for the November 2002 elections. Republican electoral interests, then, might be part of the explanation for the war, but they are not decisive. In fact, Karl Rove warned Bush that polls conveyed the public's doubts about war. Bush did not care.[28]

The third thesis was the stuff of antiwar chants. The war was about oil. Iraq had it; the United States wanted it. Alan Greenspan thought so, and he supported the war.[29] Kevin Phillips and Nelson Mandela agreed, and they disapproved of the war.[30] Reflecting its obvious, commonsense appeal, a substantial chunk of public opinion likewise subscribed to the oil thesis. The United States launched war against a country whose two main assets were oil and proximity to other oil producers, ostensibly to eliminate weapons that the oil-producing country turned out not to possess. The decision was made by an administration that was headed by an oilman; his father was an oilman too; and the decision was seconded—and maybe orchestrated—by a vice president who just had completed a stint as head of the country's foremost oil services company. Besides, the counter to the war-for-oil thesis—that the United States did not consider the economic and strategic significance of oil in making the decision—is less plausible than the alternative that it is meant to debunk. If the administration really did not assess the impact of war on oil supplies, it was guilty of monumental dereliction of duty. Plus, neoconservatives already were setting up Saudi Arabia as a future target.[31] With means, motive, and opportunity, the verdict seems clear.

There are two versions of the war-for-oil thesis. In the first, the United States went to war for the advantage of the petroleum industry. Some evidence upholds this version. Paul O'Neill, Bush's treasury secretary, reports that the Defense Intelligence Agency effectively assigned specific Iraqi oil fields to specific foreign oil companies.[32] Similarly, the British government discussed exploiting

Iraq's oil reserves with petroleum companies in the year before it joined the "coalition of the willing."[33] L. Paul Bremer, appointed by Bush to administer Iraq a month after the invasion, promptly called for privatizing state assets and opening Iraq to foreign investment, which was a tactful way of proposing to sell Iraq's oil fields to international companies.[34] The collapse of civic order, the eruption of insurgency and civil war, the opposition Iraqi politicians, and the disintegration of state administration frustrated Bremer's plans, but that does not rule out the possibility that Bush hoped for advantageous deals for favored companies.

In the second version of the war-for-oil thesis, national security bureaucracies grabbed an essential and depleting resource. As Michael Klare develops this idea, oil is destined to become scarcer as economic growth in Asia causes demand to soar at an "unsustainable rate." With about 65 percent of known petroleum reserves located in the Middle East, only Saudi Arabia holding greater reserves than Iraq, and states across the globe subject to "mounting pressure to solve the problem at any cost," the life-and-death competition between states for oil took military form.[35] Invading Iraq enhanced American national security and prosperity, conferred control over a strategic asset, and reversed the leverage that exporting countries had established over the United States.[36] The argument makes sense in power politics terms. Why would the United States not want more influence over much of the world's oil supply?

John Mearsheimer and Stephen Walt, prominent realists, dismiss the idea that the war was excited by the prospect of controlling vast reserves of oil. Oil companies, they maintain, could not have gotten war even if they had wanted it.[37] They lacked the power. Daniel Yergin, a specialist in energy markets, lodged a different objection in the run-up to the war. "If oil is the question, Iraq is not the answer."[38] Due to years of mismanagement and underinvestment, Iraq did not have enough production to warrant war. It would take a decade, he predicted, to double production from the 3 percent of the world's total that Iraq was producing at the time of the invasion (a prediction, ironically, that was too optimistic: a decade later, Iraq produces 3.35 percent of world output).[39] "It requires several leaps of logic," Yergin wrote, "to conclude that the current Iraq crisis is *all* about oil. No U.S. administration would launch so momentous a campaign just to facilitate a handful of oil development contracts and a moderate increase in supply—half a decade from now."[40] The risks of war were high, the gains from seizing Iraqi oil were paltry, and besides, the United States had alternative sources in Russia, the Caspian Sea, Central Asia, and West Africa.

There is another problem with the first version of the oil thesis. It assumes a pliant state. The thesis has oil companies dictating and the American government merely registering their demands. The American state, however, is vastly more complex and autonomous than that. The White House, Congress, and national security bureaucracies had their own interests and assessments of Iraq, and were not agents of oil companies. Still, the Bush administration was tied intimately to energy interests, and energy interests did press their priorities aggressively. The administration weakened environmental regulation, gave tax benefits to energy producers, blocked ratification of the Kyoto Protocol, belittled global warming, resisted calls for fuel-efficient vehicles, increased oil and gas exploration and production on federal land, called for opening Alaska to more oil drilling, and in general favored production over conservation.[41] The administration had multiple reasons for adopting each policy, but pressure from energy interests was persistent, influential, and public. Yet these interests did not issue public calls for action in Iraq. Perhaps they were silent because they feared recriminations if they were seen to be causing a war. But perhaps they were silent because war in Iraq, while not a matter of indifference to them, was a low priority.

Critics of the war-for-oil thesis register telling objections, especially to the claim that the war was launched for the benefit of oil companies. It is easy, however, to take criticisms of both versions too far. While the monocausal claim that the war was all—or mainly—about oil is unconvincing, it is also unconvincing to conclude the war had little or nothing to do with oil, especially about its value to national power. Indeed, Cheney intimated that oil played a role when he accused Saddam of seeking to use control of the region's oil as a geopolitical weapon.[42] If energy were a weapon, why would Cheney not want the United States to acquire it?

About the time when direct American military involvement in Iraq was ending, Timothy Mitchell published a book about the role carbon energy—first coal and then oil—has played in fostering Western ways of life, forms of government, and class struggles. Arguing that the rise of coal favored democracy and the working class in the West and that the rise of oil weakened them, Mitchell sustains one deep insight into the motivations of oil companies across time and place. Whether oil companies are blamed for causing the war in Iraq or are exonerated, critics and defenders alike take them to have been interested in acquiring Iraq's oil reserves. Either oil companies wanted to take Iraq's oil to market for their own benefit, as critics charge, or companies were not tempted because they did not need Iraq's supplies, as Yergin has it. Mitchell disagrees with both. His point of departure is that from their infancy, international oil companies and states in oil-consuming countries were devoted to suppressing, not increasing, production.

Yergin exonerates oil companies because they lacked compelling reasons for urging war with Iraq, inasmuch as they had better sources of supply at hand. But Mitchell, in reversing the interests of petroleum companies, unsettles the foundation of Yergin's defense. Markets had plenty of oil; that was the problem for suppliers. Although Mitchell's oil companies did chase sources across the globe, the purpose was not to drill, refine, and ship to thirsty markets but to "sabotage" supply. Facing gluts that would cut prices, oil companies aimed to control supply so that they could keep oil off the market. If Mitchell is right, oil companies might have backed the war precisely because they had secured other sources of supply. In this spirit, Mitchell's treatment of Iraqi history is replete with details of oil companies preventing new supplies from getting to the market. Summarizing British Petroleum's role in Iraq, Mitchell reports that it

> delayed the completion of the pipeline to export the oil, deliberately drilled shallow wells to avoid discovering additional supplies, and plugged wild-cat wells that yielded large finds to conceal their existence from the government. Although Iraq's reserves were comparable to those of [Iran, Saudi Arabia, and Kuwait], its production in the 1950s and 1960s was kept at about half the level of the others, or less. BP and its partners used Iraq as the swing producer, with a large undeveloped capacity that was increased only to meet exceptional demand.[43]

Mitchell's thesis is plausible for both empirical and theoretical reasons. Empirically, he shows oil companies suppressing supply; theoretically, he confirms textbook economics. Monopolies, oligopolies, and cartels maximize profits by reducing supply. Mitchell does not deploy his insight to explain the war in Iraq, which he attributes to American frustration with the tenacity of Iraq and Iran in the face of American pressure. The United States went to war, he writes, because "two decades of war, sanctions and covert operations had failed to bring about the collapse of either the Islamic Republic in Iran or the Ba'athist state in Iraq."[44] But Mitchell's interpretation of the interaction of oil companies, the American state, and oil-producing governments also invites an additional (and consistent) explanation for the war.

Oil cartels increase profits by suppressing production, and they suppress production by weakening the states in producing countries if they can.[45] The economic sanctions slapped on Iraq as punishment for invading Kuwait in 1990 were ideal, therefore, for both oil companies and other producing states. By keeping Iraq's oil off the market, sanctions buttressed prices. Mitchell does not draw the inference, but he suggests the clue to one of the striking anomalies of the war. Contrary to the standard behavior of hegemons and the putative interests of global petroleum companies, both of which would seem to favor stable states to facilitate oil exports, the United States squeezed the Iraqi state during Saddam's reign and undermined it after he was ousted. If the American government and the companies preferred to discourage the production of oil in Iraq, behaviors that seem irrational become rational. State weakness in Iraq, in other words, becomes consistent with American oil interests.

Critics of the war-for-oil thesis, then, defeat the monocausal thesis. They show that oil interests were unlikely to obtain substantial supplies of oil, assuming contra Mitchell that they wanted to market oil, and they win the point that the war was not all about oil. But the critics also allow that oil interests might have augmented the coalition in favor of war—that they might have signed on to a war that could bring advantages even though acquiring oil in Iraq was of secondary importance to them. Critics of the war-for-oil thesis establish, in other words, that oil was not a dominant card in going to war, but they do not rule out that it was a meaningful card.

The fourth thesis is that the war was fought at the behest of Israel, a position that is advanced most controversially by Mearsheimer and Walt in *The Israel Lobby and U.S. Foreign Policy*. By their account, American neoconservatives, who are fired by an "almost theological belief in the transformative power of freedom,"[46] conceived the idea of using war to bring democracy to the Muslim Middle East, beginning with Iraq, for the advantage of Israel. Although neoconservatives were too weak and isolated to get American policy-makers to bite on the idea, they enticed Israel's lobby of politicians, contributors, and opinion-makers into exerting its unmatched influence over American foreign policy to get American elites on board. Without the Israeli lobby, the "war would almost certainly not have occurred." "Pressure from Israel and the lobby was not the only factor behind the Bush administration's decision to attack Iraq in March 2003, but it was a critical element." The lobby was the "driving force."[47]

Mearsheimer and Walt score major points. First, they recognize that establishing democratic government was not, as frustrated hawks later imagined, concocted as a post facto justification after the Bush administration discovered that Saddam had no WMDs. It was the objective in Iraq from the start. Second, Mearsheimer and Walt appreciate that national security bureaucracies were skeptical of the war. Whatever gains might have ensued from the war, the uniformed military, State Department, and CIA doubted they would justify the risks. The war was not favored by those charged with fighting it. Third, Mearsheimer and Walt understand that, precisely because the risks exceeded the gains, the war cannot be explained in conventional terms. The choice was not made on its merits, and it is that anomaly that traps them. Mearsheimer and Walt believe simultaneously that the war was counterproductive (a point they made at the time),[48] that states are the dominant actors in international relations, and that states are self-interested and rational when their national security is at stake. If the United States was behaving irrationally on matters of national security, then another rational actor must have intruded into the decision.

Mearsheimer and Walt's final, and main, point features the special relationship between the United States and Israel in explaining why the United States ditched its security interests by electing to fight Iraq. Although the thesis generated considerable anger, it is fair to note that friends of Israel routinely stress the special relationship. "The role of the president of the United States," Ann Lewis assured the United Jewish Communities forum on behalf of Hillary Clinton during the 2008 presidential primaries, "is to support the decisions that are made by the people of Israel."[49] Mearsheimer and Walt elaborated the logic of this kind of commitment, and they were associated with anti-Semitism.[50] But in impugning the integrity of Mearsheimer and Walt, the critics overlooked the actual weaknesses in *The Israel Lobby*. What compromises the argument is not that Mearsheimer and Walt emphasize that Israel hoped the United States would depose Saddam, or that they find Israel's views to carry special significance with American policy-making elites, especially when war and peace in the Middle East are concerned. The weakness is that Mearsheimer and Walt downplay American support for regime change independently of Israel's lobbying, infer Israel's motives from the passions of neoconservatives, and project American objectives onto Israel. Israel might have encouraged the United States to attack Iraq, but it was the United States, not Israel, that expected democracy.

Israel did want to get rid of Saddam. A standing provocation, he had built a large army, awarded bonuses to the families of Palestinian suicide bombers, and, like other Arab leaders, fanned hostility to Zionism as a tactic for maintaining power. Besides, deposing Saddam, who had launched missiles against Israel during Gulf War I, was a useful object lesson to Israel's other enemies. Best of all, ousting Saddam might set Sunnis and Shi'as against each other in Iraq and the region, and if they were fighting each other, Muslims were not uniting against Israel. But the flaw in attributing the war to Israeli agency is that Israel, as Mearsheimer and Walt note, was preoccupied with *Iran*, not Iraq, and therefore was positively *opposed* to the war's objective. Democracy amounted to empowering Iraq's Shi'i majority, and Shi'i government in Iraq amounted to converting Iraq from Iran's staunchest enemy into its potential friend. It is easy, therefore, to explain Israel's support for war to depose Saddam, but it is tough to explain Israel's support for the war's objective. If democracy in Iraq was likely to yield a Shi'i government, and Shi'i Iraq was likely to align with Shi'i Iran, why would Israel want democracy in Iraq? And if the war's objective, as Mearsheimer and Walt appreciate, was to establish democracy in Iraq, then how can Israel be construed as the prime mover? The objective disproves the explanation.

The curiosity of their interpretation is that it is wholly out of character for Mearsheimer and Walt. Theorists of power politics, they postulate that power is the foremost, if not the sole, influence on states. As Mearsheimer puts the point elsewhere, "calculations about power lie at the heart of how states think about the world around them. Power is the currency of great-power politics, and states compete for it among themselves. What money is to economics, power is to international relations." "A state's ultimate goal is to be the hegemon in the system."[51] States are coherent, self-interested, and rational actors that pursue security interests to the detriment of all other concerns. The fact that no sovereign rules over states that are sovereign, which is what realists call international anarchy, requires states to depend only on themselves, on self-help, for security in a dangerous world. States do not, therefore, sacrifice their security interests to do favors for friends. When their security is at stake, and it always is in jeopardy, states must act selfishly and ruthlessly. Yet Mearsheimer and Walt throw off their precepts when they explain American involvement in Gulf War II. The war "was motivated at least in good part by a desire to make Israel more secure."[52] That is, the United States invited terrorist reprisals, antagonized important allies in the midst of its campaign against Al Qaeda, and compromised its geopolitical position—all for the purpose of helping another state. In their hands, the United States becomes hapless, bullied, and disinterested in the war it started. America for Mearsheimer and Walt is less the aggressor than the cuckolded.

Mearsheimer and Walt set aside their theoretical model when they explain Israel too. When assessing the national interests of states, realists differentiate themselves from liberals precisely by disregarding forms of government. States, in Mearsheimer's characterization, are like "billiard balls."[53] Responding only to external force, their internal composition does not matter. Mearsheimer and Walt's theoretical model, in other words, asserts that Israel had neither normative nor strategic reasons for caring whether Iraq was a democracy or a dictatorship. But Israel did have reason for caring about who controlled Iraq. If Shi'as, due to their sympathy for and assistance from Iran, were to capture state power in Iraq, then Israel would suffer a major reversal. Israel wanted to deprive Iran of allies, Iran's allies in Iraq were Shi'as, and Shi'as were the majority of Iraq's population. Israel, therefore, was disposed against democracy in Iraq.

Mearsheimer and Walt resort to democratic peace theory, which explains war and peace through forms of government, to fend off these objections. Democracies in this model live peacefully with other democracies, but coexist hostilely with dictatorships.[54] Although realists habitually disparage democratic peace theory, Mearsheimer and Walt nevertheless deploy it to explain why the United States wanted to implant democracy in Iraq. Israel is a democracy; Israel wants security; and democracies live peacefully with like-minded democracies. The United States, therefore, wanted democracy in Iraq for the purpose of enhancing Israel's security. America's commitment to democratizing Iraq was "inextricably linked to concerns about Israel's security," and Israel's security entailed transforming "the Middle East by spreading democracy."[55]

Mearsheimer and Walt have the United States motivated to seek democracy in Iraq for the sake of Israel. But in invoking democratic peace theory to provide Israel with the motivations for, and the objectives of, the war, they run into logical and empirical problems. Logically, Mearsheimer and Walt not only have Israel instigating a train of events that ultimately benefits Iran, which they identify as Israel's primary enemy. They also endow the United States with the very security interests that their argument requires that it lack. If democracies live peacefully and prosperously with kindred democracies, and only with democracies, then the logic of democratic peace theory endows the United States with security and commercial interests of its own for democratizing Iraq. Mearsheimer and Walt no longer need Israel to explain the war.

The war's objective for Mearsheimer and Walt proves Israel's influence. Wanting democracy in Iraq for the reasons recounted by democratic peace theory, Israel induced the United States to impose an elected government on Iraq. Empirically, however, Israel views the prospect of democracy in Arab societies apprehensively. Knowing that Arab public opinion rejects Zionism, and knowing from its own experience that democratic states are stronger than despotisms, Israel openly opposes democracy in Arab societies, not just in Iraq. For example, Israel backed Hosni Mubarak's dictatorship against the democratic movement in Egypt in 2010–2011. Israel trusted the dictator; it feared the people. Why, then, would Israel bet its national security on a proposition—that Arab democracy would live in peace with Israeli democracy—that empowers its enemies? Mearsheimer and Walt are right in pointing to the influence of Israel's friends in marketing the war in the United States. But they mistake Israel's purposes. Israel did not want to bring democracy to Iraq, and the American objective of democracy shows the limits of Israeli influence.

Bush's Thesis

The fifth thesis for why the United States elected to attack Iraq is implied by the doctrine of preemption, also known as the "Bush doctrine," which was elaborated by the National Security Council in *The National Security Strategy, September 2002*. The Bush doctrine made an assertion of fact, linked it to a speculative possibility, culminated in a far-reaching solution, and insinuated a comprehensive explanation for war with Iraq. Specifically, Bush asserted that

Saddam held WMDs, speculated that he might share them with terrorists due to their common hatred of America and liberal values, proposed to solve the problem by spreading market liberalism to Iraq, and explained the war as America's defensive response to the threats posed by anti-liberal regimes pursuing WMDs for the purpose of destroying America and its values. The war, therefore, was meant not just to remove Iraq's alleged WMDs but also to secure America by liberalizing and marketizing Iraq.

Bush claimed that Saddam's alleged WMDs endangered America's very existence. Americans, he warned in October 2002, "must not ignore the threat gathering against us. Facing clear evidence of peril, we cannot wait for the final proof, the smoking gun that could come in the form of a mushroom cloud."[56] Confronted with the prospect of annihilation, the United States was compelled to act first, preemptively. By the time Bush announced the commencement of hostilities with Iraq in March 2003, he had unmixed his metaphors. But he offered the same explanation. "The people of the United States and our friends and allies will not live at the mercy of an outlaw regime that threatens the peace with weapons of mass murder. We will meet that threat now, with our Army, Air Force, Navy, Coast Guard and Marines, so that we do not have to meet it later with armies of fire fighters and police and doctors on the streets of our cities."[57]

The war, according to the Bush administration, was necessary and defensive. Unless the threat was met in Iraq, the United States would suffer attacks on the "homeland" later. The hysteria was audible from the beginning. When in August 2002 Cheney unveiled the public campaign for war, he presented his unfounded fears as if they were imminent realities. "Armed with an arsenal of these weapons of terror, and seated atop ten percent of the world's oil reserves, Saddam Hussein could . . . be expected to seek domination of the entire Middle East, to take control of a great portion of the world's energy supplies, directly threaten America's friends throughout the region, and subject the United States or any other nation to nuclear blackmail."[58] Notice that Cheney, in accordance to Klare's argument, conceived of oil as a geopolitical weapon. But that was not what Bush picked up. Instead, he made explicit the logic that had been implicit: "Our best defense is a good offense."[59] Uncharacteristically, Bush was understating the point. His real point was that aggressive offense was the *only* defense.

The administration's account highlighted awful weapons and terrifying threats. It also invoked implausible scenarios. Even if Saddam had acquired nuclear weapons, the United States would not have lived at his sufferance or been subjected to his blackmail. The United States had passed through and prevailed in the Cold War, when the Soviet Union (and China) owned actual nuclear weapons and the delivery systems to strike American territory. Tacitly recognizing the absurdity of its claims, the administration refined the charge. The threat that necessitated the war did not really issue from WMDs. After all, important allies harbored more-dangerous weapons without threatening American security, world peace, or civilized values. The underlying claim was that intolerable dangers issued from the *intersection* of the weapons and rogue regimes. Eliminating WMDs, therefore, would not achieve security, because outlaw regimes incorrigibly seek to acquire destructive weapons to do their evil. Bush's solution, it followed, was to eliminate the illiberal states and closed economies that crave the dangerous weapons.

The diagnosis implied the solution. If the United States faced existential danger from evil *regimes,* Bush was justifying attacks on regimes that not only had not attacked the United States but that lacked the means to launch attacks. The conclusion remained implicit, but in conferring the United States with the right to prevent threats from gathering and in associating threats with illiberal, outlaw regimes, the Bush doctrine was obligating the United States to abolish regimes that were both illiberal and hostile. Officials got the point. Douglas Feith, Bush's undersecretary of defense for policy (and the source of much inaccurate intelligence about Saddam's weapons), later wrote, "If the proper top priority of U.S. action was to prevent the next attack . . . then the enemy was not just the particular group responsible for the 9/11 hijackings. It was the wider network of terrorists and their backers that might organize additional, large-scale strikes against the United States."[60] New targets, notice, are created by shifting, first, from the instigators of the 9/11 attacks to potential perpetrators of future attacks; second, from the potential perpetrators of future attacks to backers of future attacks; and, third, from actual backers to prospective backers (which is why the reach of preemption hinges on the word "might"). "U.S. military action should aim chiefly to disrupt those who might be plotting the next big attack against us."[61]

The doctrine of preemption tied concerns with WMDs, Al Qaeda, terrorism, market liberalism, and national security into one coherent package. But before he could apply the doctrine against Saddam, Bush had some explaining to do. It was not self-evident why Saddam threatened America's existence or even its power in the Middle East. His state, after all, was leeching off an economy that had been reduced by sanctions to about a fifth of its previous size. He lacked effective control over substantial chunks of his own territory in Kurdistan and endured no-fly zones over 40 percent of his territory, and his military had lost more than 80 percent of its fighting capacity since Gulf War I, when it had been routed in four days.[62] It was also unclear why deterrence and containment, which had succeeded against the inestimably more formidable military might of Soviet Union, would not deter Saddam.

Bush's answer was Al Qaeda. Saddam, the administration warned, might provide weapons to Al Qaeda, and Al Qaeda might sneak them into the United States. Wielding the specter of nuclear weapons exploding in the homeland, the administration claimed to be aborting the *potential* threat of Saddam allying with Al Qaeda.[63] But the doctrine did not stop with casting offensive acts as defensive. Because dictators inexorably jeopardize freedom, overturning one particular despot would not bring real security to the United States. Americans, in Bush's calls for war, are a people whose ideals and values are entwined with their interests. "The U.S. national security strategy," it was said in the document that announced the doctrine of preemption, "will be based on a distinctly American internationalism that reflects the *union* of our values and our national interests."[64] Threatening American values, therefore, threatens American interests; and securing American interests—and, according to Bush, survival—entails universalizing American values. With expansionist liberalism thus enshrined as both a strategic necessity and a moral imperative, the only sure way of preventing illiberal states from allying with the evil-doing terrorists that threaten American security and values was to convert enemies into friends—that is, to make them liberal. "[W]e are ultimately fighting," Bush said, "for our democratic values and way of life."[65]

The Bush doctrine required a threat to trigger the preemptive attacks, but it brushed aside actual *conduct* in assessing what qualified as a threat. Feith confides, "No one I know of believed Saddam was part of the 9/11 plot."[66] The value of the Bush doctrine to American power interests, then, is that it rendered Saddam's noninvolvement in 9/11 irrelevant. It licensed the United States to project power if it felt threatened, and the doctrine expanded what qualified as a national security threat to include threats to liberal values and institutions. What was relevant, according to the doctrine, was what *could* happen if freedom is attacked, which is why it featured the *threat* of the alliance between Saddam and Al Qaeda. The United States did not need to justify attacks on Al Qaeda. Osama Bin Laden provided all the justification American and world opinion required on 9/11. But the United States did need to justify war against Iraq, and the doctrine of preemption found justification in the prospect that Saddam *might* make common cause with Al Qaeda against their common enemy, the United States.

If the attack on Iraq was to be legitimated by the right of pre-emption, Saddam had to be linked to Al Qaeda. Unifying them attributed the misdeeds of the one to the potential of the other, thus raising Iraq into an immediate and imminent threat, not a potential and prospective one. Preemptive war, which under certain circumstances may be legal in international law, requires an imminent danger; preventative war, which is illegal, aims at the prospect of future dangers.[67] If the United States was claiming that Iraq might pose a threat down the road and was seeking to prevent the threat from gathering, it was conceding that the threat had not gathered yet, making the war preventative (and, therefore, unjustified under international law). But if Iraq was giving—or might be feared to be giving—nuclear weapons to Al Qaeda, then attacking Iraq might become preemptive. It meant getting Iraq before Al Qaeda got the United States, as when Israel launched preemptive attacks on Egypt and Syria in the Six-Day War. The specter of Al Qaeda is what converted the war from preventative to preemptive.

According to the Bush doctrine, then, the United States was attacking Iraq not because Iraq actually had WMDs or Saddam actually had ties to Al Qaeda. It was attacking on the basis of the speculative possibility, not the empirical fact, that Saddam's weapons, in league with Al Qaeda's record, constituted a threat to American security, which includes liberal values, and that the threat warranted offense in the name of defense. The United States was Al Qaeda's enemy, and the United States also was Saddam's enemy. On the grounds that an enemy's enemy is a friend, Saddam and Al Qaeda *might* have allied against the United States or its values.[68] That was the explanation. The cause of the war, by the administration's logic, was the American *fear*—warranted or not—that attacks *might* issue from the alliance that Saddam *might* form with Al Qaeda. Put differently, the United States regarded Saddam as a threat and responded accordingly, by threatening him. Therefore, the United States gave Saddam incentive to ally with Al Qaeda. Therefore, the United States was justified in removing him. At bottom, then, the Bush administration's explanation for the war was that it wanted Saddam removed from power because he was in America's way. The danger is undemocratic, illiberal, anticapitalist tyranny; the solution is universal, market liberalism. "We fight, as we always fight, for . . . a peace that favors liberty."[69]

What would disconfirm the administration's thesis that it waged war because it believed Saddam was a security threat due to the illiberalism of his regime? First, the doctrine works as explanation, as opposed to rationalization for ulterior motivations, only to the extent that senior officials sincerely believed that Saddam might arm terrorists with WMDs. By this measure, the administration's explanation is suspect. Before 9/11, Bush disregarded Clinton's warnings about Al Qaeda, deemphasized the priority of terrorism by demoting Richard Clarke, ignored the CIA's briefing about the intensifying Al Qaeda threat in August 2001, and assigned a low priority to terrorism.[70] Bush's answer, of course, was that he learned otherwise on 9/11, that it "changed everything." It caused the administration to take terrorism seriously and exposed the danger of Saddam allying with terrorists. The problem is that 9/11 did not change Bush's designs on Saddam. The administration wanted to attack Saddam when it came into office, and it wanted to attack him after 9/11. The doctrine of preemption, in other words, explains a constant with a variable. The variable was the insecurity exposed on 9/11 to terrorists. The constant was the goal of attacking Saddam.

The second problem with explaining the war in terms of preemption is that preemption requires actual threats, not imaginary ones. As some critics suspected at the time and as was confirmed subsequently, Saddam did not have nuclear or biological weapons.[71]

Actually, he did not have chemical weapons either. But preemption, if it was to achieve credibility in world opinion, had to be applied with a steady hand. "Fear" could be deployed to justify any attack, and given that threats are the stuff of international relations and that the doctrine broadened American security interests to include American values,[72] the doctrine was ready-made for justifying attacks against whatever country the United States wanted to attack for whatever reason. In fact, the value of the doctrine was that it legitimated aggression. All the United States had to do, really, was to identify a target. When the target reacted defensively to American threats, the United States could interpret measures that were taken in self-defense as threats to American values and security.

The point is not that the doctrine of preemption promoted American interests. As a foreign policy document, it was supposed to be self-interested. Blaming the Bush doctrine for representing American interests self-interestedly is like blaming the pope for being Catholic. The point is that the doctrine rose from being the agent of power to being its master. It seduced policy-makers into believing, first, that their offensives were defensive and, second, that Iraqis agreed with them. That is, the Bush doctrine allowed the United States to do almost anything because bad regimes, in repudiating American values, also jeopardized American security. Having given the United States license to attack and eliminate illiberalism, the Bush doctrine then wished away the prospect of resistance by construing Iraqis as receptive to the liberal values the American invasion would bring.

The question, then, is whether the United States went to war because the Bush administration really feared Saddam would give WMDs to terrorists in their common war against liberalism, or whether the administration said it feared Saddam might give weapons to terrorists because it wanted license for a war it was bent on fighting anyway. Did the doctrine motivate American behavior, or did it merely justify preexisting ambitions? Conveniently, the doctrine did produce war against a target that already was in its cross-hairs, did express the instinctive drive of hegemonic states to acquire always-more power, and did aim at an obstacle to globalizing neoliberal capitalism. But the Bush doctrine did more than legitimate preexisting ambitions. It also decreed a far-reaching and ultimately self-subverting objective—regime change.

2

Bring 'Em On

MAKING THE WORLD SAFE FOR DEMOCRACY

Do you want to know what the foreign policy of Iraq
is to the United States? . . . Fuck the United States! . . .
That's what it is—and that's why we're going to get him!

George W. Bush

The theses centered on Bush, Republicans, oil, and Israel overlook the most perplexing problematic of the war. Each identifies a particular interest that called, or might have called, for the war, and then explains why the war benefited that particular individual, party, or constituency. But none of these theses provides a cause, occasion, or purpose that explains what it purports to explain. Yes, the president controlled the bully pulpit; yes, he was immensely popular in the wake of 9/11; and yes, many Democrats were afraid to challenge a popular president on a matter of national security in the year after terrorist attacks on the "homeland." Yes, too, Israel and oil interests stood to benefit if the war was prosecuted successfully. But while this points to how Bush got the political backing he wanted, it says little about *why* he, along with most of the political and foreign policy establishment, chose war with *Iraq* from the menu of possibilities that was available in the aftermath of the 9/11 attacks.

The fifth thesis, as implied in the Bush doctrine, has problems, but it does operate on a level that is equal to explaining what must be explained. The war was about America's place in Iraq, the region, and the world; the status of capitalism and neoliberal economic institutions; and American power interests. In addition to encompassing the ambitions of oil interests and Israel in the larger objective of remaking the political, economic, and regional order in the Islamic Middle East, the Bush doctrine also opened room for expressing presidential character and pursuing partisan advantage. The point of the war, as the doctrine implied, was to project American power into Iraq and the region, to liberalize the Iraqi state and marketize its economy, and, in the process, to use liberalism in Iraq as an example to sell to the Muslim Middle East. The war, however, was a big bet. Why, then, did policy-makers make it; why did they get wrong the stakes they were wagering and the odds they were facing; and why did they misunderstand the value to the United States of democracy in Iraq?

The sixth—the idealizing of interests thesis—outlines the answer. The geopolitical motive for the war was to entrench American power, and the neoliberal motive was to implant global capitalism in Iraq and its neighbors. But the key to the decision to go to war is that American policy-makers did not recognize their interests *as* interests or their ideals *as* ideals. Instead, they translated geopolitical and neoliberal interests into ideals, and then expected Iraqis would embrace the interests that they idealized as the answer to universal stirrings in the human spirit. Thoroughly befogged by this idealization, American policy-makers then lost sight of the very interests that spawned the ideals at the outset. In other words, the United States bumbled into a self-subverting war because policy-makers, in an atheoretical, unexamined, obvious-beyond-notice kind of way, conflated American interests and ideals, associated American ideals with universal values, and then imagined that the power they had idealized was a godsend to the world (and sincerely expected Iraqis to concur). When Iraqis disagreed, the United States had no fallback position. It had planted the flag in quicksand.

The war originated in conventional national interests. The American state aimed to eliminate the obstacle of Saddam, enhance its influence and access to oil, increase leverage over states that imported Middle Eastern oil, and help its friends and clients while hurting its enemies. Detecting an opportunity in Saddam's blustering to increase its standing in the region and maybe control some oil in the bargain, why would the United States not act like a hegemon? It could acquire military bases in Iraq (and move them from Saudi Arabia, where they were controversial); take another step toward encircling Iran (in combination with existing bases in Afghanistan and, at the time, Uzbekistan); eliminate a pest who insulted American pride and threatened regional peace; get sway over a key, and hitherto hostile, oil-producing state; and repay friends in the Israeli lobby by helping Israel. More fundamentally, the United States wanted power because states crave it, as if genetically.[1] Bush put the geopolitical point crudely when he vowed "to kick [Saddam's] sorry motherfucking ass all over the Mideast."[2] But his meaning was clear. By chasing Saddam out, the United States would let itself in.

In addition to wanting power for conventional reasons of state, the United States also was committed to extending the capitalist order to Iraq and the region, to globalizing neoliberalism. As the "organizer and manager" of the neoliberal order, to use John Ikenberry's term, the United States builds the structures of the global capitalist system.[3] Because global capitalism is not just there, waiting to express itself, it must be constructed through states and institutions—national and international, political and economic. Unlike the usual national security actors, such as militaries, intelligence agencies, and grand strategists, globalizers are cosmopolitan, professional, and financial—neoliberal. They impose the legal regimes that define, regulate, and unleash capital, labor, and financial markets, batter opponents of free trade into submission, and marketize areas of the world and arenas of life that hitherto were governed by nonmarket forces and authorities. Neoliberals do not "free" markets directly; they reorganize the state, which then designates markets as the authoritative source for allocating resources. In Gulf War II, accordingly, globalizing neoliberals meant to free Iraq from Saddam and Iraqis from the burden of the statist economy.

To these ends, Paul Bremer, Administrator of the Coalition Provisional Authority of Iraq, tried to reorganize the Iraqi state along neoliberal lines in the months after Saddam was deposed. With the old state prone, Bremer issued orders that proclaimed trade liberalization and the independence of the central bank; set rules for the new currency and securities markets; declared policies for trademarks, patents, copyrights, public contracts, and debt resolution; and privatized state enterprises, thus establishing the basic conditions for the neoliberal political economy that the United States meant to launch in Iraq. As Wendy Brown summarizes the "Bremer orders," they "mandated selling off several hundred state-run enterprises, permitting full ownership rights of Iraqi businesses by foreign firms and full repatriation of profits to foreign firms, opening Iraq's banks to foreign ownership and control, and eliminating tariffs."[4] Saddam was targeted, in other words, not only because he defied American geopolitical power but also because he obstructed the neoliberal regime of free trade, privatization, and marketization.

The geopolitical and neoliberal motivations represent a basic truth: there were gains to be won through war in Iraq. But simple self-interested explanations for the war are dashed by the brute fact that, viewed coldly, the incentives for avoiding the war outweighed those for fighting it, a disparity that was—or should have been—obvious at the time. In retrospect, of course, it generally is accepted that the war was unsuccessful. Iraq had no WMDs, not even old-fashioned chemical ones, and the United States utterly failed to improve its power position in the region or to institute the regime of global capitalism inside Iraq. Although a few die-hards disagree, the bulk of both elite and public opinion concurs that the United States would have been better off if it had avoided the war altogether.[5] But just because the war came to be regretted does not mean that it was ill conceived or that its purposes were unattainable when it began. The costs of Gulf War II exceeded the gains, but this does not prove that it was a bad idea, and it certainly does not prove that the war *obviously* was a bad idea when it was hatched. It might have been a good idea gone wrong. Why, then, suggest that it was, or should have been, obvious at the time the decision to go to war was made that the costs and risks of the war would exceed the plausible gains?

The answer is that the crisis in Iraq was foreshadowed in the confused and contradictory objectives that policy-makers declared publicly. The United States wanted credible friends for Israel and Saudi Arabia as well as for itself; a liberal capitalist order; and, according to hawks outside the administration, something akin to a Reformation of Islam. The differences among these objectives and the mismatch between the later two, which would require decades, generations, or centuries to achieve, and the expectations of the quick, in-and-out war of the sort that administration officials thought they had concluded in Afghanistan, were set forth in plain view. According to the public statements of American officials, the United States either was interested in changing the leadership in Iraq while leaving the rest of the society unaltered or was embarking on a project to change the trajectory of Iraqi history, and the United States would achieve these half-considered and largely inconsistent objectives readily, easily, and cheaply. Deputy Secretary of Defense Paul Wolfowitz, who was committed to transforming Iraq, estimated during testimony to Congress that Iraqis would pay for reconstruction themselves.[6] With senior policy-makers disagreeing about their goals, often not recognizing the import of their disagreements, and failing to align their military means to their political ends (whatever those would turn out to be), how could the United States *not* fail?

Civilian policy-makers envisioned an easy transition, but military and intelligence agencies were reserved in their endorsement and open in their skepticism about war in Iraq.[7] In fact, the lone senior figure in the Bush administration to signal reservations about the war was Secretary of State Colin Powell, former chair of the Joint Chiefs of Staff. Undeterred, civilian elites were confident the US military would liberate Iraq—Saddam would fall, and after a short interval of American custodianship, Iraqis would commence self-government, only now they would adopt democratic institutions, such as elections, and these would yield liberal outcomes. In fact, American civilians, as opposed to military officers and intelligence officials, habitually equated the liberal and the democratic.[8] Their confidence was warranted insofar as most Iraqis probably did want government that respected the rights of the governed. It was one thing, however, to recognize that Iraqis wanted rights for themselves, and it was another to assume that Iraq's minorities would accommodate themselves to the power of majority, that popular sovereignty would yield liberal values, institutions, and practices in Iraq, or that Iraqis agreed on the content of the rights they wanted.

Administration regime-changers sometimes spoke of the difficulties they would face in changing Iraq, but in practice they took it for granted that everybody, Iraqis included, can become liberal, that becoming liberal is not contingent on securing prior historical, social, and cultural developments, and, therefore, that elections in Iraq would yield liberal outcomes spontaneously and naturally. Instead of recognizing that liberal institutions arise from complicated and distinctive historical processes, and might be unavailable in a society that had not passed through them, liberalism was taken to be Iraq's evident destination. History, in the refrain of the time, had ended and

American liberalism had won.[9] Once Saddam was deposed, therefore, hawks implicitly imagined that individualistic, instrumentally rational, modern liberals would crawl from the cubbyholes where Saddam had forced them to hide, and commence acting *liberally*— like the *Homo economicus* that animates economistic models of human behavior.

The arguments for war, therefore, screamed danger. Papering over risks (but not always costs), the United States put regional stability and American lives, credibility, and unlimited budget into the pot. The bet would pay off if, and only to the extent that, liberalism was achieved in Iraq and Iraq's new liberal values and institutions aligned the interests of Iraqis, the region, and the United States. If this trajectory was assumed, Saddam was standing in the way of history and the United States probably would win its bet. If, however, the viability of liberalism is contingent on prior historical developments and would not issue spontaneously from the intersection of human nature and a new regime, then the United States was making a bet on a prospect that was unlikely to be achieved.[10] Plus, the bet carried no stop order.

The assumption of historic inevitability—that history was over and liberalism had won—made the war promising, but it also conceded that the war ultimately would add little value. Once liberalism is posited as universal in scope and inevitable in outcome, then the war was reduced to a mere accelerant. It brought sooner what history was destined to deliver later. If, however, the destination of history is not written and market liberalism was not ordained as the inevitable outcome of the war, the calculus turned upside down. Under more skeptical assumptions, the United States first was disordering the oil patch, and then was jumping headfirst into the sinkhole it was opening. If hawks were promising gains that were destined to accrue anyway, why incur the costs and the risks? The United States went to war because, instead of totaling the benefits and then subtracting the costs of war realistically, policy-makers idealized American interests in accordance to two axioms and one deduction that guide American foreign policy.

Two Axioms and One Deduction

The first axiom of American foreign policy is that American interests and ideals always are associated, usually are intertwined, and often are equivalent. Uniquely among the countries of the world, America's interests in seeking power and security promote the ideals of freedom, rights, and markets. Other states are mired in zero-sum competitions with each other. But the United States is exceptional, according to the first axiom, because its ideals also are interests and its interests also are ideals. American interests are advanced when its ideals are spread, and American ideals, which also incorporate its interests, positively liberate, better, and enrich all they touch, inside and outside the United States, due to "the union of our values and our national interests" that the NSC observed in the document that announced the doctrine of preemption.[11] Capturing the spirit of the first axiom on the occasion of his second inaugural, Bush proclaimed that advancing the ideal of freedom "is the urgent requirement of our nation's security, and the calling of our time."[12]

Actors from three influential political-ideological traditions—neoconservatives, liberal hawks, and neoliberals—backed Bush's call for war in Iraq, and all took the first axiom as their point of departure. Each group introduced its own distinctive twist. Neoconservatives highlighted the military dimensions and transformative purposes of American power. Liberal hawks, close cousins to neoconservatives, invoked universal morality. Neoliberals emphasized that markets instill prosperity and freedom. But the foreign policies of the three traditions stem from the same seed. Achieving America's security and economic interests promotes its values and, conversely, America is secure when, and only when, liberal values are secure. American foreign policy for regime-changers, therefore, is inherently idealistic. With American security interests contained in its ideals, spreading liberal ideals becomes a core security interest. Bush drew the conclusion: "The survival of freedom in our land increasingly depends on the success of freedom in other lands."[13]

The marriage of interests and ideals is attacked from both sides. From the side of interests, *realists* object that it is self-subverting to burden the serious business of pursuing vital, sometimes life-and-death, interests in the dominate-or-be-dominated world of international relations with ethical diversions and fanciful delusions about win-win outcomes. Taking for granted that power interests and moral values are distinct and usually adversarial principles, realists stand on the interest side of the continuum. From the side of ideals, *idealists* agree that choices must be made, that interests and ideals usually are either-or, one-or-the-other options. But idealists make the opposite choice. Where realists fake their commitment to American ideals, idealists from the antiwar wing of the Democratic Party fake their commitment to pursuing American power interests. Unable to admit that they would subordinate national interests to universal ideals, they pretend that they believe interests and ideals are interconnected. But secretly they agree with realists that choices must be made. The difference is that idealists choose ethics over power.

Neoconservatives, liberal hawks, and neoliberals—the three traditions that allied to urge war for regime change in Iraq—seem to occupy the intermediate positions between the realist and idealist endpoints. Actually they inhabit a wholly different plane of politics. Where realists and idealists are dualists that agree on the necessity of choosing between the alternatives of interests and values (or, maybe, of combining portions of each), regime-changing hawks invoke *American exceptionalism* to preempt the need to choose. They declare they want to unite what is right and what is self-interested, that the United States can do well by doing good. In other words, regime-changers postulate as articles of faith that respecting and promoting American values satisfies core American interests, and that what is good for all also is advantageous for America. Rejecting the zero-sum world of realists and the hostility to power-interests of idealists, regime-changing exceptionalists escape the interest–ideal continuum of both realists and idealists by assuming that international affairs can be organized on the basis of American values. Regime-changers believe, in other words, that they can unify, and not merely combine, America's interests in accumulating power and America's liberal values. What makes America exceptional is its singular ability to have its cake and to eat it too.

Interests and ideals for neoconservatives, liberal hawks, and neo-liberals are complementary and linked. To use the example that is the model for much of such thinking: The freer the markets, the wealthier the economy; and the wealthier the economy, the more liberal the society and the greater its freedom.[14] Whether the United States seeks to do well for itself or whether it seeks to promote liberal values does not ultimately matter. They become different ways of understanding the same practices, much as pursuing individual advantage and serving the general interest became one and the same for Adam Smith. As the NSC set forth the Bush doctrine, "A strong world economy enhances our national security by advancing prosperity and freedom in the rest of the world."[15] Performing the indispensable spadework of harmonizing American power with world prosperity and human freedom, the "hidden hand" encourages policy-makers to advance the general interests without compromising their particular interests.[16] A force for good, American power is purposeful, liberating, and edifying. "America's vital interests and our deepest beliefs," Bush declared, "are now one."[17] Tony Blair made the same point after meeting with Bush to plan the war. As he told Americans, "We shouldn't be shy of giving our actions not just the force of self-interest but moral force. And in reality, at a certain point, these forces merge. . . . We are defending what our nations believe in: freedom, democracy, justice, tolerance and respect towards others."[18]

The second axiom of American foreign policy is that "American values," in the words of Condoleezza Rice, "are universal."[19] American internationalism, as the NSC says in the doctrine of preemption, aims "to help make the world not just safer but better. Our goals on the path to progress are clear: political and economic freedom, peaceful relations with other states, and respect for human dignity. And this path is not America's alone. It is open to all." The language is platitudinous, but it sets forth the classic liberal claim, dating from Woodrow Wilson, about American foreign policy. American values of rights, markets, and democracy, liberals affirm, apply universally. Although they originate with Americans, liberal values are not restricted to them. They extend—or can be made to extend—everywhere, just as the Declaration of Independence proclaims. The "principles enshrined in the Declaration of Independence," wrote the NSC, "are a lifeline to lonely defenders of liberty."[20] Belonging everywhere and helping everyone, the reach of American ideals transcends territorial boundaries. Naturally, therefore, the deepest aspirations of Iraqis coincided with American ideals. American values are liberal, and liberal values are universal.

The second axiom is imbued with the spirit of American exceptionalism, but of a particular sort. In most exceptionalist traditions the United States is separated from lesser countries by its Anglo-Scottish heritage of dissenting Protestantism, or its assimilation of immigrants into one people, or its lack of a peasantry, a feudal past, a socialist movement, or class-based politics, or its innate liberality.[21] For regime-changing hawks, on the other hand, America is exceptional because of the nature of its identity. Of course, every national identity is unique in substance, which is why there are multiple nation-states across the globe. If all identities were the same, they would not require separate states. But America is unique for regime-changers because its identity is made not by culture, history, or blood, but because, in the words of neoconservatives William Kristol and Robert Kagan, America is "rooted in universal principles."[22] The United States is exceptional because it is better than other societies, because it is more moral, more free, and more prosperous, and, most of all, because it, and it alone, rises above having to choose between the requirements of self-interest and universal morality. Uniquely, America escapes contradictions between the advantageous and the good.

Samuel Huntington set forth the counterposition in *Who Are We?*, a critique of combining loose immigration policies and multicultural politics. Huntington agreed with exceptionalists that the United States is unique. But he disagreed that it is uniquely unique. Instead of representing abstract, open-ended, and unbounded liberal possibilities, Huntington's America consists of a "core Anglo-Protestant culture" that produced the "political Creed of liberty and democracy."[23] Believing themselves to be a "chosen" people,[24] Americans from their conception as a people articulated a republican identity that was both distinct and inclusive. It was distinct in possessing a unique content; it was inclusive in allowing outsiders to become Americans, provided that newcomers assimilated into the values of the Anglo-Protestant dissenters who defined the nation and what it meant to be American.[25]

Huntington's America is open to immigrants who assimilate, but it is not cosmopolitan. "America was *different,* something special, the city on the hill, devoted to liberty, opportunity, and the future. People became American by embracing these distinctive characteristics, abandoning their previous attachment to another nation, culture, and belief, and rejecting . . . the old world."[26] The nationalist's America, by virtue of its special content, is inherently particular and fundamentally different from the rest of the world. It interacts and negotiates with other countries, and it may project power or go to war against them. Huntington was neither an isolationist nor a pacifist. But the nationalist's America cannot become, and does not aspire to become, universal. The United States is not the world; the world is not the United States; and nationalists live in the difference.

Regime-changing exceptionalists agree with traditional nationalists in insisting that the United States is unique, superior, and endowed with a special destiny.[27] But regime-changers diverge from nationalists on the critical divide of what it is that makes America unique. They do not regard the United States as normal in its differences, in the way every country is unique. Instead, regime-changers identify America with the cause of freedom; their America performs singular, transformational purposes. Freedom originates in America, but it also is an uncontainable spirit that grows constantly. America is exceptional because, uniquely among countries, it embodies the *liberal idea*. Although it is an actual country with specific boundaries, its ideals, principles, and values speak of rights, which are human and inalienable; of freedom, which is God-given and natural; and of property and markets, which are inherent in human nature *(Homo economicus)*. The commitments that define America for regime-changing exceptionalists, in other words, are not restricted to Americans. Applying to all peoples, they are *universalizable*. Expansionism follows in step. America is the liberal idea; liberal ideas are universal, traveling and belonging everywhere; and universal values promote the universal interest of humanity in freedom and markets. The more free-trading and liberal is international society, the better for everybody. It is the union between what is good for the world and good for itself that makes the United States exceptional. The United States is special, according to exceptionalists, precisely because all societies, including Iraq, may replicate what is most dearly American. Ideals travel without passports. For nationalists, on the other hand, the United States is separated by metaphor from the rest of the human world. The city on the hill, America may be admired but it cannot be replicated.

The liberal premises and universal telos of the second axiom madden realists as well as nationalists. The traditional rival of liberals in debates on American foreign policy, realists represent a disposition that treats politics as competition for power, advantage, and security, and as a zero-sum game. Liberal foreign policy likewise is a disposition as much as it is a doctrine, and liberals agree with realists that states compete. But liberals, including the Democratic elites that backed the war, hold also that common interests and ultimate destinations can supersede conflicts, and that what states and their people share surpasses what divides them. History progresses, states cooperate, and what is good for one can be good for all (which is why liberals can be exceptionalists). Politics becomes a positive-sum venture. Instead of "seeing" power when states interact, liberals discern interdependent human rights, prospects of mutual advantage, and, most importantly, interests that ultimately are harmonious.[28] Believing that the interests of all (liberal) states are congruent, liberals escape the realist obsession with violence, coercion, and competition and they tell themselves that their disinterested commitment to universal values and interests elevates them above crass power politics. But their high-mindedness carries one distinctive risk. Liberals are prone to displacing their interests in accumulating power onto their commitment to realizing liberal values. The liberal belief in the universality of American values, in other words, is liable to disguise the pursuit of power, interest, and advantage, and the disguise is more likely to fool liberals than those they purport to be helping.

Bush planted himself thoroughly in the mainstream of liberal American political and foreign policy elites by invoking the two axioms. But he distinguished his administration by relishing the deduction that liberal hawks and neoliberals prefer not to speak. It follows either way, but Bush deduced it relentlessly. If American power interests are embedded in American ideals, and if American ideals are universal, bettering and uplifting every society they touch, then by the transitive property it follows that American *power* must become universal too. As the NSC explains, "These values of freedom are right and true for every person, in every society—and the duty of protecting these values against their enemies is the common calling of freedom-loving people across the globe and across the ages."[29] The United States, in other words, must universalize its power not for reasons of crass self-interest, as is the case for lesser countries, but to discharge its moral obligation to humanity.

The Bush doctrine implies the point clearly. "In keeping with our heritage and principles, we do not use our strength to press for unilateral advantage. We seek instead to create a balance of power that favors human freedom: conditions in which all nations and all societies can choose for themselves the rewards and challenges of political and economic liberty."[30] All people yearn for freedom, and American power delivers it. Universalizing freedom, therefore, entails universalizing American power. Rice, in drawing the lesson explicitly, divulges why seasoned policy-makers did not register the manifest costs and risks of the war. "Power in the service of freedom is to be welcomed, and powers that share a commitment to freedom can—and must—make common cause against freedom's enemies."[31] Because Iraqis sought America's gifts, they were expected to experience conquest and occupation as liberation. Once idealized, American power banished the prospect of resistance. Who resists their freedom?

The axioms thrive because in the eat-or-be-eaten competition that is international relations, they—usually—abet American power. If doing right for the world produces good for America, then it is easy to reverse the formula unconsciously. Doing good for the United States becomes the same as doing right for the world. But intoxicated by the brew that converts American power into a universal good and that entices them into feeling altruistic while pursuing power interests, policy-makers suppressed the fundamental insight of America's Madisonian constitutional tradition—that power naturally counters power. Barely contemplating the possibility that Iraqis would resist the liberty that America was bestowing onto them, Wolfowitz pronounced himself "reasonably certain that they will greet us as liberators."[32]

The Interests That Are Idealized

The interests that are idealized via the axioms begin as standard state interests. The United States wanted raw power, as was displayed in the demeanor of Bush ("Bring 'em on") and the boasts of neoconservative cheerleaders. Naming the organization they established for the purpose of promoting the war "The New American Century," neoconservatives admired Theodore Roosevelt for single-handedly starting the Spanish-American War, called for "benevolent global hegemony," pressed the United States to recognize itself as "a global empire," and craved opportunities to celebrate military power.[33] Reveling in the assertion of power ten weeks into the war, *New York Times* columnist Thomas Friedman urged: "What [Muslims] needed to see was American boys and girls going house to house from Basra to Baghdad and basically saying, 'Which part of this sentence don't you understand. You don't think . . . we care about our open society. . . . Well, suck on this.' That . . . was what this war was about. We could have hit Saudi Arabia . . . we could have hit Pakistan. We hit Iraq because we could."[34] "Liberal imperialism," Max Boot pronounced, "is needed today to deal with the most troubled regions of the planet."[35]

Hawks began with blunt interests—as the bellicosity of Bush, neoconservatives, and Friedman make clear—and their ideals reflected the interests that spawned them. Illiberal regimes in Pakistan, Saudi Arabia, and the oil sheikdoms were exempted from regime change. Friedman might have wanted to send them a message, but for geopolitical and commercial reasons they were friends. Conventional foreign policy interests, in other words, began as the independent variable and liberal ideals as the dependent variable. If the United States had an interest in targeting a particular enemy, then liberal ideals were deployed; if not, they were ignored, just as power politics would counsel. In Iraq, which it had reasons to covet, the United States saw that Saddam was wounded, belligerent, isolated, vexed with abundant enemies at home and nearby, begging to be portrayed as a threat, and sitting atop vast reservoirs of oil, which made Iraq significant strategically and economically. Why would the United States not, in the standard fashion of hegemons, exploit the opportunity to depose an enemy and insert a client regime, particularly in the wake of 9/11?

Leading insiders support the idea that the United States was engaged in a power grab. Publicly hawks stressed the security threat posed by WMDs, but privately they regarded Saddam's real offenses as ideological and political. Wolfowitz, the administration's foremost hawk, admitted the point. "The truth is that for reasons that have a lot to do with the U.S. government bureaucracy we settled on the one issue that everyone could agree on, which was weapons of mass destruction as the core reason."[36] CIA director George Tenet concurred. "The United States did not go to war in Iraq solely because of WMDs. In my view, I doubt it was even the principal cause. Yet it was the public face that was put on it." Invoking Britain's MI6, Tenet has Bush being driven by "bigger issues, such as changing the politics of the Middle East."[37] "Intelligence and facts," according to British intelligence, "were being fixed around the policy."[38] The chair of the US Joint Chiefs of Staff, Hugh Shelton, agreed. He tells of hawks in the administration "working backward to sell their case." "What was bogus was the link that was created between Saddam and any terrorist threat to the United States, but it presented the best opportunity to garner support for an Iraqi invasion."[39]

By the account of insiders, then, hawks featured Saddam's alleged WMDs and terrorist ties as the pretext for getting the war they wanted. Why doubt, then, that the United States took what it wanted and then used liberal idealism to lure gullible publics in the United States and Iraq to feel good about themselves? And why, if the United States was manipulating fears of WMDs and Al Qaeda, would it not have been manipulating ideological language too? Inasmuch as hawks took few substantive steps that actually made Iraq more liberal, and inasmuch as the American political tradition frowns on wars that are instigated for avowedly aggressive purposes, why not conclude that the ideological professions really repackaged aggression as liberation? The answer is that the United States *was* pursuing conventional military, political, and commercial objectives, just as would be expected from a war that was conducted by such mainstays of the military establishment as former secretary of defense and then–vice president Cheney, second-time secretary of defense Rumsfeld, and former chair of the Joint Chiefs of Staff and then–secretary of state Powell. Besides, when Bush pronounced that the best defense is a good offense, he was allowing that the United States really was taking the offensive. The point of the idealizing of interests thesis is not, therefore, to deny that the United States was projecting power aggressively. It is to explain why it acted to the detriment of its power interests.

How the Axioms Favored War

The problem with featuring the power politics objectives to the exclusion of liberal values in the decision for war is that the axioms lured policy-makers into idealizing American interests, as is indicated by the differing objectives in the two wars with Iraq. Bush I fought Gulf War I for conventional power politics reasons. Iraq's 1990 invasion of Kuwait jeopardized oil supplies, upset the regional balance of power, transgressed an important international boundary, and endangered the security of Saudi Arabia. If the administration had had its druthers, the United States and its allies would have driven Saddam from Kuwait, then the Iraqi army or secret police would have ousted Saddam by a coup d état, and ultimately a new strongman would have emerged to maintain the (Sunni) bulwark against Iran. But when Shi'as in southern Iraq rose in insurrection upon Saddam's surrender in March 1991, Bush I was forced to choose between accepting what a popular revolution would produce or putting up with Saddam. Bush I preferred Saddam, providing he was disarmed, because his rule contained Iran and maintained Sunni ascendancy in the oil patch. Popular revolution, on the other hand, portended Shi'i government in Iraq, opportunities for Iran, and trouble for Saudi Arabia.[40] Not subscribing to the axioms, Bush I abstained from regime change because it would have compromised conventional power objectives. By contrast, Bush II fought Gulf War II to enact regime change because he and his coalition took the truths of the axioms for granted.

The axioms made four kinds of contributions to the choice for and the objectives of Gulf War II. First, they divided regime-changing hawks from doves. Regime-changers disagreed among themselves on important issues, including the status of international organizations and international law. But what united regime-changing hawks, and what separated them from doves, was their conception of the relationship between interests and ideals. For regime-changers, American interests and ideals depend on each other for completion. Doves, whether the semi-pacifist, antiwar idealists on the left of the Democratic Party or the ostensibly amoral, self-interested realists in the Republican Party and the academic discipline of international relations, disagreed.[41] The two kinds of doves differ philosophically on most everything. Idealists agree with liberal hawks in favoring multilateralism, valuing international law, and doubting whether mere national interest justifies war ethically. Representing a wholly different sensibility, realists take war as part and parcel of the international system, respect the principle of self-help, dismiss international law, and subordinate justice to the imperative of national interests. Wars for realists are smart or stupid, well advised or ill advised, prudent or reckless; they are not just or unjust. But idealists and realists do converge on the very point that differentiated both from regime-changing hawks. Both refused to fuse American interests and ideals.

Realists and idealists reject the fusion of American interests and liberal values for different reasons. For realists, the very notion of universalizing national interests is nonsensical. International relations are organized through the clash of interests that are, by definition, *national*. They cannot be universal. States exist amid other states, and for one state's interests to prevail in the zero-sum game that is international relations, another's must be subordinated. Therefore, the quest for universal power, which follows from the two axioms, is revolutionary and dangerous.[42] It not only attacks the integrity of the state system; it also is doomed to futility. Attempts to establish universal domination are like pushing down one end of a teetertotter. They inevitably organize coalitions that rise in the opposite direction. For realists, therefore, it is foolish to believe in universal values, and it is foolhardy to try to realize them.

Idealists refuse to equate national interests with liberal values for opposite reasons. Idealists object not to the idea of universal values, which they treasure, but to the claim that they are distinctly American properties. Regime-changers embraced American power as intrinsically moral, as a force for unalloyed good. Idealists disagreed. Convinced of the corrupting effects of power on ethics and refusing to equate American power with moral right, idealists resuscitated one classically realist insight. At their core, idealists agree with realists that power ultimately is power, and they behave accordingly. Rejecting the notion that power is different when Americans exercise it, they deny the defining claim of exceptionalist foreign policy. Idealists, in other words, object to the *power* in American power. By installing universal standards *above* American interests and calling upon American power to answer to them, idealists reject realism by calling on the United States to abjure its self-interest, not to assert it. But they agree with realists—and disagree with regime-changers—in believing that states in international relations must choose between doing good and doing well. Only fortuitously—in World War II, say—can they do both at the same time.

Second, the axioms informed justifications of the war. The Authorization of the Use of Military Force Against Iraq, which was passed by both chambers of Congress, itemized upwards of two-dozen reasons for war. Some were large (allegations of Saddam's WMDs, his nuclear programs, and Al Qaeda's presence in Iraq), some were small (Iraq's failure to return property that was seized in Kuwait after it invaded in 1990), and most were unconnected. The axioms, however, bundled the many particulars into a moral cause. Promising that the United States would restore "international peace and security to the Persian Gulf Region,"[43] hawks equated the pursuit of particular American interests in Iraq and the region with the achievement of peace and security. Instead of having to choose between one and the other, the United States could achieve its particular interests by achieving the general good. In asserting its interests, the United States promoted peace; and in promoting peace, it achieved its interests—just as the axioms decreed.

Third, the evidence that the axioms were not merely justificatory, as power politics realists would expect, is that they skewed cost-benefit calculations about the advisability of the war. If the liberal talk had played no role in assessing the pros and cons when policy-makers opted for war, then policy-makers would have viewed promises of transformative gains warily. But by idealizing American interests, the axioms enlarged the gains policy-makers anticipated and minimized the risks they foresaw from the war they were contemplating. On the pro side of the ledger, policy-makers not only argued that American victory would yield regional peace; they also predicated their decision on the expectation that the war would transform the region to the general advantage, thus enhancing American power. Then, on the con side, policy-makers defined away risks because they believed, and did not merely pretend to believe, that Iraqis would embrace America's cause. The axioms, in other words, both inflated gains and deflated risks.

The official army history described the evidence that shows that policy-makers took their rhetoric seriously.

> The most unexpected aspect of the campaign was the emergence of an organized and lethal insurgency. The surprise exhibited by both the Coalition military leadership and the Soldiers in Iraq stemmed from widespread assumptions about probable Iraqi reactions to war and liberation. Before the war, few United States Government officials had expected this type of resistance in the absence of the Baath Party's rule, and that consensus ultimately contributed to the attitudes of military planners tasked to design the overall war plan.[44]

In other words, the US military did not plan for resistance because civilian policy-makers ruled out the possibility, and they excluded resistance because they believed that Iraqis had no reason to refuse the gifts the United States was bringing them.

Regime-changers did not wish away all problems. Liberal hawks and neoliberals, in particular, were apprehensive about the disruptions that might flow from the collapse of Saddam's government. They worried about disruptions that might cause disease, refugees, food shortages, and about breakdowns in law and order. But their concerns, by focusing on the perils of implementing regime change amid tumult, actually support the idealizing of interests thesis. By concentrating on the hazards of the transition, regime-changers effectively narrowed the challenges they would face to enforcement issues. They took the terms of the new order as given, uncontroversial, and welcome because, having universalized the appeal of liberal values, regime-changers assumed the fundamental issues as resolved. As Clinton said when he signed the Iraq Liberation Act, "I categorically reject arguments that this is unattainable due to Iraq's history or its ethnic or sectarian make-up. Iraqis deserve and desire freedom like everyone else."[45] In his second inaugural, Bush echoed Clinton: "Americans, of all people, should never be surprised by the power of *our* ideals. Eventually, the call of freedom comes to every mind and every soul."[46]

Three Images of Regime Change

The fourth, and the most important, evidence of the idealization of American interests were the objectives of the war. Although the meaning of regime change was not clear, all hawks said they favored it. But they meant different things by "regime change." National security bureaucracies implied a minimal conception, whereas civilian regime-changers imagined expansive meanings. In all, three distinguishable and sometimes contradictory versions of regime change circulated among policy-makers, and the several meanings were used promiscuously and interchangeably in spite of important differences among them.

In the first image, regime change was conceived as *decapitation*. The regime consisted of Saddam, his two sons, and their forty-nine associates whose faces also were put on the decks of playing cards that were distributed to the American soldiers who were charged with hunting them down. By this definition, which was that of national security interests in the uniformed military, CIA, and State Department, regime change would be complete when Saddam and his cronies were ousted and replaced by the next strongman. Doubting that Iraq was fertile terrain for cultivating democracy, decapitationists were content to stitch a new head onto the body of the old regime. The army "assumed that after the removal of Saddam, the Coalition would recall the Iraqi army to help with both the maintenance of order and the reconstruction of the country while removing only the highest echelon of the Baathist leadership."[47] The rest of Saddam's regime would endure and continue with the business of stamping out democratic embers. Change would occur only at the very top, which is why decapitationists were *not* regime-changers. The regime would survive.

Rumsfeld's ambitions were modest because he reckoned that the prospects for liberal democracy were dim. He set forth the logic of decapitation in his memoir: "A nation that had suffered under decades of dictatorial rule was unlikely to quickly reorganize itself into a stable, modern, democratic state. Deep sectarian and ethnic divisions, concealed by a culture of repression and forced submission to Saddam, lurked just below the surface of Iraqi society. I hoped Iraq would turn toward some form of representative government, but I thought we needed to be clear-eyed about democracy's prospects in the country."[48] Wanting "an Iraqi face" for American administration, he continued:[49]

> Our strategy was not to create (for the first time in its history) a noncorrupt, prosperous democracy, with all the protections afforded by due process. Such goals were desirable, but not within the limits of American capabilities or patience. Because Iraq would be plagued for years by some level of violence, ethnic tensions, and a poor economic infrastructure, I thought our strategy should be to try to contain those problems and build up the abilities of Iraqis to deal with them so that they could manage their own affairs and not be a security problem for the region, the United States, or our allies.[50]

Translated, Rumsfeld expected that Iraqis would have to be repressed after Saddam was deposed, and he meant to leave the job to the apparatuses that Saddam had devised for that purpose.

A year and a half into the war, National Security Advisor Condoleezza Rice articulated the same vision. "The concept was that we would defeat the army, but the institutions would hold, everything from ministries to police forces. . . . You would be able to bring new leadership but that we were going to keep the body in place."[51] Tony Blair, who at various times endorsed the other two visions of regime change too, alluded to the decapitationist vision when he later was called to explain his policies to a parliamentary committee. "[Y]ou would remove the top level but you would have a functioning system underneath it."[52]

Stephen Hadley, Rice's successor as national security advisor, explained what went wrong with decapitation a few years after the invasion: "[T]he administration has discovered that changing regimes was a lot easier than changing habits."[53] Regimes in this view are distinct from culture, society, and institutions—what Hadley calls "habits"—and changing them involves simply peeling away a thin stratum of people. Bush and Tenet voiced a similar understanding when they characterized the attempt to kill Saddam by surgical bombing attacks at the opening of the war as a stab at regime change.[54] So did the US military when it described the attacks on Saddam that launched the war as an attempt at "decapitation."[55] Essentially, Rumsfeld, the CIA, the National Security Council, and senior military officers wanted to fire the coach and keep the team, which would have allowed the United States to minimize its commitments, maintain regional stability, and make few waves.

Decapitation would be followed by recapitation, the attaching of a new head onto the old body. The CIA, according to Under Secretary of Defense for Policy Douglas Feith, argued that Saddam "should be replaced by another Baathist military strongman."[56] "Without someone strong," wrote Chief of Staff Shelton, "the Kurds, the Sunnis, and the Shia would immediately be at one another's throats and the place would turn into a rabble; it would break out into civil war."[57] The CIA and military reflected serious intellectual traditions about the sources of liberal democracy. The absence in Iraq of the usual preconditions of liberal democracy—a tradition of constitutional government, rule of law, and individual rights; middle classes that were independent of the state; common national identities; and an economy organized on the basis of markets—weighed against instituting liberal democracy successfully. Plus, the power politics of the region, according to national security bureaucracies, favored installing a strongman who would perform the essential services of warding off the Shi'i theocracy in Iran and reassuring the Sunni regime in Saudi Arabia. Another Sunni government was sure to be received poorly by Iraq's Shi'i majority, but paradoxically its very unpopularity would reinforce the strongman's dependence on his American patrons. Trapped, he would have no alternative but to "preserve Sunni authoritarianism," reassure the Saudis, and blunt Iran's ayatollahs.[58]

Decapitationists got the power politics of indirect control. The more accountable the new government was to the Iraqi people, the less responsive it would be to American interests. If the end of the invasion was to serve particular constituencies, as the oil and Israeli theses have it, then the national security bureaucracies had to keep the new government dependent on American patronage. Distinguishing between stability and democracy, tough-minded, unsentimental decapitationists made the realistic choices. They were interested in achieving security, not in spreading liberal values, and in deposing Saddam, not in universalizing America. They were undone, however, by the contradictions between their strategy and their objective. They aimed to preserve the Ba'athist state because they counted on it to uphold order. But the decapitationist strategy required the four-fifths of the population that was disposed against the decapitated state on sectarian or national grounds to submit to what remained of the Ba'athist state after military defeat had snapped its power. The decapitationist conception of regime change, in other words, was naive.

The second image of regime change was *liberal*. Liberal hawks agreed Saddam had to go; that was their point of convergence with decapitationists. But the liberal image did not condense the regime into a single individual. Saddam was evil and intolerable, yes. He endangered American (and Israeli) security, defiled liberal values, and violated human rights, yes. But the problem was not personal, and neither was the solution. The solution to the illiberal dictatorship and the statist economy was, as Clinton, Bush II, and Blair agreed, liberal markets, institutions, and values. Regime change for liberals meant removing Saddam's oppressive government, reorganizing the economy, and establishing representative government. "Change inside Iraq," according to Clinton's national security advisor Sandy Berger, would "make it easier for its people to focus their energies on commercial cooperation."[59] It was not enough, therefore, to replace Saddam with a milder, more pro-American and less anti-Israeli autocrat, after the fashion of Rumsfeld, Rice, and the CIA. As the Iraqi Liberation Act had drawn the picture in 1998, "the policy of the United States [is] to support efforts to remove the regime headed by Saddam Hussein from power in Iraq and to promote the emergence of a democratic government to replace that regime."[60]

The liberal sense of regime change pictures Iraqis as raring to govern themselves once Saddam's instruments of domination were dismantled. Answering universal stirrings for freedom, liberal regime change equates democratization with liberalization and marketization. It cast the well-nigh-universal desire for popular sovereignty as equivalent to the substance of Western liberalism, and eased liberals into believing that because Iraqis wanted power, humane government, and human rights, they also wanted market capitalism, individualism, and secularism. Blair invoked this image a week into the war. "I have no doubt at all that the vast majority of ordinary Iraqi people are desperate for a better and different future, for Iraq to be free, for its government to be representative of its people, for the human rights of the people to be cared for. And that is why, though of course our aim is to rid Iraq of weapons of mass destruction and make our world more secure, the justice of our cause lies in the liberation of the Iraqi people. And to them we say, we will liberate you. The day of your freedom draws near."[61] Although Blair's statement sounds like boilerplate cheerleading—he hardly would expound on the virtues of the Ba'athist generals that he intended to install in power in his decapitationist moments—Blair was cheering for a war that he elected precisely because he expected it to liberalize Iraq. It never occurred to him, Blair later confessed, that Iraqis would reject their liberation.[62]

The decapitationist and liberal images were used interchangeably by some hawks, even though they differed in sensibility and ambition. But the two versions did agree that Saddam's dictatorship could be removed more or less surgically. Although Saddam was malignant, he had not metastasized throughout the Iraqi body. Either the leader could be replaced and the state mostly preserved, as per the decapitationists, or the state could be changed without rupturing society, as per the liberals. In this spirit, Bush treated the decapitationist and liberal conceptions of regime change as one and the same when he spoke about his plans for Afghanistan: "We would put boots on the ground, and keep them there until the Taliban and al Qaeda were driven out and a free society could emerge."[63] By marked contrast to the first two images of regime change, neoconservatives envisioned transforming Iraqi society, culture, and economy along with the Iraqi state. Change had to be in root and branch, thorough and institutional. Iraqi civilization was to be remade from top to bottom through what neoconservative Norman Podhoretz (in an article titled "World War IV") called the "benevolent transformation of the Middle East."[64] Neoconservative regime change had to issue from without, from Americans, because neoconservatives regard regimes as values and Iraq's values were malignant. Neoconservative regime change meant changing Iraq's values.

Neoconservatives did not explicate their image of regime change. It reeked of imperial overreach and would have enraged world opinion, scared the American public, and spooked policy-makers if it had been spelled out by its advocates and grasped by their audiences. It implied a darker, unspoken vision. More ambitious, activist, and radical than the other images, the neoconservative conception of regime change insinuated that Iraqi culture and religion were the real sources of Iraq's problem. Liberals, although expecting regime change to free Iraqis, allowed that Iraqis might need to learn how to cope with freedom after the horrors of Saddam and might need help in developing institutions to coordinate their spontaneous energies. But these were transitional issues that would be solved through experience. The point of the neoconservative image was that Iraqis could not be trusted to express themselves freely. The source of Iraq's problem was not Saddam or his government. It was Iraqi culture and Muslim civilization. Americans had to remake both before Iraqis could be allowed to govern themselves democratically.

Neoconservatives said they wanted liberal democracy, and most probably believed their rhetoric. But they also said that Arab societies were diseased, rejected modernity, and, in the refrain of the time, "hate us for who we are." Bush II, like Clinton, pronounced Muslim societies as wholly compatible with democracy,[65] and insinuated that those questioning the suitability of liberalism to Muslim societies were bigoted. Yet beneath the surface, neoconservatives presented Islam as inimical to liberal society and implied that radical cultural transformation was the precondition of instituting liberal democratic capitalism in Iraq. David Frum, Bush's speechwriter and the author of the phrase "axis of evil," and Richard Perle, the patron of the neoconservative foreign policy establishment and a bridge between neoconservative policy-makers and ideologues, pressed the neoconservative charge in a 2004 book they wrote together. By their diagnosis, "the Islamic world has lagged further and further behind the Christian West; since 1948, it has repeatedly been humiliated even by once disdained Jews. These defeats and disasters have been more than a wound to Muslims. They have directly challenged the *truth* of Islam itself."[66]

Frum and Perle open with a plausible historical point. Islamic societies, especially in the Middle East, did lose power to secularized Christian powers. Once powerful players in parts of Europe, Islamic powers were defeated, colonized, carved into pieces, and humiliated in the nineteenth and twentieth centuries. They remained weak even after they attained independence, according to Frum and Perle, not because of the misdeeds of the West but because of Islam. Islam for them was not a trait the weak societies happened to share. It was what made them weak. "[T]he roots of Muslim rage are to be found in Islam itself."[67] Islam, moreover, was not the only problem vexing Arabs. Frum and Perle indict Arab nationalism too.

Although they do not spell out what follows logically, the conclusions are clear. If Arab nationalism and Islamic culture are the sources of Arab failure, and if Arab failure fuels violence against the United States, then representing Iraqis in a democratic government must endanger American security. The liberal image of regime change is representative in character; the neoconservative is transformative. For liberals, government represents people and interests that arise in society, culture, and economy. For neoconservatives, however, Islam causes the failures that the United States must rectify. Therefore, Iraq could not be changed from within. Radical Islam grows not only in oppressive societies but in liberal ones too. "All the available evidence," Frum and Perle write, "indicates that militant Islam commands wide support, and even wider sympathy, among Muslims worldwide, including Muslim minorities in the West."[68] To excise the malignancy, the United States must eradicate whatever obstructed liberalism, and that, as shown by prevalence of illiberal Muslims in the liberal West, was not just despotic Arab regimes but Islam itself.

Not wanting to admit the burdens they were imposing on the United States, Frum and Perle looked to Iraqi exiles for help. "Saddam's terror drove a generation of Iraqi intellectuals and political leaders into exile. There they saw that almost every Arab political grouping supported their persecutor. . . . The effect was to alienate many of the Iraqi exiles from the rest of the Arab world—and liberate them from its dogma: not only Baathism, but also Marxism, Islamism, even nationalism."[69] Neoconservatives, in other words, favored government by exiles precisely because exiles were estranged from Arab political traditions, because, as outsiders, they were *unrepresentative* of Iraqis. It remains unexplained, however, how exiles whose primary virtue was that they had severed their connections with Iraqi traditions would govern, how they would garner support, and how they would induce obedience.

Frum and Perle, then, assert that failing Arab societies "challenge the truth of Islam." They note that "no nation poses a more comprehensive challenge to the vision and ambition of radical Islam than the United States."[70] They also regard the United States as threatening not only Islamic radicals, but also the whole rotten, failing, Islamic, Arab nationalist order. If, therefore, the United States had installed a government that represented Iraqi society in classically liberal democratic fashion, it would have failed Iraqis and reproduced the threat to America. The conclusion of the neoconservative argument laid undeveloped, exerting its influence fitfully but forcefully. Regime change required neutralizing effective self-government in Iraq and increasing American power. Whatever goals they professed, neoconservatives instigated a train of events that, by breaking state power in the middle of the oil patch, created the need for prolonged American occupation of Iraq. During the run-up to the war, Colin Powell had invoked the "Pottery Barn" rule. If the United States breaks Iraq, he warned, it would own it.[71] In effect, neoconservatives turned Powell's logic around. Although they said they wanted democracy, their policies broke Iraq and required ongoing American governance.

Blinded by the Light

Regime-changing hawks, especially liberals and neoconservatives, regarded themselves as committed democrats and tough-minded masters of power. Actually they were captives of the axioms. Having postulated American ideals as universal and liberalism as naturally and spontaneously ordering, regime-changers broke Iraq's civic order, already fragile and unpopular, but without realizing the import of their actions. The official army history puts the point blandly. "Few, if any, in the White House, Department of Defense, or the US Army foresaw the impending struggle to create a new Iraq in place of the Saddam regime as the greatest challenge of [Operation Iraqi Freedom]."[72] Bush made the point more colorfully. "The degree of difficulty compared to Afghanistan in terms of the reconstruction effort, or emerging from dictatorship [in Iraq], is, like, infinitesimal."[73] That is, the US government implicitly assumed the can opener of political order in the absence of state power.

American policy-makers, of course, paid little attention to the deep logic of arguments for war. Focused on the immediate, they thought in terms of WMDs, Al Qaeda, and the dislocations that would result from the invasion, not the broad swath of Iraq's historical development or the implications of American ideology. Except for some neoconservative ideologues, hawks were not aiming to de-state Iraq by undermining the capacity of the Iraqi state to monopolize legitimate violence and control administration. The intent was not conscious. But abolishing the defining features of the Iraqi state was part and parcel of regime change. If it was to be remade by the United States, the Iraqi state had to lose its sovereign capabilities; and if it lost these, it was not much of a state. But immersed in their delusions, hawks never saw the consequences that flowed from their commitment to regime change. By the terms of the case hawks mounted against him, deposing Saddam would fracture state power; yet apart from problems of dislocation and transitions, they expected civic order to grow stronger because Iraq would become more liberal.

The United States, in other words, attacked the defining attributes of the Iraqi state, expected to withdraw militarily without the burden of having to occupy Iraq, and then registered sincere surprise when order collapsed from 2004 to 2008. The United States made these assumptions because atheoretical, matter-of-fact, pragmatic exceptionalists assumed that civic order arises from liberal forms and that the United States is the fount of the liberal. Policymakers, at bottom, took it for granted that American ideals, being universal, would order Iraq naturally, because liberals regard order as incipient in society prior to and independently of state power. Upon this understanding, it was routine for American policy-makers to calculate troop numbers on the basis of law enforcement requirements, as if law would be present in postinvasion Iraq to be enforced.[74] Iraq might require guidance and the United States might stay longer than expected. But the complications would arise from the execution, not the design, of regime change because, by axiom, American power ordered the society even as it was disordering the state.

The United States had standard reasons for being tempted to invade Iraq. It had better reasons for not invading. Acquiring oil, establishing energy markets, helping Israel, improving its geopolitical position, and imposing the conditions of the neoliberal regime were tempting. If the United States had achieved this agenda, or even if it had offered plausible scenarios that would explain why achieving the agenda was likely, the self-interested case for war might hold. But instead of pursuing its geopolitical and economic interests in Iraq directly, the United States pursued them under the guise of universal liberal values. Ideology, alas, turned against its master.

Originally policy-makers wanted power in Iraq for conventional geopolitical and neoliberal purposes. But in idealizing American interests policy-makers both changed the content of the interests and blinded themselves to the import of their values.

Logically, if American values are interests and interests are served by spreading values, then it should not matter whether the United States sees itself as acting on its interests or on its values. They already had been pronounced to be one and the same. But politically the two are worlds apart. By asserting that universal ideals coincide with particular American interests, the United States confused its self-interest with universal values, and then it translated its acts of self-interest into gifts to the world. Exceptionalist alchemy, therefore, interpreted the paraphernalia of expanding American power—such as going to war—as the means of American altruism. Thoroughly idealized, policy-makers never anticipated that American power would be resisted. In fact, the axioms so blinded elites that they could not understand what went wrong in Iraq even when they had the benefit of hindsight. The axioms bushwhacked American policy-makers.

3

What Went Wrong

THE DECAPITATIONIST CONSENSUS OF WASHINGTON ELITES

Worldly wisdom teaches that it is better for reputation
to fail conventionally than to succeed unconventionally.

John Maynard Keynes

At first the war in Iraq seemed to be going swimmingly. Within weeks the United States captured Baghdad with few casualties, Iraq's army melted away, Saddam ducked into hiding, the United States declared victory, Bush staged a celebratory landing on an aircraft carrier, and neoconservatives debated publicly whether the next target for regime change should be Iran or Syria. Saudi Arabia was mentioned too. Soon, however, victory turned into "fiasco" (to use the title of an influential book on the subject). As dreams of regime change in Iraq soured from 2004 to 2007, political and foreign policy elites drew on military and intelligence assessments of the cause of the failure to formulate a clever, plausible, and flexible consensus about what went wrong, why it had gone wrong, and who was—and was not—to blame. Their views, which will be called Elite Consensus (EC), can be boiled down to ten tenets.

The first tenet is that the war should have been won. In some versions, it was won. But the administration, to quote the title of another book, squandered victory.[1] Not all versions of the EC agreed that the war should have been fought, although most did. But the price of admission into the Consensus was agreeing the war would have succeeded if senior officials in the Bush administration had listened to the advice of security elites. Thomas Ricks, the most trenchant journalistic critic of the period between the decision to go to war and the implementation of new counter insurgency (COIN) strategies in late 2006, begins his book *Fiasco: The American Military Adventures in Iraq* with the proposition that the war was winnable. "The U.S.-led invasion was launched recklessly, with a flawed plan for war and a worse approach to occupation. Spooked by its own false conclusions about the threat [of WMDs and Saddam's nexus with Al Qaeda], the Bush administration hurried its diplomacy, short-circuited its war planning, and assembled an agonizingly incompetent occupation. None of this was inevitable."[2] James Fallows, a critic before the war was launched, agreed that the outcome could have been different. America's political and military leaders "let the occupation fail."[3] Larry Diamond, an expert on the processes of democratization who had been dispatched by Condoleezza Rice to Iraq in early 2004 to help build democracy, observed that the situation was "difficult" but not "hopeless."[4] It was salvageable. Fareed Zakaria, a hawk turned critic, recited the shibboleth: "The chaos in Iraq was not inevitable."[5]

CIA Director George Tenet (a Clinton appointee whom Bush retained) wrote that the "true tragedy of Iraq is that it didn't have to be this way."[6] "The opportunity to take hold of the situation," claimed Ricks, "slipped between the fingers of the Americans."[7] The insurgency was "not preordained," according to Michael Gordon of the *New York Times* and General Bernard Trainor.[8] John Edwards, the Democratic nominee for vice president in 2004 and a candidate for the Democratic presidential nominations in 2004 and 2008, concurred. If "the war in Iraq [had] been executed the way that it should have been executed, I think there would be a much greater likelihood of there being a democratic Iraq."[9] The point of departure was implicit but understood. If the way the war was fought and the way the occupation was conducted are what turned victory into defeat, then the problem was not *that* the United States went to war.

The second tenet is that the occupation failed because the United States did not *plan* for it. The trouble began, according to Ricks, with "perhaps the worst war plan in American history. It was a campaign plan for a few battles, not a plan to prevail and secure victory. Its incompleteness helped create the conditions for the difficult occupation that followed."[10] Expecting to be greeted as liberators, the United States was unprepared for adversity.[11] According to Gordon and Trainor (a *New York Times* hawk and a retired general), the Defense Department did not bother with what it would do after it got rid of Saddam. "Bush, Cheney, Rumsfeld, and Tommy Franks," they wrote, "spent most of their time and energy on the least demanding task—defeating Saddam's weakened conventional forces—and the least amount on the most demanding—rehabilitation of and security for the new Iraq."[12] Franks, the general in charge of planning and conducting the invasion, did not think that it was his job to plan for governing Iraq after the invasion; the responsibility belonged to someone else.[13] "Instead of making plans to fight a counterinsurgency, the president and his team drew up plans to bring the troops home and all but declared the war won."[14] Peter Galbraith, a hawk from an impeccable liberal lineage, sang the same song: "The Bush Administration assumed the transition from Saddam Hussein's Sunni Arab dictatorship to a stable new order in Iraq would be easy—so easy, in fact, that no real planning would be required. Many of the United States's present difficulties in Iraq are the direct consequence of the failure to plan for the day after U.S. troops entered Baghdad."[15]

British intelligence's Downing Street memo, which was written in July 2002, reported that "there seemed to be little deliberation among the Americans of what to do after Saddam was toppled."[16]

Powell complained to Bush before the war that too little planning had been devoted to the aftermath of the invasion.[17] Alastair Campbell, Tony Blair's former communications chief and close advisor, agreed. "I don't think the aftermath was as well planned as it should have been."[18] Galbraith, who served as an advisor to the Kurds, complained about the "casual—almost lackadaisical—approach to the staffing of the U.S. occupation."[19] "The Administration prepared so little for postwar Iraq that it had no idea what it didn't know."[20] Echoing the point, Tenet writes: "What never happened, as far as I can tell, was a serious consideration of the implications of a U.S. invasion. . . . [T]here was precious little consideration, that I'm aware of, about the big picture of what would come next."[21] Larry Diamond concluded that "the truly cardinal sin was going to war so unprepared for the post war. . . . [T]his was negligence on a monumental scale, what is called in the law 'gross negligence,' or 'criminal negligence.' I do not use the terms lightly."[22] The US military, according to Ricks, did not prepare a "road map for attacking the insurgency" until August 2004—more than a year after invading.[23] Geoff Hoon, the United Kingdom's minister of defense, conceded, "We didn't plan for the right sort of aftermath."[24] The official army history agreed. Some tensions "were going to be released as soon as Saddam Hussein's ironclad grip on Iraqi society was destroyed, regardless of Coalition military or political actions. . . . Nevertheless, it is clear that the United States did not sufficiently plan for . . . post-Saddam Iraq."[25] Mitt Romney, in his 2008 campaign for the Republican presidential nomination, said the same thing. "I think we were underprepared and underplanned for what came after we knocked down Saddam Hussein."[26]

The third tenet is that the United States committed too few troops to secure Iraq after defeating Saddam. Neoconservatives and liberal bloggers, politicians and writers, all hawks and many doves, Republican presidential candidates in 2008 and the Democratic presidential nominee in 2004, and, most influentially, senior officers

in the US military blamed American failures in Iraq on the shortage
of American troops. Bob Woodward, the oracle of conventional wisdom in Washington, said so.[27] So did Larry Diamond and L. Paul
Bremer, who was put in charge of the political side of the occupation a month after the fall of Baghdad.[28] Bremer wanted to double the number of troops.[29] The uniformed military, along with Colin Powell and John McCain, demanded more troops, especially
officers on the ground. Said James A. (Spider) Marks, who had
served as the chief intelligence officer for the land war, "My position is that we lost momentum and that the insurgency was not
inevitable. . . . We had momentum going in and had Saddam's forces
on the run. But we did not have enough troops."[30]

Early hawks, like liberal George Packer and neoconservative
Robert Kagan, made the point repeatedly.[31] Josh Marshall, another
erstwhile hawk, concurred. "For what it's worth, I think substantially more troops would have made a big difference earlier on."[32]
Thomas Friedman drew the obvious link between the second and
third tenets (and contributed a dose of helpful stereotyping). The
"Bush team [arrived] in Iraq with too few troops and no plans. . . .
And therefore the natural tribalism of Iraqis surfaced and the minimal trust between citizens needed to forge a real democracy never
emerged. Now we have a tit-for-tat civil war."[33] "Clearly," according to the army history, "the Coalition lacked sufficient forces on
the ground in April 2003 to facilitate, much less impose, fundamental political, social, and economic changes in Iraq."[34]

The fourth tenet pins blame, and starts with Donald Rumsfeld.
Delighting in recounting incompetence after incompetence, Consensus accounts saddled Rumsfeld with the responsibility for "undermining the formulation of the war plan," "the lapse in the planning," and allocating too few troops.[35] "In Washington," according
to his biographer from the *Washington Post,* "much of the blame
for the mess in Iraq has fallen on Rumsfeld. He had failed to plan
adequately for the occupation, was slow to develop a counterinsur-

gency campaign, and had alienated too many people with his combative, domineering personality."[36] He also was blamed for ignoring expert advice, preventing the United States from establishing "order on the ground," misjudging the power of insurgency, and assigning troops to defend only the oil ministry during the mass looting that followed the fall of Saddam. Then, after having concentrated as much power as possible in himself, Rumsfeld lost interest within a year.[37] "The US effort," in Ricks's assessment, "resembled a banana republic coup d' état."[38]

McCain agreed. "Rumsfeld will go down in history, along with McNamara, as one of the worst secretaries of defense in history."[39] The British made the same point. Lady Morgan, a close associate of Blair, charged: "The operation of the war and post-war planning was Donald Rumsfeld and I don't think President George Bush was running Donald Rumsfeld in the end."[40] American neoconservatives joined the chorus. Kenneth Adelman explained why his predictions of an American "cakewalk" turned out wrong: "I'm very, very fond of [Rumsfeld], but I'm crushed by his performance."[41] Rumsfeld insulted American allies, and then he expected to get more international assistance from "old Europe" because he did not want to inconvenience the American people with the costs of war.[42] Rude, abrupt, abrasive, and disrespectful, Rumsfeld humiliated senior officers in front of their subordinates. Retired officers retaliated publicly.[43]

Rumsfeld failed, according to the Elite Consensus, because he was more interested in military transformation,[44] which centered on "missile defense and space weapons," than in occupying Iraq.[45] Captivated by the shock-and-awe stage of initial combat, Rumsfeld was indifferent to the aftermath. Wanting to build the military around speed and technology, Rumsfeld did not want American soldiers ferreting out suicide bombers. Denouncing calls for more troops as the "product of old thinking, and the embodiment of everything that was wrong with the military," he recommended

125,000 troops, a number that "seemed to be pulled out of thin air."[46] "It was ludicrous," he said, "to think that it would take more forces to secure the peace than win the war."[47] Rumsfeld wanted the battle plan to favor the army he envisioned, not validate the army he was aiming to transform. Instead of confronting his dogmatism, senior officers—Franks in particular—devised strategies to flatter his vision of war and to disarm his critics. The point for Rumsfeld was to defeat the enemy; the catch is that his enemies inhabited the Joint Chiefs of Staff, the State Department, and the CIA. As Rumsfeld said during the planning for the war in Afghanistan, "Every CIA success is a DoD [Department of Defense] failure."[48]

The fifth tenet also blames L. Paul Bremer, Administrator of the Coalition Provisional Authority of Iraq from May 2003 to June 2004. He was portrayed as a loose cannon, a control freak, and a micromanager. According to Diamond, "Bremer was the captive of the same imperial hubris that had landed the United States in Iraq with a democratizing mission but no real sense of how to accomplish it."[49] Whereas his predecessor, the decapitationist Jay Garner, had spoken about packing up and clearing out within a few months, Bremer seized executive, legislative, and judicial powers for himself. He rejected talk of transferring government to Iraqi politicians, returning exiles mostly, and boasted, impoliticly, that he was the "paramount authority figure."[50] As Rajiv Chandrasekaran reported, "Bremer insisted on approving every substantive CPA [Coalition Provisional Authority] policy. . . . One staffer remarked . . . that history was repeating itself: Saddam signed off on even the most insignificant decisions because nobody else wanted to, lest they mistakenly contradict the dictator's whims. 'Nothing's changed,' the staffer said. 'We can't do anything without Bremer's okay.' "[51]

Bremer was blamed mostly for two strategic blunders. First, he de-Ba'athified the state—that is, fired members of the Ba'ath Party, ostensibly just senior ones—from thousands of state jobs. Saying he was ridding the state only of a small number of bitter-enders and violent wrongdoers,[52] Bremer's policy opened the way for Shi'as and Kurds to get rid of Sunni officials in the name of removing Ba'athists. Two problems resulted from the purge. For one, it weakened the state by removing essential personnel just when the United States was assuming responsibility for maintaining law and order, liberalizing the economy, and operating infrastructure. For another, the Ba'ath Party favored the Sunni minority and drew the bulk of its support from it. Removing Ba'athists from the state, therefore, amounted to attacking the power of Sunnis. Bremer himself conceded that his policies effectively disenfranchised Sunnis. "Almost all politically active Sunnis had been co-opted into Saddam's security services or Baath Party, or killed as traitors."[53] Doubling the bet, Bremer assigned Ahmed Chalabi—a Shi'a, the favorite of neoconservatives, the source of fabricated intelligence before the war, and, according to the CIA, a conduit to Iran—with the task of cleansing the state. Around 50,000 officials in the top four ranks were fired, out of the 900,000 or more civil servants that Saddam is estimated to have employed.[54]

Bremer's second strategic blunder, according to the Elite Consensus, was dissolving the Iraqi army in spite of furious objections from Jay Garner, the CIA, and the American military command. In abolishing the Iraqi army, Bremer repudiated promises US commanders had made to Iraqi officers that "if . . . they refused to fight they would be taken care of afterward,"[55] erased the leading symbol of national unity,[56] and eliminated the main instrument for enforcing order. In combination, de-Ba'athification weakened state administration and ruined what little remained of the economy after the double blow of Saddam's malfeasance plus international sanctions; and disbanding the army funneled disgruntled, savvy, desperate, and trained organizers into the burgeoning Sunni insurgency, which is why the British government also objected to both measures.[57] Zakaria summarizes the indictment: "During those first crucial months, Washington disbanded the Iraqi Army, fired 50,000 bureaucrats, and shut down the government-owned enterprises that employed most Iraqis. In effect, the United States dismantled the Iraqi state, creating a deep security vacuum, administrative chaos, and soaring unemployment. Iraq's Sunni elites read this as not just a regime change but a revolution in which they had become the new underclass."[58]

The sixth tenet highlights the role neoconservatives played in conceiving the war, pressing the issue before 9/11, and bungling the occupation from their perches in the Defense Department and the vice president's office. Neoconservatives were chastised for their naiveté and zealotry, for letting their passion for democracy get the better of them, and for being too idealistic. Neoconservatives, reported the liberal hawk George Packer, were motivated by "democratic idealism,"[59] and Ricks agreed. "Wolfowitz and his fellow neoconservatives [were] essentially idealistic interventionists who believed in using American power to spread democracy."[60] Jacob Weisberg, editor of the neoliberal *Slate,* called neoconservatives "freedom-sowing idealists." Graham registered their "democratic idealism," and the repentant liberal hawk Peter Beinart commended their commitment to democracy and their "moralistic" foreign policy.[61] Antiwar critics went along; James Fallows thought America fought "for largely idealistic reasons."[62]

A few critics did question whether neoconservatives were motivated by democratic idealism. Ahmed Hashim doubted neoconservatives really wanted an "economically vibrant, politically mature, free" Iraq.[63] General Anthony Zinni, retired commandant of the Marines, likewise questioned neoconservative altruism.[64] But these sentiments do not belong in the Consensus, which attributes neoconservative failings to high-mindedness. According to the Consensus, neoconservative arrogance proved their principles. As the lapsed neoconservative Francis Fukuyama put it, "There was a tendency among promoters of a war to believe that democracy was a default condition to which societies would revert once liberated from dictators."[65] Neoconservatives should have been more skeptical about Iraqis, but it was not in their nature. True believers, they were too idealistic to learn the ways of the world.

The seventh tenet faults Iraq's sectarianism for ruining America's gift. The neoconservative Charles Krauthammer blamed ancient hatreds (which he overlooked when he demanded war) for Iraq's failure. "Iraqis were given their freedom, and yet many have chosen civil war. . . . Iraq is their country. We midwifed their freedom. They chose civil war."[66] Senator Hillary Clinton picked up the point in her 2008 presidential campaign. "Our troops did the job they were asked to do. They got rid of Saddam Hussein. They conducted the search for weapons of mass destruction. They gave the Iraqi people a chance for elections and to have a government. It is the Iraqis who have failed to take advantage of that opportunity."[67] Krauthammer concluded at a time when neoconservatives were buckling, "We have given the Iraqis a republic, and they do not appear able to keep it."[68] Thomas Friedman agreed: "[W]hen people are that intent on killing each other there's not much we can do. As bad [sic] as we've performed in Iraq, what Iraqis have done to each other, and the little that other Muslims have done to stop them, is an even bigger travesty."[69] Bad people do bad things. Therefore, bad things are done because the people doing them are bad.

The eighth tenet chastises the military for lacking counterinsurgency (COIN) doctrine. Criticisms were guarded for fear of saying anything that smacked—or could be interpreted as smacking—of criticism of the troops, but military sources initiated most of the criticisms. Ricks catalogs them in his two books on the war and occupation. Injected into the EC through General David Petraeus and younger officers experienced in Iraq, the critique argued that American strategies and tactics were ill-suited to fighting the Sunni insurgency in Iraq. The problem, military critics maintained, was that the United States was conducting the occupation through conventional military means instead of deploying counterinsurgency methods.[70] Committed to minimizing American casualties, the US military treated Iraqi civilians as potential enemies and soon created more enemies than it eliminated. With every "success," the United States lost ground. Petraeus's critique of American military methods served the needs of the EC perfectly. In ascribing American failures to defective *techniques* and in advocating the adoption of COIN strategies, Petraeus glided over the decision to go to war (although he let journalists divine that he seriously questioned it).[71] Accepting the fact of war (as was his duty under the US Constitution), he concentrated on methods, procedures, and policies for fighting it. What mattered was the how of the war, not the what.

The EC reached its crescendo in the ninth tenet. It blamed the fiasco on Bush (and later Cheney) personally. Bush suppressed essential questions about troop levels, planning, and objectives. He appointed the officials that mismanaged the war. He tolerated debilitating bureaucratic infighting and confusion. He did not know the differences between Shi'as and Sunnis. Frank Rich castigated Bush's "avoidable bungling of Iraq."[72] Bush was a "plunger," wrote the neoliberal Jacob Weisberg.[73] A decade later Maureen Dowd praised Bush's motives but repeated the refrain about his incompetence. "President George W. Bush meant well when he tried to start a domino effect of democracy in the Middle East and end the awful hypocrisy of America coddling autocratic rulers. But the way he went about it was naïve and wrong."[74]

Neoconservatives jumped aboard. A year into the occupation, Robert Kagan complained that Bush "continues to tolerate policymakers, military advisors and a dysfunctional policymaking apparatus that are making the achievement of his goals less and less likely. He does not seem to demand better answers, or any answers, from those who serve him."[75] Richard Perle explained, "Huge mistakes were made, and I want to be very clear on this: They were not made by neoconservatives, who had almost no voice in what happened, and certainly almost no voice in what happened after the downfall of the regime in Baghdad."[76] William Kristol agreed. He snipped about one administration decision, "Because it's the Bush administration. Maybe you haven't noticed—they're not the most competent at executing the war."[77] Neoconservatives had demanded the war; the war was going badly; it could not be their fault; therefore, Bush was to blame. Democrats made the same point. Rahm Emanuel, a backer of the war in 2002 (before he entered Congress) and soon to become the chairman of the House Democratic Caucus, gave the sound bite. "The Army won the war. George Bush lost the peace."[78] Of course, in getting himself and like-minded Democratic hawks off the hook, Emanuel (legendary for his hyperpartisanship) let the Republican Party off it too.

The EC respected one sovereign imperative. The war in Iraq might have turned out badly, but elites could not be blamed. Consequently, the fiasco had to stem from the manner of execution, not from the war that they had endorsed. Joe Biden, who voted for the war when he was chair of the Senate Foreign Relations Committee, got the stakes. "I never figured on the absolute incompetence of the administration. . . . If I knew Cheney and Rumsfeld so wholly possessed the president's attention, I never would have voted for that."[79] Senator Clinton, who also had voted in 2002 in favor of a war that had become deeply unpopular in the party whose presidential nomination she was seeking in 2008, hit the same note. "[T]his is George Bush's war. He is responsible for this war. He started the war. He mismanaged the war. He escalated the war."[80] And again: "I think it's the height of irresponsibility and I really resent it—this was [President Bush's] decision to go to war, he went with an ill-conceived plan, an incompetently executed strategy, and we should expect him to extricate our country from this before he leaves office."[81] With Bush tolerating "devastating incompetence" and ignoring "paralyzing bureaucratic conflict," Packer issued the conclusion: "No one really was in charge of Iraq."[82]

Bush's decision-making processes were confused, arbitrary, secretive, impulsive, and dysfunctional. According to Galbraith, "The Bush Administration's grand ambitions for Iraq were undone by arrogance, ignorance, and political cowardice."[83] Packer, with the incidental consequence of absolving himself of culpability for selling the war, noted, "By sheer fecklessness, confusion, and ignorance, the administration in Washington and the occupation authority in Baghdad had allowed Iraq to become explosive and had then triggered the detonator themselves."[84] Frank Rich, the paragon of cultural liberalism, agreed. If Bush had been a real man, the United States might have won. "If Mr. Bush had had the guts to put America on a true wartime footing by appealing to his fellow citizens for sacrifice, possibly even a draft if required, then he might have had at least a chance of amassing the resources needed to secure Iraq after we invaded it."[85] The Consensus succeeded brilliantly in proving that the occupation was mismanaged totally and in blaming Bush personally. Even Bush said so. "I think history is going to look back and see a lot of ways we could have done things better." "Well, no question [our] decisions have made things unstable."[86]

The tenth tenet finds salvation from the fiasco in the strategy of counterinsurgency warfare and its application in the Surge. Through improved methods, COIN salvaged America's pride, Iraq's stability, and the elite's reputation. Petraeus's purpose during his command in Iraq in 2007 and 2008 was not to rescue the reputations of hawks, but in showing how the war could be won he repaired them all the same. If Petraeus was right and the war was winnable, then blame for losing affixed to Bush and his appointees. Hawks became culpable only for assuming basic proficiency from the American government. Victory was available all along, if only Bush's team had conducted the war professionally. Of course, the acquittal comes with a codicil. If COIN was required to succeed and yet the doctrine had not been formulated when the United States went to war, then America was destined to lose the war at the time the decision was made. But the EC was not looking gift horses in the mouth.

The success of the Surge—or, more precisely, the belief of political, foreign policy, and national security elites that it was the Surge that defeated the Sunni insurgency—completed the circle of the EC. By proving that inventive strategies, flexible methods, and technical expertise could save the situation in Iraq, the Surge proved that inadequate planning, inappropriate doctrine, and bad techniques caused the fiasco. Once the United States got the how of the war right, the United States recovered. The source of American problems in Iraq, therefore, was not the war, which elites supported, but the conduct of the war, which Bush, Rumsfeld, and Bremer hijacked. The grip of the Surge on the Consensus and of the Consensus on Washington was so tight that the legend of the Surge popped up at inexplicable moments. Early in President Barack Obama's first term, for example, Maureen Dowd introduced a column on his recreational plans and the criticisms they were receiving from Republicans by invoking the EC. What doomed the United States in Iraq, she wrote, was "going to war with a phony justification, inadequate troop levels, insufficient armor, an inept Defense secretary and an inability to admit for years, deadly ones, that you needed counterinsurgency experts."[87]

The Elite Consensus proves that the Bush administration fouled up the occupation miserably. But its inference that incompetence was the decisive factor in American failures implies a prior, unacknowledged, and unwarranted assumption. It assumes the United States would have succeeded if only Bush had not failed, that the taproot of failure was not the objective of regime change in Iraq, with whatever that entailed, but merely the administration's inept efforts. Necessary conditions, however, differ from sufficient conditions, and the Elite Consensus erases the difference. Yes, good planning might have been a necessary condition of success; and, yes, bad planning might have been sufficient to cause failure. But while bad planning could ruin a potentially successful enterprise, good planning was not sufficient to guarantee success. If the enterprise was misbegotten from its conception, then concentrating on the means is misleading and incomplete.

The EC, by highlighting the administration's manner of making and implementing decisions, preempted questions about the import of regime change. Making the process of enacting it supreme, the actual substance receded into insignificance. Correct procedures—listening to experts, weighing alternatives, reviewing evidence, planning, proceeding pragmatically, and holding final meetings that actually decide on the course that was to be adopted—produce successful outcomes. Bad procedures produce unsuccessful outcomes. Futility in Iraq proved, therefore, that the processes were flawed. It was as simple as Bush. The United States had the winning hand; Bush misplayed the cards. The ascension of Petraeus, who personified technical expertise, and the ensuing improvement in security, proved the EC.[88]

Why the Elite Consensus Fails

If the judgment, integrity, and status of elites were to be rescued from the fiasco, the Consensus must establish that good decisions were there for the taking and that Bush did not take them. Without that foundation, it cannot be concluded that the administration's incompetence was decisive in defeating American dreams of regime change, only that amateurism made the situation worse. Bush and his officials become culpable for fracturing civic peace through wanton incompetence only if civic order was achievable before their incompetence subverted it—only if, in other words, Iraq's descent into civil war resulted from the manner of the occupation and not from the project of regime change. Unless the EC establishes the viability of alternative political strategies for the United States, the war for regime change becomes the prior cause of Iraq's grief, and hawkish elites, instead of being exonerated, become Bush's co-dependents. So what was the EC's answer?

The EC's conception of regime change, reflecting the politics of its military and intelligence sources, is decapitationist. It assumes the purpose of the war was to remove Saddam for acquiring, or striving to acquire, WMDs. That is why Ricks opened his book by observing that the Bush administration rushed to war because it took reports of Saddam's WMDs too urgently. The war for the military and CIA—and, therefore, for the EC—was about disarmament. Consequently, disbanding Iraq's army and de-Ba'athifying its state were diversions from the essential mission. But the EC suffers a major empirical shortcoming. Its predicate was that the war was meant primarily to disarm Iraq, that disbanding, de-Ba'athifying, and democratizing—the three Ds—were extraneous to the real purpose, that, in other words, regime change meant decapitation. But this version ignores both the disputes inside and outside the Bush administration about the logic of the indictment of Saddam and the case for war.

Feith records debates within the administration about the war's goals. The CIA argued with neoconservative civilians about "whether 'regime change' should mean merely a coup against Saddam Hussein or a more thorough removal of the Baathist government."[89] The CIA, the State Department, and, attesting to the utter confusion in the administration, Rumsfeld (but not his senior assistants) favored preserving Sunni hegemony, both to buttress the Saudis and other allies in the oil sheikdoms and to contain Iran. Neoconservatives countered with warnings about the risks of cozying with the remnants of the defeated regime. If the United States defeated Saddam and then "failed to take serious action against the Baath Party," neoconservatives predicted, "Iraqis who detested the regime would feel betrayed. Their outrage could give rise to an anti-Baathist bloodbath led by Kurds and Shiites, in defiance of the coalition."[90]

Debates about disbanding and de-Ba'athifying reflected underlying disagreements about whether the regime that was targeted for extinction consisted of Saddam and his cronies or, more broadly, the whole Ba'athist state that suppressed liberal rights, economic freedom, and democratic governance. It is convenient for the EC, given the interests of the political and foreign policy elites that signed on to it, to depict Bremer as inventing from thin air the idea of disbanding and de-Ba'athifying. Certainly he shocked important actors both in Baghdad and in Washington when he issued his edicts. But the ideas had circulated among policy-makers before Bremer announced them and, in fact, were discussed and debated before he even was appointed. Prior to the war, Feith had briefed Bush on the pros and cons of disbanding, and Tommy Franks had attended meetings that were meant to "clarify the policy of 'deBaathification.'"[91] Most importantly, Bremer claims that the White House, the State Department, and the Department of Defense agreed to de-Ba'athification.[92] The EC, in other words, was wrong empirically in attributing the policies of disbanding and de-Ba'athifying wholly to Bremer. Not only had they been discussed independently of Bremer, but they also were implicit in the liberal and transformative conceptions of regime change.

The EC suffers a crippling political problem too. If elites are to be exculpated for Iraq's descent into violence in the mid-2000s, the EC must establish that the Sunni insurgency was avoidable, and that it was not the predictable reaction against regime change. Accordingly, the EC depicts disbanding and de-Ba'athifying as wholly volitional, unexpected, and impulsive decisions; separates them from confusion about the meaning and content of regime change; and, most of all, ignores the possibility that the power politics of the occupation forced disbanding and de-Ba'athification onto the United States. The EC criticized de-Ba'athification, disbandment, and, later, democratization for threatening the power, status, and resources of Sunnis, and for thus provoking their insurgency. It follows, if the Sunni insurgency was the main problem and the three Ds caused it, that Bush could have avoided the insurgency by maintaining Sunni power in the state and military.[93] The EC's indictment hinges, therefore, on the political viability of conserving the essentials of Ba'athism after Saddam's demise, of decapitation.

Decapitation was infeasible for two specific reasons. First, it required the essential institutions of the Ba'athist government to cohere and sustain control over Iraq in spite of the demise of Saddam. But Saddam, as a condition of the despotism that had ruled Iraq for over twenty years, blocked viable institutions from evolving in the state, society, and, most of all, in the security apparatuses that decapitationists were looking to use for their purposes. Institutions require internalizing standards of integrity that stand independently of powers outside them. If an organization is an institution, it is not merely the instrument of power. Yet Saddam, in stuffing the military, secret police, and party leadership with his dependents, cronies, tribesmen, and relatives, deliberately thwarted the evolution of independent institutions. That was the point. As long as Saddam's clients retained his favor, they kept their positions or advanced; without it, their competence was immaterial. In fact, the very idea that appointments should be made on the basis of merit, that criteria besides Saddam's approval should count, implicitly undercut the terms of his regime. It assumed that Saddam's power was limited. Yet in spite of Saddam's penchant for using terror to enforce obedience (and to preempt institutionalization) in the organs that decapitationists meant to maintain, the EC's critique assumed that Saddam's officials could have retained their powers after the invasion snapped his powers. The puppets would govern after their puppeteer's downfall, just as Rumsfeld and Rice had hoped.

The EC faced a second, not unrelated, problem when it criticized Bremer for burying the body of the state after the head was decapitated. The core of the EC's critique was that the three Ds fanned Sunni resentment by dispersing their power. Implicitly, therefore, the EC recommended preempting the Sunni insurgency by preserving the centers of Sunni power. What the EC's sources in the military and CIA did not explain, however, was how the United States could protect the power of Sunnis without creating reactions from Shi'as and Kurds. The EC's strategy for avoiding the Sunni insurgency assumed that Shi'as and Kurds would be released from Saddam's despotism and then would disappear politically when Saddam's henchmen assumed his powers, consolidated their positions, and restored the hegemony of the Sunni minority. Yet the EC not only failed to explain why Shi'as and Kurds would forego the opportunity to seize control once the structures that had dominated them were ruptured. It also failed to recognize that the question required an answer.

The Bush administration, contrary to its depiction by the EC, did comprehend what was at issue in disbanding, de-Ba'athifying, and democratizing. Suspecting that Shi'as and Kurds would not defer to a Ba'athist restoration, and doubting that the defeated state and army could be restored anyway, the administration owned up to the choice facing it. The cleavages were not clean. Sunnis, Shi'as, and Kurds were divided internally, and none acted cohesively. Some Iraqis rejected communal politics. But even though the three largest groups were fragmented, few political parties straddled the sectarian divide between Arab Sunnis and Arab Shi'as or the national divide between Arabs and Kurds. More ominously, the militias that burgeoned after the collapse of the regime also operated within, patrolled, and embittered communal boundaries. With political loyalties tracing sectarian (or, in the case of Kurds, national) identities, the Bush administration faced a blunt choice. Either it could antagonize Sunnis, who composed about one-sixth of Iraq's population, or it could antagonize Shi'as and Kurds, who composed upward of 80 percent.

Bremer, backed by Bush, made the realistic choice. Better, it was decided, to empower Shi'as and Kurds at the risk of provoking Sunnis than to provoke the majorities that had been unshackled from Saddam.[94] Disbanding, de-Ba'athifying, and democratizing augured badly for the Sunni minority, but they addressed political realities in post-Saddam Iraq, as Bush understood. "Had the Shia concluded that we were not serious about ending the era of the Baath Party," he wrote in his memoirs, "they may have turned against the coalition, rejected the goal of a unified Iraqi democracy, and aligned themselves with Iran."[95]

The EC was articulated by national security interests that shared the priorities of Bush I. The senior Bush had refrained from marching to Baghdad after expelling Iraq from Kuwait in Gulf War I in part because the UN had not authorized the American-led coalition to overturn Saddam's regime. But Bush I held back mostly because he mistrusted Shi'as due to their affinities with Iran and Kurds due to their secessionist preferences. Both portended instability in the region. Thus, even though Shi'as answered Bush I's appeals by rising in insurrection in southern Iraq in March 1991, he refused to support them. When Gulf War II was launched twelve years later, senior officials, including the secretary of defense, senior military officers, and the CIA, clung to the old strategy of using Saddam's security apparatuses as stabilizing forces, which is why they opposed the three Ds.

In envisioning post-Saddam Iraq as a bulwark in Iraq against Iran and as an ally for Saudi Arabia, national security bureaucracies took for granted that decapitation was the war's objective. Rumsfeld's memoirs, as if intent on confirming the EC's portrait of him, dismissed Bush's talk of democracy as uninformed. "Bringing democracy to Iraq had not been among the primary rationales. It was hard to know exactly where the President's far-reaching language about democracy originated. . . . Bush often expressed his belief that freedom was the gift of the Almighty. He seemed to feel almost duty-bound to help expand the frontiers of freedom in the Middle East."[96] Oddly, many liberals agreed with Rumsfeld. In spite of the record to the contrary, they later accused Bush of endorsing democracy in Iraq only *after* Saddam was shown to have disarmed before the war. John Ikenberry summarizes their point. "As the Iraq war turned into a protracted and costly struggle, both the rationale for the American presence in Iraq and the aim of the war on terrorism shifted substantially. The Iraq war was less about relinquishing Iraq of its weapons of mass destruction than about bringing freedom and democracy to the Middle East."[97] But this account overlooks what Mearsheimer and Walt recognized. Democracy was baked into the administration's sense of regime change from the outset.

Take, for example, Bush's speech to the UN General Assembly on September 12, 2002, which made clear both his intent to go to war and his objectives. "The United States has no quarrel with the Iraqi people, who have suffered for too long in silent captivity. Liberty for the Iraqi people is a great moral cause and a great strategic goal. The people of Iraq deserve it and the security of all nations requires it. Free societies do not intimidate through cruelty and conquest and open societies do not threaten the world with mass murder. The United States supports political and economic liberty in a unified Iraq."[98] A month later Bush reiterated his commitment to installing liberal values and institutions in Iraq: "America believes that all people are entitled to hope and human rights, to the non-negotiable demands of human dignity. People everywhere prefer freedom to slavery; prosperity to squalor; self-government to the rule of terror and torture. America is a friend to the people of Iraq. Our demands are directed only at the regime that enslaves them and threatens us. When these demands are met, the first and greatest benefit will come to Iraqi men, women and children."[99]

In invoking the conjunction of outlaw regimes and WMDs as the danger and in identifying democracy, markets, and liberal values as the answer, Bush was reading from both the doctrine of preemption and from his predecessor's speeches. Clinton likewise invoked WMDs in calling for regime change when he explained why he ordered military strikes against Iraq in December 1998. "The best way to end that threat, once and for all, is with a new Iraqi Government, a government ready to live in peace with its neighbors, a government that respects the rights of its people. . . . . And mark my words, he will develop weapons of mass destruction. He will deploy them and he will use them."[100] Bush and Clinton, then, spoke not of decapitating the head of the oppressive regime while preserving its body. They said that they meant to abolish the regime that sought the WMDs, that violated the basic rights and liberties of the Iraqi people, and that prevented peace in the region. The war's "strategic objective," as the official army history records, "was to destroy the Baathist regime."[101]

The EC, in other words, got Bush's intentions exactly wrong. It accused him of conjuring democratic justifications because he came up empty-handed in searching for WMDs. Actually his moral case for war—and much of his political case too—stood independently of the national security case. By Bush's logic, the United States should have gotten rid of Saddam even if his WMDs were not threatening Americans directly because he was killing hundreds of thousands of "his" people, was destabilizing the region, was thwarting democratic transformation, and, therefore, was endangering America in the most fundamental sense. Bush's charges about the dangers that Saddam's WMDs posed, or would have posed if Saddam had acquired them, presented a war that was meant to project American power and to facilitate liberalism as defensive. Deploying the specter of WMDs convinced public opinion that Saddam imperiled Americans. But the deeper threat by Bush's logic was the regime's illiberalism. Getting rid of Saddam's regime meant, therefore, getting rid not just of him personally but also of the regime that blocked freedom—understood liberally—in Iraq.

Consequently, the EC's explanations for why political and foreign policy elites were innocent of responsibility for the fiasco—that Bush redefined American objectives and eviscerated the Iraqi state unexpectedly and unnecessarily because he discovered Saddam already had dismantled his WMDs—actually implicate the very elites that the EC was shaped to exonerate. Not only did Bush justify the war all along on the grounds that illiberal regimes with WMDs endanger American security, and not only did Bush (and Clinton) call explicitly for liberal regime change, belying EC claims that American policy spun in unimagined directions, but indicting the Bush administration for disbanding, de-Ba'athifying, and democratizing implies that Ba'athist rule was sustainable after Saddam's power was broken.

If eliminating Saddam's WMDs was the real aim of the war, then the war was winnable, the objectives were achievable, and the conflicts engendered by disbanding, de-Ba'athifying, and democratizing were unnecessary. But the conflicts were avoidable only if regime change clearly meant decapitation, and even then only if Shi'as and Kurds could have been empowered without threatening Sunnis or disempowered without threatening the occupation. If, however, Shi'as were bent on demanding their share of state resources, or more, and Kurds on demanding their cut too, and if both Shi'as and Kurds were committed to reorienting Iraq's national identity from the Arab nationalism that Sunnis expected, which allied Iraq with Sunni states and reflexively opposed Iran, then Shi'as and Kurds were destined to resist decapitationist policies. And if decapitation was unsustainable in practice, the EC fails as explanation. What went wrong was not fundamentally the manner by which the war was fought. It was the project of regime change.

Narrowing the Lessons

The Elite Consensus described what went wrong in Iraq in rich detail and with acuity. As description, it is compelling. As explana-

tion, it is deficient. Inhabiting a world devoid of unintended consequences, its method was to identify a problem and then insinuate
that different policies would have averted that problem (and, apparently, all others too). When the invasion was launched, the US
military lacked counterinsurgency doctrine, a point lamented by
the EC. Conducting the occupation like a standard military operation, the US military shifted risks to Iraqi civilians as a consequence
of minimizing American casualties, used maximum available (as
opposed to minimum necessary) force, and ignored the niceties of
Iraqi customs, including gender norms. Until Petraeus revived and
rewrote American COIN doctrine in 2007, the American manner of
fighting the war antagonized Iraqis, as the EC recognized. Yet the
EC adamantly demanded more troops even though more troops
acting in the absence of proper COIN doctrine and training would
have meant, by the logic of counterinsurgency doctrine, more inci-
dents with Iraqi civilians, more reprisals against Americans, and
more counterreprisals against Iraqis.

The contradiction between recommendations for more troops
and the EC's larger critique that the United States lacked effective
COIN doctrine is a particular instance of the general conceptual failure. All three versions of regime change identified Saddam with the
state, and all aimed at his ruin. They implied, therefore, that deposing Saddam meant breaking state power in Iraq. Yet even though
Consensus accounts plotted the dots, they did not see the picture.
They record deliberate American policies. Packer observed, "One
of the most hierarchical, top-down state systems on earth had
been wiped out almost overnight, and no new system had yet taken
its place."[102] Galbraith made the same point. "In 2003, the United
States . . . smashed Iraq's army and then legally dissolved the Iraqi
military, security services, and Ba'ath Party."[103] Tenet conceded, "The
critical missing element was an Iraqi government that could have
helped us. We decided instead to have Americans administer Iraq."[104]
Gordon and Trainor recognized "how much of the United States
postwar strategy was the product of careful deliberation. The failure

to organize a civilian constabulary for immediate duty in Iraq was not an oversight."[105] " 'Stability,' " Ricks concluded, "wasn't [the administration's] *goal*, it was their *target*." One of his generals ruminated, "It's almost as if, unintentionally, we were working . . . to create the maximum amount of chaos possible."[106] Yet the EC, as it relates the specifics, cannot see the general logic of destruction. It recounts particular instances of statelessness, but sees them as bugs in the execution, not features in the design, of regime change.

The EC, therefore, did not see the deep causes of the fiasco. Because it was committed to rationalizing away the responsibility of the foreign policy establishment, Congress, the media and pundits, and both political parties for advocating and endorsing war for regime change, the EC necessarily narrowed the import of the war and the lessons that were learned from it. If incompetence and mismanagement caused, or were agreed to have caused, failure in Iraq, then it follows that competent management would have brought success. Implicitly the EC counseled the United States to avoid wars for regime change that are led by inattentive and incapable leaders. But by the EC's logic, wars that are led by qualified professionals are likely to succeed. Provided that future leaders know the difference between Shi'as and Sunnis, arm themselves with good plans, and respect technical expertise, the EC vindicates interventionism.

The Obama administration demonstrates the point. Obama was elected president in large measure because of his early opposition to the war in Iraq. Yet the antiwar president rejected the obvious lessons of the misadventure in Iraq when he decided first to escalate in Afghanistan and then to intervene in Libya. In setting policy in Afghanistan, he went along with, even if he was not wholly convinced by, the claims that were made on behalf of COIN.[107] If technical mastery was the key to defeating insurgencies, and if COIN provided the techniques, then the United States could apply the methods it had honed in Iraq to defeat the Taliban in Afghanistan. Thus, after ordering an assessment of the situation in Afghanistan,

Obama went along with arguments for adopting COIN methods, endorsed escalation, and, before long, appointed Petraeus himself to lead the effort. New methods and new leadership in Afghanistan, alas, yielded familiar results. Instead of reversing the Taliban's growth, as the EC implicitly had promised when it endorsed the Surge as the solution in Iraq, the United States remained bogged in Afghanistan.

The diplomatic circumstances surrounding intervention in Libya were different from Iraq. America's European and Arab allies publicly pressured the United States to intervene in support of insurgents that were fighting Muammar Gaddafi. But Gaddafi's regime, like that of Saddam, concentrated power in the leader, repressed independent political organizations, and corroded ties among people. Thus, after tipping the balance of power toward the insurgents, the United States confronted a situation in Libya that was eerily similar to what it had beheld in Iraq. In Iraq, rival militias rose to fill the security vacuum; in Libya, militias that had allied to vanquish Gaddafi turned against each other soon after they succeeded; and in both, the state's monopolies on violence and administration were denied and violence ensued. As Libya's militias compete for control of people, territory, and oil revenue, they fight rivals that threaten to curb their independence, especially the state that wants control for itself. The pattern should have been familiar from Iraq, yet American policy-makers were caught unaware when the newly constituted Libyan state, which controlled neither violence nor administration, could not subdue the militias, establish civic order, and govern. In spite of America's experience in Iraq, in other words, the Obama administration assumed the can opener of civic order in the absence of the sovereign state.

The EC, then, acquitted political and foreign policy elites of responsibility for the fiasco in Iraq, but with costly consequences and via bad logic. The costs were exemplified in the futile escalation in Afghanistan and the unsuccessful intervention in Libya. The logic concluded that regime change failed because it was managed incompetently. But the conclusion rested on the *post hoc ergo propter hoc*—"after this, therefore because of this"—fallacy. Mismanagement in Iraq preceded failure in Iraq, but that does not mean mismanagement caused the failure. If the fallacy encouraged more futile interventions, that was the price of absolving hawks, redeeming the interests that favor wars for regime change, and refusing to think about what the real regime-changing traditions—neoconservatism, liberal hawks, and neoliberalism—meant by regime change.

4

What Were Neoconservatives Thinking?

"When *I* use a word," Humpty Dumpty said, in a
rather scornful tone, "it means just what I choose it to
mean—neither more nor less."

Lewis Carroll

What went wrong in Iraq? Incompetence and mismanagement, as
politicians, media, and foreign policy elites say? The chorus accused
the Bush administration of squandering the smashing victory the
US military won in March and April 2003. Ineptitude, according to
political and foreign policy elites, converted the resistance of a few
die-hard Saddamists into an insurgency that was supported by the
bulk of Sunni Arabs, precipitated sectarian civil war, and caused
Iraq to spiral out of control. But blaming the Bush administration
for mismanagement and incompetence obscures the prior questions: Did the Bush administration go wrong by mismanaging the
war or by *initiating* it? Was the problem with *how* the war was
waged or with *what* it was about? More fundamentally, was Iraq's
civil war of 2004–2008 an inadvertent consequence of weakening
of the state or did the neoconservatives require the dissolution of
Iraq's state and society if Iraq was to be ordered along the lines they
envisioned? If so, did the neoconservatives who demanded regime

change recognize consciously what their conception of regime change entailed actually?

Decapitationists in the national security bureaucracies were skeptical about the war, and neoliberals accepted it dutifully, but it excited neoconservatives and liberal hawks. Almost as soon as Bush I refused in March 1991 to exceed the United Nations mandate by advancing to Baghdad to depose Saddam, neoconservatives commenced grumbling. When the coup against Saddam failed to materialize, they complained about American irresolution in Iraq and scouted for fresh opportunities to display American strength. They called for intervening in Bosnia and for challenging China aggressively. They did let some opportunities pass. As they were mocking Clinton in the late 1990s as cowardly for his caution in the face of Saddam's brutality, central Africa was engulfed in war and chaos. Around 5,400,000 people, mostly in Congo, perished in the convulsions and the starvation and disease they caused from 1998 to 2003. Yet the *Weekly Standard*, a reliable guide to neoconservative priorities, published just two stories on Congo during these years. In the same time span it published 279 articles on Iraq. Neoconservatives were bent on projecting power in the Middle East, not on engaging in humanitarian do-goodism.

Always, neoconservatives returned to Iraq. They pronounced that regime change was strategically necessary, morally obligatory, and politically imperative. They worried about Saddam because he was repugnant, and also because timid and irresolute American elites were so concerned with international opinion that they renounced their rightful role of world leadership. By neoconservative reckoning, America beheld a unique opportunity for demonstrating national resolve in the 1990s. Having won the Cold War, the United States was in position to define what was right, prohibit what was wrong, and enforce both without regard to the opinions of others. But America's material power was worthless without the will to use it. For neoconservatives the point of war with Iraq was to change

Iraq's regime, whatever that meant; but it also was to fortify America's will to greatness, to change the regime of American restraint, chickenheartedness, and self-loathing. By unsheathing its warrior spirit in Iraq, America's appetites would grow, its doubts would recede, and its greatness would be unloosed.

Both amoral realists and pusillanimous multilateralists counseled the United States to dishonor, to fail its fleeting moment to write its interests and principles into the new world order. But neoconservative mania for power was permeated by streaks of irrational despair. If the United States did not seize the opportunity, neoconservatives fretted, it faced doom and disaster. Either the United States asserted its will or its nemeses would assert theirs. Fears of potential Hitlers loom large for neoconservatives because, having belittled the importance of materiality in their glorification of political will, they were left with no material counters to strongmen—like Saddam—who stare down the faint of spirit. Thus, during the years between the end of Gulf War I and the beginning of Gulf War II, neoconservatives swung from dreams of world domination to fears of dissolution. They compulsively identified enemies that were on the verge of destroying Western civilization and then, opportunistically, enlisted the dangers they were concocting to justify their ambitions. In projecting their own lust for universality onto minor despots, such as Saddam, neoconservatives were guided by one constant purpose. Whether they were motivated by dreams of grandeur or night frights, neoconservatives confronted Americans with a choice. Either Americans imposed their universality on the world, or they faced global barbarism.

William Kristol and Robert Kagan set forth the core principles, priorities, and arguments for neoconservative foreign policy in a *Foreign Affairs* article they wrote during the 1996 election campaign. Kristol and Kagan had opposed the realism of the Bush I administration, with its obsession with stability and order, alliances with oil sheikdoms, quarrels with Israel, and predilections for power politics over moral crusades. But they were not liberated to advocate aggressive foreign policies and berate the Republican foreign policy establishment until Clinton was elected in 1992. Wanting to establish America's "benevolent global hegemony," Kristol and Kagan envisioned a "foreign policy of military supremacy and moral confidence."[1] Confidence was key. "[T]he main threat the United States faces now and in the future" was not foreign enemies or even Saddam. It was "its own weakness."[2] Material power without the will to use it, they believed, was useless; and judging from their fear of Saddam, the will to power was formidable even if it was not backed by material power.

Manipulated by the Third World, paralyzed by moral relativism, and compromised by delusions of interdependence, America's power was evaporating because its will was enervating. Most Democrats and Republicans, in spite of their putative ideological and foreign policy differences, were alike in having chosen comfort, commerce, and capitulation over national greatness. Confronting this crisis of the American spirit, Kristol and Kagan demanded that the United States display will, what the classical Greeks called *thumos*. "The first objective of U.S. foreign policy should be to preserve and enhance [strategic and ideological] predominance by strengthening American security, supporting its friends, advancing its interests, and standing up for its principles around the world."[3] The United States, in other words, must assert itself partly to improve its geopolitical and ideological positions, but mainly to restore its ability to act manfully. Like Vito Corleone slapping Johnny Fontaine (the Frank Sinatra character) in *The Godfather,* neoconservatives demanded: "You can act like a man!"

Kristol and Kagan answered Bush I–style realists, who were no better than Clintonian vacillators, with the first axiom. Challenging realism directly, Kristol and Kagan denied the dichotomy between power and principles. America's "moral goals and its fundamental national interests," they observe, "are almost *always in harmony.*"[4]

Realists favor the practical over the utopian, the interest over the ideal, the friend over the value, and order over risk. But Kristol and Kagan knew better. The United States, alone among countries of the world, is not compelled by circumstances to decide between what it wants and what it values, between its interests in expanding its power and its regard for its principles. It is exempted from having to choose by "American exceptionalism."[5]

America is exceptional for two reasons. First, American power interests blend with liberal principles. The United States can devote itself to spreading its principles without impairing its power. When its principles travel, its power increases; and when its power increases, its principles soar. Acquiring power, therefore, is elevated into a normative good. But—and this is what separates neoconservatives from liberal hawks—American power is good not because universal abstractions say it is good. American power is good because *American* principles say so. Neoconservative America is not liberalism's avenger. America for neoconservatives is liberal, but not absolutely. Asserting liberal values is the occasion for asserting American power. Neoconservative America advances liberal principles because they are written into its interests, not because America is bound by universal norms. America for neoconservatives acts self-interestedly, and exceptionalism tidies up the consequences.

Second, America is exceptional for neoconservatives because the world needs American, and *only* American, values. American interests are embedded in its principles (and its principles are embedded in its power), and, as the second axiom provides, all countries benefit when America extends its principles (or its power). But America is exceptional really because its principles coincide with and serve interests that are universal. By neoconservative accounts, all people benefit when American principles are exported, much as liberals say. But neoconservatives engorge themselves on the deduction. All mainstream foreign policy traditions favor projecting American power; otherwise they could not become mainstream. But neoconservatives relish the deduction that obligates American power to expand. Dreams of conquest become "benevolent hegemony."

Up to this point Kristol and Kagan are in substantive agreement with liberals on policy. But neoconservatives are not fully liberal; they certainly are not democrats; and they absolutely are not liberal democrats on steroids, and not only because they thrill in imperialism. Liberals have imperial impulses of their own, as shown by their will to universality. Neoconservatives are not democrats because they refuse, as a corollary of their willfulness, to defer to decisions that are made democratically but that yield outcomes they reject,[6] and they are not liberal because they mean to *reverse* the trajectory of history. Liberals know that history backs them, a point Francis Fukuyama made to considerable acclaim as the Cold War was winding down. In his influential article announcing "the end of history," Fukuyama argued that the ideological conflicts that had caused unprecedented death and destruction in the twentieth century had been resolved once and for all. Fascism, Communism, and lesser ideologies lost, and market liberalism won resoundingly and permanently. Holdouts might remain. The North Koreas, Burmas, and Iraqs of the world might make nuisances of themselves. But that was beside the point for Fukuyama. What signaled the end of history is that world opinion finally agreed that the holdouts were losers. Nobody emulated them. The ideological and political triumph of liberalism was complete, and only a little mopping up remained.[7]

Fukuyama saw himself, and was seen by his associates, as a neoconservative. But the partnership, which collapsed acrimoniously over the war in Iraq, was mismatched from the beginning.[8] The point of neoconservative polemics is to induce insecurity. Fukuyama, however, bore the diametrically opposite effect. By telling Americans that they had won the ideological wars of the twentieth century, and, even better, that they never would have to fight another, Fukuyama deepened the very complacency that was anathema to neoconservatives. Convinced that history was on America's side (or America was on history's side), Fukuyama resembled Clintonian neoliberalism more closely than fearful, bipolar, dominate-or-face-extermination neoconservatism. Conflicts would continue for Fukuyama, but they would occur within the framework of liberalism. Neoconservatives, on the other hand, require pervasive danger, and their dangers are *existential*. They threaten the very existence of liberal civilization. As Donald and Fredrick Kagan, mainstays of the neoconservative foreign policy network (and, respectively, father and brother of Robert), wrote in the opening sentence of their 2000 book, *While America Sleeps: Self-Delusion, Military Weakness, and the Threat to Peace Today:* "America is in danger."[9]

Neoconservatives thrive on enemies, and the inextricability of American power interests and values provided plenty of them. Writing of the "elevated patriotism that joins interest and justice,"[10] they turned into moral imperatives the conventional interests in increasing power, helping friends, and nurturing commercial ties. By the same token, Kristol and Kagan turn adversaries, whose pursuit of power and advantage for themselves compete with American interests, into moral threats. Conflicts of interests become clashes of values. Kristol and Kagan accent themselves to be heard as saying that American power serves the good. But they also may be accented as saying that what serves American power is deemed as the good. Morality ennobles, renames, and glosses American power interests, but for neoconservatives what is deemed as universal right does not dictate to American power interests.

American interests promote American values, and American values promote the world's interests. America's ideal is liberal, capitalist democracy, and the world's interest is establishing liberal, capitalist democracies. Therefore, American principles fit the world's needs. This is the flattering formulation for neoconservatives, and it is widely accepted.[11] But the formula can be reversed, and then different implications surface. If the world's interests converge with American principles, and American principles reinforce American interests in acquiring more power, then it follows that the world has a deep interest in the expansion of American power. Democracy, which already has been made coterminous with American power, now becomes the idiom of United States imperialism. Because the people of the world want democracy, they need American military supremacy.

Neoconservatives, however, glide over a key link in their causal chain. They proceed as if American ideals are universal in applicability. Yet they recognized—albeit implicitly—that the people whom they affect to be liberating often reject American values, American principles, and American liberalism. Neoconservatives, in other words, maintain that American principles converge with the *interests,* but not necessarily with the *values,* of the people of the world. Kristol and Kagan write as if they mean to align countries everywhere with American principles for the good of all. But their existential fears, their incessant calls for more military spending, and their constant demands for military action expose the fiction. The real problem for neoconservatives, and the one they meant to correct, is the misalignment of American values with those of the people neoconservatives say they are liberating. Regime change means changing values to American specifications.

Leo Strauss and Regime Change

What did neoconservatives mean by "regime change"? They invoked the idea repeatedly, advocated war with Iraq to inaugurate it, and yet they were lax in spelling out what they meant by it. In fact, they seemed positively averse to defining it. But neoconservatives did invoke the term frequently and they did write extensively about why their targets were subjected to regime change, and this provides clues for teasing out what the term meant for them. Neoconservative regime change encompassed both the decapitationist removal of Saddam and the liberal emancipation that, as Paul Wolfowitz explained, was "trying to remove the shackles on democracy."[12] It is, perhaps, confirmation of the Elite Consensus's incompetence thesis that Wolfowitz, the administration's senior neoconservative and most zealous regime-changer, assumed the can opener of liberal democracy and never got the radicalism of the conception of regime change that he absorbed from neoconservative thinkers.

Regime change for neoconservatives meant radical transformation. It was not a matter of peeling off a layer or two of senior officials, inserting more amenable leaders, and heading home. Nor was it a matter of writing a new constitution, declaring new institutions, marketizing the economy, and letting Iraqis get on with the business of governing themselves, Wolfowitz notwithstanding. Neoliberals expected that unloosing markets would eat away at Iraqi traditions, cultures, and religion, and that Iraqi ways would bend to market realities. But neoliberals had *Iraqis* changing their society by acting economistically within structures that regime change would institute, not enacting American power interests. Neoconservatives, by contrast, drew their idea of regime and regime change from the political philosopher Leo Strauss. If they had read him carefully, however, neoconservatives might have noticed that Strauss foretold their failure in Iraq.

By the standard American account, Saddam maintained power through arbitrary violence, systematic torture, and pervasive fear. His police state was detached from Iraqis, oppressing them from without. It was because the Bush II administration conceived of Saddam's regime as standing over the people that it thought it could fight a war versus Iraq without harming Iraqis. Without that assumption, Iraqi civilians were the battlefield, and not the bystanders that Rumsfeld had announced them to be on the day after he launched hostilities. "This is not a war against a people. It is not a war against a country. It is most certainly not a war against a religion. It is a war against a regime."[13] In Rumsfeld's usage, Saddam's regime was separate and apart from Iraqis, alien to them. Because Saddam's regime prevailed only by virtue of the physical fear it instilled in its subjects, it followed that it would disintegrate the moment it lost the power to instill fear. The regime would recede into history, and Iraqis would be free. That is what Wolfowitz had in mind when he spoke of regime change as removing the shackles on Iraqi democracy. The essential idea was that the regime existed outside Iraqis, and that it coerced Iraqis to act against their wishes.

Strauss's writings, ironically, expose the impoverishment of American versions of Saddam's regime. When Bush and Rumsfeld pictured Saddam's government as external to Iraqis, they took for granted that Iraqis had not internalized the regimes that they were targeting. But regimes for Strauss are more than officials, secret police, and armies. People live *in* regimes, not under them. Allan Bloom, the influential Straussian political philosopher, called the regime "the soul of the city."[14] The regime is the spirit that makes each polity distinctive and unique, that endows it with a character of its own, that steeps its subjects in its purposes and meanings, and that educates them in what they should value, esteem, and want to become, entering into and inhabiting people.

Strauss borrowed the notion of "regime" from the classical Greek idea of *politeia*:

> We shall translate *politeia* by "regime," taking regime in the broad sense . . . of the Ancien Regime of France. . . . The character, or tone, of a society depends on what the society regards as most respectable or most worthy of admiration. . . . [E]very society regards a specific human type . . . as authoritative. . . . In order to be truly authoritative, the human beings who embody the admired habits or attitudes must have the decisive say within the community in broad daylight: they must form the regime.[15]

Strauss's regime defines what counts as good, inculcates admiration for the qualities it esteems and the figures who embody them, and promulgates the standards into which people and society are molded. "[E]very political society derives its character from a specific public or private morality . . . and this means from what the preponderant part of society (not necessarily the majority) regards as just."[16] Changing regimes, therefore, changes what counts as moral, changes who decides what is valued, and changes why some qualities are valued as moral and others are despised. In Saddam's Iraq, brutish deportment was admired; compassion was loathed as womanly. Regime change, properly understood, meant changing all that. "[T]hrough a change of regime the political community becomes dedicated to an end radically different from its earlier end."[17]

Changing regimes, Strauss understood, is more arduous than the Bush administration, neoconservatives included, recognized. Not just snapping shackles, it revamps the ends of, and the reasons for, both individual and collective life; alters all domains of society, economy, culture, and values; and changes who people are and who they aspire to become. Moreover, regime change issues from the state and those it designates as authoritative, be they thugs, financiers, or holy men. Thus, instead of aligning government with society and market, Strauss's state remakes society, economy, and culture. By Strauss's understanding of what regimes do, Saddam's brutality, sadism, willfulness, and impulsiveness had infected every nook and cranny of Iraq. The import of full neoconservative regime change, therefore, was to sweep away the old regime as part of redefining public and private standards, to define new purposes and values for individuals and peoples, and to teach and instill respect for the new regime throughout society. Whatever particular neoconservatives thought, their project of regime change took as its point of departure the fact that Iraqis were not, and could not be, incipient liberal democrats who were waiting to be uncaged from Saddam's prison. Liberals wanted Iraq's new government to represent society; neoconservatives reversed liberal causality. Changing regimes meant changing Iraq's soul.

The Subtext of the Happy Talk

David Wurmser, who was affiliated with the American Enterprise Institute before moving into the Bush II administration and eventually becoming Vice President Cheney's Middle East advisor, outlined his thoughts on regime change in a 1999 book. Flashing the standard neoconservative hysteria, he foresaw America's "looming strategic defeat" in the Middle East and discerned that Saddam could send the United States into a "free fall" [in] the Middle East.[18] In opting for regime change as the alternative to imminent American defeat, Wurmser targeted not just Saddam and the Ba'ath Party, but (like Frum and Perle) the whole Arab nationalist and Islamist orders. Saddam, by Wurmser's reckoning, was evil; Ba'athism was evil; the Arab nationalist state that produced Saddam and Ba'athism was evil; and the ayatollahs' regime in Iran was evil too. Meaning to abolish the Arab state not because Saddam perverted it but because he perfected it, Wurmser aimed at the Ba'athist version of Arab nationalism as the first ball in a combination shot. By displaying its resolve against Saddam, America next would cause the Islamist state in Iran to "wilt."[19] "Launching a policy and resolutely carrying it through until it razes Saddam's Ba'athism to the ground will send terrifying shock waves into Teheran."[20]

Bush I feared that empowering Shi'as in Iraq would benefit Iran. Wurmser knew better. It would *undermine* Islamism in Iran.[21] When Iraq's Shi'as achieve self-determination, Wurmser promised, they will "present a challenge to Iran's influence and revolution."[22] "Iran must be severed from its Shi'ite foundations. And this can be accomplished by promoting an Iraqi Shi'ite challenge."[23] In other words, Wurmser reversed the logic of decapitationists. They worried that empowering Shi'as in Iraq would provide Iran with allies. He answered that "unleashing Shi'ism in Iraq would threaten Iran's Islamic revolution more than it would threaten Saudi Arabia."[24] Wurmser never established why Iraq's Shi'as would show Iran the way forward, but he seemed to recognize them as incipient liberal secularists, who were just waiting for the opportunity to fulfill themselves.

According to Wurmser's plan, the United States would overthrow Saddam in Iraq, cut the legs off the ayatollahs in Iran, and both countries would reject both nationalism *and* Islamism. Then Wurmser took an abrupt U-turn. Instead of ushering Iraq into liberal democracy, Wurmser's regime change was to denationalize, demodernize, and deliberalize Shi'i Iraq. The assumption that Iraq's Shi'as were liberals-in-waiting, having served the purpose of silencing the geopolitical risks of war against Saddam, was abandoned. Scouring history for examples, Wurmser found his model for Iraq in the pre-nationalist, pre-Islamicist, "decentralized, loosely bound nations" of Lawrence of Arabia's time.[25] The Great Arab Revolt of 1916–1918, which was memorialized in the film, became Wurmser's "hope for the future." That is, Wurmser ditched modern liberalism in Iraq and harkened to Arab traditionalism. Freedom in the new liberal democratic Middle East was to consist of tribal leaders resuscitating the "old, traditional, and established."[26]

Of course, neoconservatives sensed that resurrecting the rule of tribal leaders across the Arab world was unfeasible, that a century of history could not be undone by an act of American will. But the significance of Wurmser's fantasies about the Arab Revolt is the ambitions they disclose. Wishing away organized political and military power in Arab world, rejecting broad, encompassing identities ("Iraqi," "Iranian," "Arab," "Muslim"), and dissolving the Iraqi people as they had evolved under the Iraqi state, Wurmser would return Arabs to their tribes, rather like apartheid had hoped to do with Africans in South Africa. The key organizations of the modern state (armies, parties, and bureaucracies) would be abolished and, not incidentally, the Middle East would be left ripe for plucking. The point of the fantasies, in other words, was the policies that ensued from them. With states broken and Arabs (and Iranians) disarmed, Middle Eastern societies would be rendered politically impotent, defenseless. Stripped to its basics, Wurmser's "freedom" amounted to imposing conditions that allowed foreign interests to act without impediment in the Muslim Middle East. It excavated the underside of the first axiom: American power interests were packaged as high democratic principles.

Bernard Lewis and the Import of Regime Change

Neoconservatives picture themselves as the intellectual vanguard of the conservative movement. Although they defer to economists on economic issues, they feature themselves as authorities on what they regard as the more sublime matters of culture, morality, and foreign policy. Their intellectual accomplishments, alas, rarely warrant their self-regard. Neoconservatives mostly work in think tanks or as pundits or journalists, often for the Murdoch media empire (with whatever constraints that imposes). They network assiduously. Their books are published by ideological presses and preach to the choir. The Kagans depart from the pattern—Donald Kagan is a distinguished authority on the Peloponnesian War and the two sons write serious histories—but the most conspicuous exception is Bernard Lewis.

After a lifetime in academics, in which he won renown as the foremost English-language historian of Islam and the Ottoman Empire, Lewis published two short, influential, and deeply political books for general readers soon after the 9/11 attacks. Both books draw on similar histories, make similar arguments, and propose similar policies. Both maintain that Islam is troubled, is struggling to adapt to modern ways, and is preoccupied with memories of the splendor it has lost. More than a religion or a culture, Islam for Lewis is a civilization, and it is failing. Other civilizations, of course, also have struggled to adapt successfully to modernity, but Islam is unusual because it once stood at the pinnacle of world civilization. Now, however, Muslim societies have been eclipsed not only by the West but also, to their unbearable frustration, by the East.

> It was bad enough for Muslims to feel weak and poor after centuries of being rich and strong, to lose the leadership that they had come to regard as their right, and to be reduced to the role of followers of the West. The twentieth century, particularly the second half, brought further humiliations—the awareness that they were no longer even the first among the followers, but were falling ever further back in the lengthening line of eager and more successful Westernizers, notably in East Asia.[27]

This disparity between Islam's illustrious history and its contemporary reality is both effect and cause of its tribulations in the modern world, and breeds particularly noxious forms of "anger," "grievance," "victimhood," and resentment at their declining fortunes.[28] "What we confront now," Lewis warned, "is not just a complaint about one or another American policy but rather a rejection and condemnation, at once angry and contemptuous, of all that America is seen to represent in the modern world."[29]

Lewis's two post-9/11 books oscillate between praise of the good Islam, as exemplified by liberally minded Muslims who are committed to learning from, and cooperating with, the West, and condemnations of the bad Islam, as exemplified by extremists, terrorists, and Osama Bin Laden. Although Lewis expressed deep reservations about what Islam has become, he also made pointed displays of sensitivity and respect. He noted that Islam contributed immeasurably to world civilization, that it treated Jewish minorities more civilly and humanely than Christian societies and rarely erupted in the paroxysms of anti-Semitism that blighted Christian history in Europe, that traditions of hospitality pervade Islamic civilization, and, finally, that Islam dignified and enriched the lives of untold millions of Muslims over the 1,400 years of its existence. If history had stopped a few centuries ago, Lewis would have crowned Islam as the champs and Christians as the chumps.

Lewis's heart roots for Western-minded liberals, but his analysis of the structure of Islam predicts that the bad Islam will prevail. As he forces himself to admit, the failures of Muslim societies, which date back three or four centuries, incite and sustain civilizational animosities. Bin Laden, from this perspective, appears as the tip of the iceberg. Islam is a failed civilization, and its root problem is not, the terrorism of some Muslims notwithstanding, how it treats other religions, but the damage it inflicts on its own. If Lewis believed that Muslim societies were failing for reasons that were independent of religion—because, for example, they had not achieved development yet or because they were disadvantaged geopolitically—he could expect them to improve their position and outgrow their anger. But Lewis implicates Islam directly. Islam is what causes Muslims to fail in the modern world.

Attributing Muslim anger to civilizational failure, Lewis takes exception to those who blame Western imperialism for the degradation of Muslim societies, most famously Edward Said.[30] Lewis does concede that Western imperialism in the early and mid-twentieth century was a "plausible scapegoat" for the decline of Islamic societies. But it was only a scapegoat. "Anglo-French rule and American influence . . . were a consequence, not a cause, of the inner weakness of Middle-Eastern states and societies."[31] Maintaining that Muslim societies were in decline before their encounters with imperialism, that the imperialist era was short and was over and done by the early 1960s, and that the United States—the main target of Islamic "anti-imperialists"—never colonized the Middle East anyway, Lewis locates responsibility for the poverty, underdevelopment, unaccountability, and corruption of Islamic societies not in the structural power of Europe and the United States but in the specific disabilities that Islam as a religion, culture, and civilization inflicts on its faithful. The fault lies within.

Lewis's Islam is dangerous because it is unhappy; it is unhappy because it lacks power; and it lacks power because it rejects, neglects, or forecloses the sources of power in modernity. Lewis cites three self-imposed disabilities in particular. First, Islam marginalizes and subjugates women, keeping them in the household and out of the public sphere. Oppressing women not only harms women. It also deprives Muslim societies of the contributions that educated, emancipated women would make to the common good. Second, Lewis's Muslims are committed to learning; they founded major universities, some of the oldest in the world. But following the interests and priorities of the Prophet Muhammad, Muslim thinkers devote themselves to the study of theology and law, and are indifferent to science and technology. If science were important, according to Lewis's interpretation, the Prophet would have pronounced on it. He had nothing to say about science; his followers emulate his example; and so Muslim societies replicate Muhammad's indifference.[32] But discounting the value of science and technology weakens Islamic societies intellectually, hampers them economically, and induces stagnation. The West cultivates science and technology. By dismissing them, Islam disempowers itself.

For Lewis, subordinating women and marginalizing science are serious impediments, but they are symptoms of the total and comprehensive view of all human life that is Islam's original failing. Contrasting the two great monotheistic, proselytizing religions, Lewis has Christianity recognizing limits on the domain of the sacred for both historical and theological reasons. Historically, the Roman Empire persecuted the church in its formative stages, forcing Christians to carve out spaces that were separate from, and beyond the jurisdiction of, the authority of states. By the same token, the

Christian church accepted that states were beyond the authority of religion. Theologically, the scriptures reinforced the lessons of history. Christians are to "render unto Caesar the things that are Caesar's and unto God the things that are God's." Islam, by Lewis's account, differs on both scores. Historically, Muhammad unified the authority of state and mosque in Mecca (and beyond) in himself. "The state was the church and the church was the state, and God was head of both, with the Prophet as his representative on earth."[33] Theologically, Muhammad taught that "there is no Caesar but only God, who is the sole sovereign and the sole source of the law."[34] Thus, Lewis concluded, Islam denies the distinction that is at the heart of Christianity.

The original differences between Christianity and Islam did not amount to much until modernity arrived, when their full implications surfaced. Whereas Christianity allows for, and even invites, the development of secular spheres that are independent of religious authorities, Islam expressly forbids them as contrary to Islam's way:

> The idea that any group of persons, any kind of activities, any part of human life is in any sense outside the scope of religious law and justification is alien to Muslim thought. There is, for example, no distinction between canon law and civil law, between the law of the church and the law of the state, crucial in Christian history. There is only a single law, the shari'a, accepted by Muslims as of divine origin and regulating all aspects of human life: civil, commercial, criminal, constitutional, as well as matters more specifically concerned with religion in the limited, Christian sense of that word.[35]

Integrating all spheres of life under its domain, Islam presides over state and society as well as mosque, tells people how to live, and prevents them from developing alternative ways of living and thinking, from outgrowing the Prophet's word. But in ruling out the secular, Islam dooms Muslim societies to poverty and weakness, and obstructs them from recovering the glories of their past.

Lewis contrasts Muslim resentment of the West's power, scorn for its cultural decadence, and refusal to learn from its successes with the lessons that East Asian societies, in spite of their greater reasons for resenting Western power, have drawn. Borrowing from the West, East Asians narrowed the gap with, or even surpassed, the West economically and technologically. Muslims too might accrue more power, produce more wealth, jobs, education, and development, and facilitate decent lives and better futures for their burgeoning populations. But they fail on all these scores because, most fundamentally, their societies do not evolve independently of religious strictures. Having reduced state, society, and economy to adjuncts of the mosque, Islam blocks prosperity, locks Muslims into poverty, consigns them to underdevelopment, and ordains civilizational frustration. These failures, moreover, are natural extensions, not distortions, of the foundational principles of Islam.

Lewis wants to absolve Islam of responsibility for the 9/11 attacks. Some extremists "have deviated very far from their [Islamic] origins."[36] But his argument implies otherwise. Having engendered the grievances that enrage Muslims, Islam does not become a mere trait that numerous societies that are in decline happen to share. As Frum and Perle learned from Lewis, Islam instead becomes the fundamental cause of decline and, therefore, of resentment and violence. It is, Lewis wrote, "precisely the lack of freedom—freedom of the mind from constraint and indoctrination, to question and inquire and speak; freedom of the economy from corrupt and pervasive mismanagement; freedom of women from male oppression; freedom of citizens from tyranny—that underlies so many of the troubles of the Muslim world."[37] Emancipating women, developing science and technology, and respecting the secular all have the effect of increasing power. Rejecting them, conversely, decreases power. Islam disempowers Muslims, and then Lewis's Muslims rage about their powerlessness.

Public opinion, neoconservatives, and the Bush administration—Lewis met with Bush II occasionally and with Cheney regularly—got Lewis's implicit conclusion.[38] The familiar refrain of the "war on terror"—"they hate us for who we are"—condensed his thesis into a sound bite. As Lewis wrote, Muslim hatred "becomes a rejection of Western civilization as such, not so much for what it does as for what it is, and for the principles and values that it practices and professes. These are indeed seen as innately evil, and those who promote or accept them are seen as the 'enemies of God.' "[39] Lewis, in fact, previewed the point in his title: *The Crisis of Islam.* The preposition is the tip-off. The crisis is not in Islam; it is *of* Islam. Instead of being contained in the religion, the crisis consumes and defines the whole religion. Lewis, therefore, set forth two stark alternatives (and warned of extremist Muslim wolves donning the sheep's clothing of pseudoliberals).[40] Either Muslims overcome their hatred of the West, which entails overcoming their actual inferiority in power and wealth, or the West must defeat the ensuing rage.

Lewis tries to sound optimistic; he wants Muslims to succeed. He hopes they could catch the West, eliminate the inequalities in power and wealth that leave them lagging behind, and shed their festering resentments. In his exuberant moods, Lewis celebrates the open-minded, liberal Muslims who are committed to modernizing their societies and participating as good citizens in the international community. True friends of the West, they embrace the promise of a new future, favor progress, reject narrow-minded prejudices, and hope for what Islam can become. "In most other countries in the region, there are people who share our values, sympathize with us, and would like to share our way of life. They understand freedom and want to enjoy it at home. It is more difficult for us to help those people, but at least we should not hinder them. If they succeed, we shall have friends and allies in the true, not just the diplomatic, sense of these words."[41] Writing in 2004 as if the good liberal Muslims might win, Lewis concluded *The Crisis of Islam* by promising that the democratic oppositions in Iraq and Iran were capable of governing their societies.[42]

However, Lewis faces two obvious problems. First, his analysis of Islam refutes the outcome he prefers. Lewis wants liberal government in Muslim societies, but he exposes, or believes that he exposes, Islam as incompatible with secularism. Lewis vacillates; he frequently points to hopeful signs and promising developments, but always, as if gravitationally, he is drawn from starry dreams back to earth. In fact, he vindicates traditionalist objections, which would include those of Bin Laden, to Muslim liberals. Agreeing that modern liberal secularists *do* reject the essence of Islam, Lewis seems to have painted himself into a corner. He said Muslims hate Western liberals for "who we are"; declared that Islam constitutes a mortal threat to the West; believed that liberal freedom is inextricable from secularism and that secularism contradicts Islam; and acknowledged that fundamentalists agree with the Muslim mainstream theologically.[43] Although Lewis tries to wiggle free, his conclusion is clear. Muslims may remain Islamic or they may become modern, but they cannot be both.

The second problem Lewis faces is that his argument about the incompatibility of Islam and secularism is unwarranted, and he had documented that fact in his previous scholarship. If it is the structure of Islam that prevents Muslims from adapting to modernity, then all Islamic societies must struggle with modernity because all must reject secularism. Universal explanations require universal effects. Lewis enforces his argument on Arabs (and Iranians), but he modifies it for Muslims in Turkey (who successfully overcame the illiberal antimodern effects of Islam).[44] Acknowledging exceptions to his argument, he allows, "We should not exaggerate the dimensions of the problem. The Muslim world is far from unanimous in its rejection of the West, nor have the Muslim regions of the Third World been alone in their hostility."[45] Lewis, then, has made two parallel arguments. His historical argument suggests Islam might be receptive to liberal changes and advises the West to help its liberal friends in Muslim societies. Lewis's theoretical argument, however, requires that Islam must reject Western reformers, and predicts that Muslim liberals must fail.

Lewis was averse to facing the conclusions that follow from his exegesis of the logic of Islam. In keeping with his historical arguments, he wanted the United States to assist Arab liberals, who are its true friends, and complained that the West ignores them. But the policy of marginalizing Arab liberals follows logically from Lewis's theoretical argument about the structure of Islam. Why back losers? Wanting to change Islam and to open opportunities for his liberal friends in keeping with his historical argument, and accepting that Islam is impervious to internal reformers as his theoretical argument concludes, Lewis did see a way of empowering liberals and of breaking down the hostility of Islam. He called on the United States to "risk the hazards of regime change."[46]

Lewis's recommendation was fraught with danger, as he knew. During the run-up to Gulf War I, Lewis argued that the West had no place in debates among Muslims, that if the West butted in where it did not belong it would compromise Arab liberals, blunt internal reforms, and constitute the United States as Islam's enemy. In 1990 Lewis recoiled from the "clash of civilizations," "the danger of a new era of religious wars," and regime change.[47] In the wake of 9/11, however, Lewis endorsed full-fledged Straussian regime change for Iraq. Meaning to change the regime of Islamic civilization, Lewis beckoned for a war of civilization.

Regime Change as Destruction

The subtexts of regime-changing neoconservatives were explicated in the citadel of the liberal establishment, Thomas Friedman's column on the op-ed page of the *New York Times*. Friedman long had espoused the neoliberal values of technology, markets, and globalization, but the 9/11 attacks intensified their significance. Before, spreading them had been a good thing. After 9/11 it became a matter of national survival. Joining neoliberal objectives with the analyses and sensibilities of neoconservatives, Friedman announced, "These terrorists aren't out for a new kind of coexistence with us. They are out for our nonexistence."[48] "Does my country really understand that this is World War III? And if [the 9/11] attack was the Pearl Harbor of World War III, it means there is a long, long war ahead."[49] Friedman cast his war broadly. He aimed not only at Bin Laden and Al Qaeda, the actual culprits, but also at *all potential* enemies, "all the super-empowered angry men and women out there."[50] Like Bush, Friedman identified as targets even those who were uninvolved with Bin Laden, the 9/11 attacks, or radical Islam. If Muslims were young, angry, and Arab—and given the poverty of Arab economies, the inequalities in Arab societies, and the unaccountability of Arab states, many young Arabs were angry—then Friedman declared them to be America's enemies in the world war he envisioned.[51]

Friedman recited Lewis's catechism. "Many of these super-empowered angry people hail from failing states in the Muslim and third world. They do not share our values, they resent America's influence over their lives, politics, and children, not to mention our support for Israel, and they often blame America for the failure of their societies to master modernity."[52] Following Lewis, Friedman recounted that "the reason they have fallen behind can be traced to their lack of three things: freedom, modern education, and women's empowerment."[53] The cause of these problems for Friedman, as for Lewis, was Islam, which thwarts modernity, disempowers Muslims, engenders dangerous resentments, and targets America. Therefore, Friedman warned, "we patronize Islam, and mislead ourselves, by repeating the mantra that Islam is a faith with no serious problems accepting the secular West, modernity, and pluralism, and the only problem is a few bin Ladens."[54] Friedman's solution was decent, accountable government and liberal capitalism.

Friedman responded to the 9/11 attacks by calling for invading Afghanistan, but his heart was not in it. He envisioned a quick in-and-out operation. He would depose the Taliban government, and then leave Afghanistan to its fate. Friedman averred that a "long war" had to be conducted and was committed to fighting it, but not there. "America needs to do its business in Afghanistan . . . as quickly as possible and get out of here. This is not a neighborhood where we should linger."[55] Freedom, modern education, and the emancipation of women in Muslim societies were compelling US interests for Friedman, just not in the country that Bin Laden had used as his staging area for the 9/11 attacks.

Iraq was a different matter. Unworried about Saddam's weapons—WMDs "was the wrong issue before the war, and it's the wrong issue [ten weeks into it]"[56]—Friedman identified America's real interest as modernizing the Muslim Middle East. "It is not unreasonable to believe that if the U.S. removed Saddam and helped Iraqis build . . . a more accountable, progressive, and democratizing regime, it would have a positive, transforming effect on the entire Arab world—a region desperately in need of a progressive model that works."[57] America's enemies, he wrote two years into the war, "know this is a war about Western powers, helped by the U.N., coming into the heart of their world to promote more decent, open, tolerant, women-friendly, pluralistic governments by starting with Iraq."[58] "America and the world have a real interest in helping Iraqis build a more stable, democratic decent government. . . . Setting up the first progressive Arab state, at the heart of the Arab world, could have a very positive effect on the whole region. It would be a *huge undertaking*, though, and *maybe impossible*, given Iraq's fractious history."[59]

Note two subtexts. First, Friedman acknowledged that US power is *intruding* into "the heart of *their* world," with the purpose of staging a heart transplant. America's values were to replace Iraqi values. While Friedman seemed to be arguing for emancipating Iraqis, his real project was to save Iraqis—and, through them, Arabs—from *themselves*. They were to be rescued not only from their state, but from their culture too. When this project was complete, the United States would have satisfied Strauss's definition of regime change. No longer would Iraqis be what they had been: "We are not 'rebuilding' Iraq. We are 'building' a new Iraq—from scratch. . . . Iraq is not a vase that we broke to remove the rancid water inside, and now we just need to glue it back together. We have to build a whole new vase. We have to dig the clay, mix it, shape it, harden it and paint it."[60] Like Kristol and Kagan, Friedman's version of democracy makes the United States into the supreme actor and Iraqis into the clay it molds. The West becomes the subject; the Arab is reduced to its product.

America must begin by destroying. It broke the vase of Arab culture for thwarting what Friedman calls democracy. Less than a year into the occupation, Friedman acknowledged that Iraq's government could not be allowed to express the will of actual Iraqis. "Our most serious long-term enemy in Iraq may not be the Iraqi insurgents, but the Iraqi people."[61] Friedman's "democracy," in other words, was not to represent the Iraqi people or express their actual aspirations. It meant, instead, remaking Iraqis in America's image, and only then, maybe, could their aspirations be allowed to be expressed democratically. But until they become like Americans, which would require prolonged wardship to teach Iraqis the ways of liberal, market, secular modernity, Friedman's talk of democracy amounted to spreading American political and economic power in the Middle East and destroying the institutions and customs that got in Friedman's way.

The second subtext derives from the first. "I am for invading Iraq *only* if we think that doing so can bring about regime change and democratization."[62] But Friedman predicted democracy would fail.

Democratizing Iraq was a "huge," "maybe impossible" undertaking. It might seem, therefore, either that Friedman was oblivious to the import of his prescriptions, that he did not know he was consigning Iraq to pointless destruction, or that he was building an escape hatch for himself in case things went wrong. But Friedman is inconsistent *only* if the invasion was meant to install democracy. If so, he was endorsing a strategy that he already had expected would prove futile. But if "democracy" meant *modernizing* Arab societies, and if modernizing Arab societies entailed dispersing, disorganizing, defeating, and banishing antimodern, illiberal forces, then Friedman's contradiction dissolves—and the full import of regime change surfaces. Friedman's counsel culminates inevitably in destruction. It was not the unpredictable consequence of an ill-considered adventure. Destruction was the point. The United States would destroy the vase and its rancid contents, and then would fail to rebuild Iraq. That, by Friedman's account, was the likely outcome of the war, and judging from his enthusiasm, much of the allure.

Friedman applauded the term "axis of evil" when he commented on Bush's State of the Union Address in 2003. Friedman knew the term was misleading and inaccurate, there being no axis among Iran, Iraq, and North Korea. But that was precisely its appeal. Irrational and unmeasured, the term implied blind rage, lashing out. Reveling in the irrationality, Friedman wrote: "[T]he 'axis-of-evil' idea isn't thought through—but that's what I like about it. . . . There is a lot about the Bush team's foreign policy that I don't like, but their willingness . . . to be as crazy as some of our enemies, is one thing they have right."[63] Friedman's sensibility might have been inauspicious for building democracy, but it suited a war of civilizations perfectly. Friedman was the liberal bull in Iraq's china shop. When the several pieces of his argument are assembled, they amount to the claim the Iraqi people must be sacrificed to save Western civilization.

The objective in world wars is to destroy enemies. When Friedman declared World War III, proclaimed that Arabs endangered the very existence of the United States, and identified with policies *because* they were "crazy," he was establishing the predicate for total destruction. The Arab Middle East's "terrorism bubble . . . had to be burst," he wrote about nine months into the war, "and the only way to do it was to go right into the heart of the Arab world and smash something."[64] What Friedman would smash, fortuitously, is what obstructed the expansion of both American national and neoliberal power. But Friedman, in keeping with the axioms, never understood regime change in terms of either national or capitalist power. Casting regime change defensively, he had the United States either imposing the American and neoliberal order on the Middle East or facing annihilation. Arabs hate Americans for who they are, and Americans must respond by affirming themselves. But Americans, according to Friedman, are people whose nature is to impose themselves over other peoples. Arabs hate Americans because "they resent America's influence over their lives," but that is what Friedman's America does. Thus, Friedman's logic concludes that, because Americans are hated for having taken an inch, they must take a mile. Coexistence is impossible because Arabs resent being controlled, and because Americans, as seekers of Kristol and Kagan's "benevolent global hegemony," insist on universalizing their ways.

Creating Anarchy

All regime-changers, neoconservatives included, repeated the same refrain. Saddam headed the Ba'ath Party; the Ba'ath Party controlled the Iraqi state; the state controlled Iraqi society; and Saddam ruled both party and state through the secret police. According to the anti-Saddam exile, neoconservative associate, and advisor to the American government on post-Saddam policy in Iraq, Kanan Makiya, Saddam's Iraq was a "chamber of horrors." "At the apex of the system of punishment sat torture"; the society was "made up of citizens who positively expected to be tortured under certain circumstances."[65] Designed to make Saddam immune to the coups that had vexed his predecessors, Saddam's system deployed the secret police to preempt potential rivals from assembling the power that might translate them into actual threats. Anyone occupying any position of power that might be used to challenge Saddam was treated with suspicion, including his close associates. They were, as Makiya stressed, liable to being tortured and killed. The purpose of torture and violence was not only to acquire information and force confessions, to intimidate and punish. Torture also was meant to sow suspicion and distrust among Iraqis, to dissolve social ties, and to extinguish the possibility of collective action against Saddam.

The main objective of the police state was to ensure Saddam's personal control. But for one man, no matter how ruthless, to assume effective control over the population of a whole country, he had to become a despot in the classical sense. Brutality and sadism were part of Saddam's formula for controlling Iraq, but the key—and the reason why indiscriminate torture was integral to Saddam's regime—was dismantling the capacity to act politically and collectively. The human connections that make collective action possible, of trust and reciprocity, of a sense of common destiny, had to be broken.[66] Saddam's regime, as *the* condition of its existence, made sure that nobody—not even family—could be trusted. As Strauss's regime defines the ideal citizen, so Saddam's "ideal citizen became an informer."[67]

Makiya's account, which neoconservatives adopted and publicized, offers a coherent and generally accurate, albeit exaggerated, portrait of Saddam's Iraq. Social cohesion was weak or absent; civil society—that is, organs outside of the state—was ineffectual, coopted, or repressed; and the state was the instrument of Saddam's cruel paranoia. Makiya described a state that closely resembled the

USSR under Joseph Stalin, much as Saddam had intended. Stalin, who was Saddam's model, assumed leadership over a conspiratorial party that already had subjugated the state. After establishing his leadership over the party, Stalin then used the secret police to consolidate personal control and subjugate the party.[68] Terrifying both party and state into submission, Stalin converted the party's dictatorship into his personal despotism. Likewise, Iraq's Ba'ath Party seized the state via a military coup in 1968 and, determined to avoid the fate of the previous Ba'athist government in 1963, which shared power for nine months and then itself was overthrown in a coup, proceeded to take control of the state by recruiting millions of party members and stuffing them into state bureaucracies during the 1970s. The Ba'ath Party reduced the state to its appendage, suppressed independent political activity, eliminated rival parties, and subordinated the military.[69] When Saddam, who controlled the secret police, forced out his patron (and cousin), Ahmad Hasan al-Bakr, and created a cult of personality around his unique genius, he took the final step in copying Stalin. As the Ba'ath (and Soviet Communist) Party used the secret police to control the state, Saddam used his control of the secret police to subject the party—and, thereby, the state—to his personal rule.

Makiya's portrait of Saddam's Iraq ignores important details. Saddam's despotism was not total. The state's control of parts of Iraq was shaky and disputed, and Kurdistan rebuffed it. Shi'i clergy maintained a modicum of independence, although at terrible personal costs, and it served Saddam's purposes to portray the Sunni clergy as independent of the state too. Professional institutions that were both indispensable to the economy and segregated from the levers of violence, such as universities, hospitals, and the oil economy, limped on. Tribes and mosques remained as sites of social connections, and Makiya ignores the substantial improvements in health, literacy, and living standards that were achieved by Saddam's spending programs in the 1970s, when oil prices were high and the economically disastrous wars against Iran and Kuwait had not been launched.

Makiya is right, however, in describing a country that lacked the actors, institutions, and political know-how that are necessary for self-government. The consummate despot, Saddam undermined social connections, isolating and atomizing Iraqis, and destroyed their capacity to act in concert for public purposes. By the time he fell, Saddam had weakened or undone ties among Iraqis, actively disorganized society, and infected tribes and families with distrust. The state had substituted itself for society; the party had substituted itself for the state; Saddam had substituted himself for the party; and the state, party, and secret police had subdued or extinguished most organs of civil society and the capacity for independent political action. The despotism of the Ba'ath Party over the state and the state over Iraq had become the despotism of Saddam over party, state, and country, just like in Stalinism. Saddam undermined law, institutions, integrity, trust, and social capital (although, to be fair, none were plentiful before his despotism). He compelled obedience, terrified officials, and issued orders arbitrarily. Officials were connected hierarchically to Saddam through their superiors; they were not connected to each other laterally.

Consider, therefore, the import of what neoconservative regime-changers imagined for Iraq. By the terms of their indictment, state power was concentrated in the person of Saddam. It was not institutionalized, and Makiya depicted Saddam as committed to disorganizing society. Makiya likened Iraq under Saddam to a prison, with Saddam as warden and chief torturer. If, however, Saddam had destroyed state institutions, corroded social cohesion, and suppressed civil society, then deposing Saddam was tantamount to instigating a national jailbreak. Makiya himself worried deeply about what Iraqis, having been traumatized by Saddam's despotism, might do with their newfound liberties.[70] He wanted to free Iraq from

Saddam, build civil society, and escape the logic he anticipated. But by the terms of his analysis, destroying Saddam, disbanding the military, and de-Ba'athifying the state—enacting the neoconservative version of regime change—would amount to unleashing anarchy.

From Goldwater and Reagan to Neoconservatives

Why, given neoconservative conceptions of regime change, did pillars of the Republican foreign policy establishment, like Henry Kissinger, George Shultz, James Baker, and Colin Powell, sign on to a war whose risks were obvious, whose goals were unreasonable, and whose salesmen were alarming? Historically, conservatives are committed to maintaining order, which is why so many conservatives are realist and realists are conservative. Fearing disorder, conservatives want to conserve the institutions, traditions, and ways that preserve civic order, which always is precarious, from the ever-present threat of chaos.[71] Epistemologically, conservatives shun risk, and worry always that the unknown is more likely to inflict costs than to offer benefits. Yet by the logic of Makiya, war with Iraq would unloose a population that had been turned into brutes, stripped of human ties, and pitted against even their own families. By the logic of Friedman, the war would let the United States smash Muslims. By the logic of Lewis, the war would target a civilization that was six times older than the United States of America. And by the logic of Wurmser, the United States would restore, or toy with restoring, something akin to Hashemite rule in the Middle East. Why, then, did the conservative political and foreign policy establishment choose to take major risks in pursuit of gains that, philosophically, they should have seen as unattainable and that, temperamentally, they should have regarded as unworthy of the risk, even on the off chance of success?

Basic stereotyping buttressed the case for war. Offering a shortcut to a prolonged war of civilization, neoconservatives promised that Iraqis would not resist American power. They would submit because, Kristol explained, the Arab world "respects the decisive use of power above all."[72] By portraying Arabs as cowering before power, neoconservatives not only called on the United States to assert itself forcefully. They also required the United States to continue fighting. Setbacks were attributed not to the immensity of the project, but to American restraint. As Iraq's violence was worsening in 2006, John Podhoretz advanced the claim in the form of a rhetorical question about inflicting civilian casualties during wars. "What if the tactical mistake we made in Iraq was that we did not kill enough Sunnis in the early going to intimidate them and make them so afraid of us they would go along with anything? Wasn't the survival of Sunni men between the ages of 15 and 35 the reason there was an insurgency and the basic cause of the sectarian violence now?"[73] The war against Islamic civilization apparently was meant literally by some.

The second, more important, answer to why the Republican establishment approved of regime change is that it had allied with, and had been redefined by, the "movement conservatives" who had arisen in the 1960s and triumphed in the Reagan administration.[74] Their victory was not total. Bush I and his senior national security team remained traditionally realist, averse to 1960s-style movement conservatives and their neoconservative successors. Not coincidentally, many of Bush I's advisors were skeptical of Gulf War II. But movement conservatives, who stemmed from Barry Goldwater in the 1960s and Ronald Reagan in the 1970s and 1980s, were ascendant in Bush II's administration, and they were reinforced by neoconservatives. Traditional conservatives—as represented by presidents Dwight Eisenhower, Richard Nixon, and Bush I—were committed to maintaining the international order while trying to improve America's position within it. In the 1950s and 1960s, they favored containment; in the 1970s they favored détente; and in the wake of the Cold War, they remained cautious. By contrast, movement conservatives rejected the status quo, averring that it imperiled America's existence, and demanded aggressive offense in the name of self-defense. Abandoning traditional conservative concerns with maintaining order in favor of eliminating enemies through military means, movement conservatives favored regime change before the term was popularized.

Neoconservatives often are associated with the Wilsonian foreign policy tradition, and not without reason. Both neoconservatives and Wilsonians scorn realpolitik as immoral, dirty, and unnecessary; both accord full legitimacy and respect only to states that accept liberal values; both incline toward the imperialism of universality; and both championed regime change in Iraq. But stressing the similarities between neoconservatives and Wilsonians—also known as "liberal internationalists," "liberal interventionists," "liberal universalists," as well as "liberal hawks"—overshadows three significant disagreements. First, neoconservatives reject international law and disdain multilateral organizations, two of the hallmarks of liberal hawks. Second, liberal hawks elevate justice above states, and they regard the pursuit of power as grubby, unseemly, and corrupting. Rules for liberal hawks apply to everyone, the United States included. Neoconservatives, on the other hand, savor American unilateralism and, rather like Thomas Hobbes's infamous sovereign, envision the United States as making rules but not having to obey them. Third, liberal hawks are heirs to the Enlightenment, and, as such, believe in the irresistible momentum of progress. They reject the neoconservative portrait of international society as perilous, worsening, and verging on the apocalypse. History is the neoconservative's enemy, but it is the Wilsonian's friend.

Neoconservatives and movement conservatives are indistinguishable, however, on the very issues that differentiate both from liberal hawks. Both demand military supremacy, entertain war as the surest means of exerting American power, mock noninterventionists and internationalists as weaklings, register challenges to American power as threats to America's existence, take the axioms for granted, and relish asserting the deduction that requires power to materialize human liberty. Striking these themes at the birth of movement conservatism, the Republican National Convention that nominated Barry Goldwater for the presidency identified American power with human freedom. "America must advance freedom throughout the world," the party platform declared, "as a vital condition of orderly human progress, universal justice, and the security of the American people. . . . That stand must be: victory for freedom. There can be no peace, there can be no security, until this goal is won."[75] America's freedom, therefore, must reign universally if Goldwater's America was to be safe, and American power must become universal if freedom is to become universal. Goldwater called the new regime free and liberal, but it also amounted to claiming American sovereignty over the world. Human freedom and American supremacy were one and the same, indistinguishable and inseparable.

Movement conservatives, Goldwater included, subscribed to much of the Cold War consensus. They held that the United States represented freedom and the USSR epitomized slavery and that the United States loved peace and the USSR prevented peace. But after concurring with the Cold War consensus in diagnosing the problem, Goldwater disagreed on the response. The consensus, taking as self-evident that nuclear war was unthinkable, accepted coexistence between the United States and the USSR as unavoidable. Unable to entertain war with its rival, and yet convinced that the USSR endangered peace and freedom, the United States settled on the strategy of containment. Designed to secure America's short- and medium-term needs without compromising long-term interests, containment bought time to allow for America's eventual victory in the Cold War. It was on this point that Goldwater broke ranks with America's Cold War consensus. He rejected the inevitability of coexistence, the effectiveness of containment, and, most of all, the confidence in ultimate victory.

Containment took many forms and encompassed many debates, as befits a strategy that guided American policy for the forty-plus years of the Cold War.[76] But the doctrine originated in and never abandoned George Kennan's insight that the Soviets, for reasons of both Russian history and Communist ideology, were fanatic, neurotic, suspicious, and paranoid;[77] that they were convinced that "the outside world was hostile and that it was their duty eventually to overthrow the political forces beyond their borders"; and that they were inherently expansionist.[78] Ultimately, however, Kennan was reassuring. Although they were locked in conflict, the United States held the stronger position and the USSR, precisely because it believed (wrongly) that it was destined by history to prevail, would avoid apocalyptic military confrontations. Kennan's USSR was compelled to seek expansion, but it was not suicidal. If the United States established barriers and enforced them firmly, containing the USSR in its sphere of influence and strategically unimportant margins of world politics, then it would force the USSR either to implode or mellow. "[N]o mystical, Messianic movement," Kennan wrote, "can face frustration indefinitely without eventually adjusting itself in one way or another to the logic of that state of affairs."[79] That is, if the USSR did not win, it would lose; and if the United States did not lose, it would win. The best American offense, therefore, was a good defense. Time, just like Fukuyama later argued, was on America's side.

Goldwater disagreed. The only viable defense was aggressive offense. In response to the nuclear-armed, Communist power that was advancing relentlessly, probing the West's weaknesses, exploiting its desire for peace, and preparing to attack, Goldwater was committed to increasing American military power instead of deterring war, as the Cold War establishment had it. Goldwater wanted the United States to build its military strength because he meant to use it; and he meant to use it because he concurred with the Soviet Union's claim that history was on *its* side. The Soviet threat "is growing day by day."[80] Because "we were losing the Cold War,"[81] Goldwater's America could not wait out the enemy by containing it. If freedom did not destroy Communism first, Communists would destroy freedom. "Our strategy must be primarily offensive in nature. . . . [W]e cannot win merely by trying to hold our own. . . . In addition to keeping the free world free, we must try to make the Communist world free. To these ends, we must always try to engage the enemy at times and places, and with weapons, of our own choosing."[82] "The risks I speak of," wrote Goldwater, "are risks on our terms, instead of on Communist terms. *We,* not they, would select the time and place for a test of wills. *We,* not they, would have the opportunity to bring maximum strength to bear on that test."[83] In the speech that endorsed Goldwater for president (and that, coincidentally, launched his political career), Ronald Reagan associated the United States of the mid-1960s with the ill-fated and reckless George Custer: "If we lose freedom here, there is no place to escape to. This is the last stand on Earth."[84]

As president from 1981 through 1989, Reagan pushed the implications of his them-or-us rhetoric when he could get away with them, notably in Central America. He implemented a policy to destabilize the Sandinista government in Nicaragua, backed the right wing in El Salvador, and detected the specter of communism haunting the region.[85] But the Reagan administration was staffed by conservative mainstays such as Secretary of State George Shultz, Chief of Staff James Baker, and Secretary of Defense Caspar Weinberger, and they respected limits when risks were high. The Reagan administration escalated the arms race with, and rhetorical attacks on, the USSR, but ultimately it dealt realistically with Soviet power. Reagan widened America's military advantages via the arms race, and then consolidated them in a cordial relationship with Mikhail Gorbachev.[86]

So what explains the discrepancy between the rhetoric of movement conservatives and the traditional conservatism of the Reagan administration? It is possible that Reagan mellowed, that he was changed by the responsibilities of office, and that he finally acceded to what elites had understood all along. It is also possible that Reagan deeply feared the prospect of nuclear war and acted to reduce it.[87] But it is plausible too that Reagan and the movement conservatives (who were shifting the center of gravity in Republican foreign policy elites) accommodated the international context because they had no choice—that Reagan deferred plans to universalize American power and values not because he had outgrown his old ambitions but because they were unattainable during the Cold War. Democrats controlled the House of Representatives, credit markets constrained deficit spending, and most of all, Soviet military power thwarted Reagan's original agenda. Thus, after increasing military spending, developing more nuclear weapons, and denouncing the Soviet Union as evil, the Reagan administration deferred to basic power realities. Recognizing that the USSR had amassed too much military power to be swept aside by a policy of rollback, to be attacked preemptively, or to be pushed from East Europe, the Reagan administration settled for advantageous arms deals and confined ideological adventures to its sphere of influence in Central America.

Goldwater's and Reagan's foreign policy rhetoric was recycled by Bush II and neoconservatives. All tied American interests with American ideals, equated American ideals with liberal values, and required expanding American power to actualize freedom and ensure national security. But whereas the Reagan administration moderated its actions, Bush II translated the rhetoric into policies. The differences in the two presidencies might be ascribed to presidential personalities or to advisors. But accentuating these factors overlooks the fact that Shultz, Baker, and Weinberger endorsed Gulf War II (and so did Kissinger). More importantly, it neglects the significance of the end of the Cold War and the dissolution of the USSR. In their wake the Bush II administration faced lower risks in asserting American power. Without the Soviets to balance

American power and exploit American adventurism, Bush II could enact the views and priorities of neoconservatives (or movement conservatives: the two were indistinguishable in foreign policy). Reagan's former key advisors backed Bush's initiatives, in other words, because history had lifted the constraints that had limited Reagan.

The end of the Cold War, the Republican assumption of control of the House of Representatives, and the trauma of 9/11 emancipated neoconservatives to do what the right wing had been promising to do since the 1960s. Ironically, the very familiarity of the fervent rhetoric—that it was them-or-us, that America's existence was in constant jeopardy, and that America must attack first or face extinction—had the effect of lulling old-fashioned status quo political and foreign policy elites into complacency. Having heard ringing words before and then seen conventional policies, they expected more of the same. Unaware of the full radicalism of movement conservatives and neoconservatives, risk-averse elites did not recognize the import of regime change. They certainly did not recognize that the neoconservative intelligentsia were aiming not only at Arab nationalist and Islamic regimes but also, closer to home, at the regime of timid, decadent, limp-wristed, cowardly American liberalism. Regime change in Iraq, in the fullest logic of neoconservatism, was meant to change the regime of American liberalism too. Regime change abroad would produce regime change at home.

Blowback

Harvey Mansfield, a leading Straussian political philosopher, published a book on the subject of manliness a few years into the war in Iraq. Elegant, engaging, provocative, serious in its purpose, and delightfully politically incorrect, *Manliness* argues in favor of compartmentalizing gender relations. Mansfield accepts, albeit reluctantly, the utility of organizing the public realm, both state and economy, without regard to what he takes as the natural fact of gender. But Mansfield also defends the natural role of gender in family life. In the end Mansfield objects less to feminism than to liberalism; it is the unnatural logic of liberalism that culminates in America's gender-neutral society. Liberalism is "the cause of [feminism's] easy victory."[88]

Mansfield acquiesces to gender neutrality in public life because he accepts parts of liberalism. But he does not accept all of it, particularly those parts that collide with natural law. Mansfield's talk of nature would seem to suggest that gender differences are indelible and that unnatural attempts to impose gender neutrality are doomed by nature to fail. But that is not what Mansfield means by nature. He fears precisely that the onslaught of feminism can efface gender. Objecting to the gender-neutral regime of contemporary liberalism not because it is unsustainable but because it is viable, Mansfield floats a compromise. Feminists may achieve complete equality in the public sphere; in exchange, they should accept the natural fact of manliness.

Mansfield knows he is asking a lot. To begin with, respecting manliness means feminists must give up their claims to universality. Gender neutrality must withdraw its claims on the family, where nature should prevail. Besides, manliness is obnoxious and hard to get along with, as Mansfield admits. As if thinking of Bush II, Mansfield presents the manly man as the male equivalent of the drama queen. The manly man is bossy and theatrical, "struts and boasts," will not shut up, "cannot abide the rational life of peace and security," and is "insistent" and "intolerant."[89] "Whereas rational control wants our lives to be bound by rules, manliness is dissatisfied with whatever is merely legal or conventional. Manliness favors war, likes risk, and admires heroes."[90]

Nevertheless, Mansfield offers three justifications for manliness. First, manly men perform necessary services. Not just useful and valuable, they are indispensable. The manly person—it is worth making explicit that most men are not manly and a few women, such as Margaret Thatcher, are manly—"takes responsibility in a risky situation."[91] "The manly man is in control when control is difficult or contested—in a situation of risk."[92] In crises, everybody needs the firemen who rushed into the World Trade Center. Second, manliness is not instrumental; it never calculates marginal utility or pursues incremental advantage. It is noble and honorable, "an act of sacrifice against one's interest."[93] Third, manliness is natural; it expresses what the classical Greeks called *thumos,* the throbbing, pre-rational violence that is nature's response to danger. Manliness rejects limits, "endlessly" risks death, and pursues honor heroically.[94] Alas, Mansfield cannot get around the stubborn fact that natural manliness also is *stupid.* Like an unguided missile or a teenage boy, *thumos* "has no natural end beyond itself; it is blind and wants only independence."[95]

Paradoxically, Mansfield's critique of manliness resembles his critique of feminism. Each has a point, each gets carried away with itself, and both need tempering—but not from each other. Mansfield is not a Madisonian. He does not envision a battle of the sexes—Hepburn versus Tracy—in which each checks and balances the other, before they reconcile in a kiss. Mansfield's manliness and feminism share the same defect; lacking true wisdom, both need philosophy to find their just place. Mansfield's strategy is to use manliness to put gender-neutral liberalism in its place and then use philosophy to tutor the warrior, just like Plato used philosopher-kings to govern warriors in the *Republic* (or, to use the Greek title, *Politeia*). Warriors—manly men—need direction from philosophers. Without it they will chase honor anywhere and everywhere.

Honor for Mansfield is directionless and "always somewhat arbitrary."[96] Manly men espouse their causes as honorable, but they are wholly undiscriminating in what they deem as good.[97] They often find honor in reprehensible causes. They thrive in war, but they are unconcerned with the justice or injustice of their wars, which is where philosophers come in. Philosophers "show their responsibility as philosophers and also as manly men by setting limits to the responsibility of active men, reminding them as if with the attitude of women that peace is better than war. They make it clear that risks should be taken not endlessly for greater advantage or thrills but for what is less or not at risk, the satisfaction of a good life that is complete in itself by not depending on other men."[98]

Mansfield does not trust manliness, but he needs it. Its enemies are his enemies. Manliness is locked in unending war with modern, rational, marginal-utility-calculating, liberal, bourgeois civilization, which must extinguish manliness as a relic of past ages. "[T]he entire enterprise of modernity . . . could be understood as a project to keep manliness unemployed."[99] "Our rational control, fearing courage more than fear, will do without manliness and will seek to supplant it and to keep it unemployed by means of measures that encourage or compel behavior to be lacking in drama. Thus we have replaced the manly man with the bourgeois, a character who has several faces, none of them manly."[100] By subjecting manliness to legal rational authority and forcing it to justify itself in terms of universal principles, liberals suffocate it. Manliness excludes, dominates, and competes. Making it answer to the standards of every person, of the unmanly, not only insults manliness—it also unmans men, suppressing the excess, vanity, self-love, and irrationality of manly men. Mansfield's manliness inevitably rips down "dull, bourgeois society lacking in both love and ambition."[101] Manliness either destroys liberal civilization or liberal civilization destroys it.

It might be thought that Mansfield's manliness, being generated by nature, is irrepressible. It is not. It evolves for the purpose of fighting war, without which it faces extinction. Manliness "cannot abide the rational life of peace and security."[102] Withering inside the enervating routines of bourgeois society, manliness needs war to live and a just cause to give it direction, which is—to return to the themes of neoconservatives—where war against "Islamic fascists" comes in.[103] The gift that keeps on giving, the war on terrorism uncorks manliness from the liberal bottles of rational control. War needs warriors; warriors need causes; and the war against Islamic fascism ties manly honor to defending Western civilization at the same time as manliness is rejecting the terms of Western civilization. The war on Islamic fascism and the war in Iraq, in other words, also aimed at liberalism.

Mansfield was not preoccupied with Bin Laden, Al Qaeda, and Saddam. He did not warn that Islamic fascism threatened the *existence* of Western civilization in the fashion of Soviet Communism during the Cold War. Mansfield's warning is that the real threat issues from the totality of liberalism, from out-of-control gender neutrality, and from liberal values that reject natural law. The main danger is the unnatural, gender-neutral, liberal regime. But in crisis is opportunity. The threat of Islamic fascism mandates war; war unlooses manliness; and manliness instinctively turns against its real enemy: dreary, unmanly, liberal rationalism. Regime change in Iraq changes America's regime at home.

Mansfield, then, answers one of the vexing questions about going to war in Iraq. Why did neoconservatives want such an *irrational* war? The reason is that for neoconservatives, war does not simply continue politics by other means. It not only is instrumental; war also requires the existential redefinition of Americans. Fighting changes men. Precisely because war is irrational, because it is the manly assertion of mastery, because it arises from man's nature, his pulsating aggression, vanity, and will to dominate, his *thumos*—precisely for these reasons, neoconservatives demanded war. War stimulates honor, and honor rejects bourgeois liberalism. It overwhelms rationality with manliness. Mansfield's interest in the war did not originate in the Middle East or in Islam, but in the need to answer liberalism's attack on natural law.

Mansfield's student understood. William Kristol wrote in his column on the *New York Times* op-ed page, "It's not easy to rally a comfortable and commercial people to assume the responsibilities of a great power. It's not easy to defend excellence in an egalitarian age. . . . It's not easy to make the case for the traditional virtues in the face of the seductions of liberation, or to speak of duties in a world of rights and of honor in a nation pursuing pleasure."[104] Neoconservative regime change in Iraq was meant to change Americans too, and certainly not in the image of the neoliberal bourgeoisie. The neoliberal is the enemy of the neoconservative. Neoconservatives meant to subordinate neoliberalism by unleashing the warrior spirit. If, however, the war was intended to disorganize and disorder the oil patch, remake Arab civilization, and then discipline liberal civilization too, why did neoconservatives find allies among liberal hawks in general and among neoliberals in particular? Why did many liberals favor the war?

5

Democratic Hawks

English-speaking peoples are past masters in the art of
concealing their selfish national interests in the guise of
the general good, and . . . this kind of hypocrisy is a
special and characteristic peculiarity of the Anglo-
Saxon mind.

E. H. Carr

Why did much of the Democratic Party sign on to a war that was
steeped in the personality, sensibility, partisan interests, ideology,
and constituencies of the Republican Party? Although some Democrats in elite political and foreign policy circles did oppose it, for
reasons of principle, prudence, or both, most endorsed the war
with Iraq. Did these Democrats agree publicly with a war they disagreed with privately, or did they favor the war sincerely? It is
widely thought that Democrats, including several who harbored
presidential ambitions, voted to authorize war in spite of their opposition because they feared being defined as weak on national security.[1] They heard the administration's talk of mushroom clouds
and madmen armed with nuclear weapons, listened to their poll-
sters and political strategists, could not figure out how to oppose
war while appearing strong, and so jumped onto a bandwagon they
could not have halted anyway.

Robert Shrum, the chief political strategist for Senator John Kerry
and advisor to Senator John Edwards, invokes political expediency

to explain their votes in favor of authorizing war. When the Senate was voting in 2002, both were positioning themselves for a presidential run in 2004, and both, against their better judgment, voted in favor. Many Senate Democrats, according to Shrum, "suppressed their doubts and [were] bullied into voting with Bush, overcompensating for their fear that otherwise, the party would be seen as weak on national security. Virtually none of the party's foremost foreign policy advisors had argued the other side."[2] Other leading Democrats admitted as much too. House Minority Leader Richard Gephardt, for example, endorsed the war with the express hope that Democrats could get the issue off the table and shift the 2002 congressional elections, which were staged a couple weeks after Congress voted, to what he thought was the more favorable terrain of the economy and health care.[3]

National Democrats broke into three camps—clear opponents (Senator Edward Kennedy, former vice president Al Gore, and House Minority Whip Nancy Pelosi), cautious supporters (Senators Kerry, Hillary Clinton, Joe Biden, and former president Bill Clinton), and passionate champions (Senators Joseph Lieberman, Dianne Feinstein, and Evan Bayh). Interestingly, the stronger the particular Democrat's national ambitions, the more likely he or she was to favor the war (although not necessarily enthusiastically). Perhaps because no Democrat who had opposed Gulf War I had been placed on the national ticket in the three intervening elections, every Democrat who voted on the question in the House or Senate and who would go on to run for the presidential nomination in 2004 or 2008—Christopher Dodd, Biden, Clinton, Kerry, Edwards, Gephardt, and Lieberman—voted in favor of authorization in October 2002. Interestingly, Senate Democrats supported the war more narrowly, 27–21, than did their future presidential candidates. In fact, if the six future presidential candidates are deducted from the count, Senate Democrats split evenly. House Democrats opposed the war by a 126 to 81 vote, although their leaders also voted for war (Gephardt and soon-to-be house minority whip Steny Hoyer) in a greater proportion than the caucus as a whole. Members of the Congressional Black Caucus voted 32 to 4 against authorization.

Shrum's explanation, which is in line with most popular accounts, performs a double disservice to Democratic hawks—it casts their convictions as cowardice, and it misinterprets their politics. And then it eclipses Shrum's more insightful observation. Democratic foreign policy elites supported the war heavily. Their support was confused, sometimes incoherent, and was muddled by complaints about how Bush was taking the country to war. They faulted his timing, methods, and priorities. But with few exceptions, senior figures in the Democratic foreign policy establishment went along with the decision, if sometimes reluctantly, for mostly positive reasons. Their criticisms were constructive in spirit. They criticized the unilateralism of Bush's march to war and his aversion to planning what would come afterward, much as they later criticized his administration's conduct of the war. But they rarely challenged the decision to use the means of war to enact the end of regime change. Electoral considerations might have clinched the case for ambitious Democrats, but most backed the war because they and their foreign policy advisors favored regime change in Iraq.

Most Democrats take the axioms on faith. In fact, liberals have advocated them over the objections of Republicans like Dwight Eisenhower, Richard Nixon, and Bush I, who were not interested in turning interests into ideals or national values into internationalist imperatives. Since Woodrow Wilson's presidency, liberals have made a point of affirming that American interests are defined by American ideals and that American ideals are universal in application. It is this morality, liberals maintain, that elevates them over their coarsely self-interested realist rivals. But by identifying moral purpose as their defining trait, regime-changing liberals built a blind spot into their foreign policies. As an article of faith, liberals believe power is different when they exercise it, that it becomes more sublime, disinterested, and softer. Power for liberals derives its meaning from the intent of those wielding it and from the objectives they seek, not from its intrinsic properties. In the hands of liberals, power does not compel people. It frees them to do what is in their best interests; it helps, facilitates, and mothers.

Liberals pride themselves on their pragmatism, not their realism. Realists see power as both the stuff and the object of human interactions, as the principle of life.[4] People want power, and they use whatever power they have to get more. Although the concept is strikingly ill-defined for a tradition that myopically sees little else, power usually is "hard" in the sense of military, political, and maybe economic, and it is zero-sum. Most of all, it is inescapable. Realists see power everywhere; it might be all they see. The imperative to dominate or be dominated permeates human interactions. Life for realists is an either-or, who-whom affair. There is no opting out of power struggles. Power can be countered or challenged, but it never can be eliminated.

The liberal counter to realism is pragmatism. Realists, in pronouncing that power is inescapable, maintain that it infiltrates actors, their objectives, and the space in between. Because power is pervasive, realists allow no pristine vantage point, no actor who exists prior to and apart from power fields or who seeks power only to implement notions of the good that, as if by virgin birth, arise independently of power considerations. Pragmatists, by contrast, conceive of power instrumentally. It is a tool, not a force field that influences all passers-through. Thus conceived, power does not contaminate the ends liberals seek or the means they use to achieve their ends. With power rendered as mere means and with means reflecting the intentions of power-holders, power is made servant to, not master of, pragmatists. Thus, where realists are obsessed with power, which is ubiquitous, pragmatists barely notice it. Power does not entangle. It is used for good by liberal pragmatists, for bad by their adversaries. Power, therefore, is not an independent force in their analyses, appearing mostly in the form of the malice of their rivals. Even when pragmatists operate inside the parameters of power, they do not see it. Calling the parameters "reality," pragmatists uphold power interests without recognizing the import of their acts as they act pragmatically. They take power as given and, like a blind person navigating in a maze, grope for openings. When they find the path of least resistance, they leave power structures standing.

The dispositions of realists and pragmatists, then, are wholly different. Pragmatists seek the highest common denominator among stakeholders in pursuit of optimal, win-win solutions. They want the most widely shared goals that can be achieved practically, paying little attention to whether power realities infiltrate their goals and whether pragmatic goals actually reinforce powerful interests. Realists, by contrast, live in a world of either/or, not both/and. Rejecting the possibility of universal interests, the realist asks who does what to whom. Pragmatists, on the other hand, assume the existence of universal interests, which is why they are a type of liberal and realists are not. It also is why pragmatists assumed that Americans and Iraqis shared common interests and why they sincerely expected Iraqis to welcome American power. By remaining unaware of the overwhelming fact of American power, pragmatists reproduced it.

Half of the Democratic hawks were pragmatic neoliberals. The other half issued from the overlapping but distinguishable tradition of liberal hawks (also known as Wilsonians). Both liberal hawks and neoliberals prize human rights, markets, globalization, multilateralism, feminism, and disinterested American leadership, which they prefer the United States to exert by force of example when possible but by force of arms when necessary. Both traditions also made alliances with neoconservatives in backing the war against Iraq, liberal hawks more happily. But both also diverged from neoconservatives on the same two scores. First, both liberal hawks and neoliberals are committed to multilateralism. They stressed the importance of receiving, or at least of being seen to be seeking, endorsement for the war from the UN Security Council. Second, both liberal hawks and neoliberals are optimistic that history is on their side. Feeling propelled by forces beyond them to expand their domain and to discount obstacles, they agree with Francis Fukuyama's talk of the end of history and the triumph of the liberal model. With history ensuring success, the challenges awaiting liberals shrink. The United States might encounter die-hards and traditionalists in Iraq, but victory was not in doubt. It is the advantage of owning the future.

Neoliberalism and liberal hawks are overlapping traditions theoretically, but liberal hawks were closer to neoconservatives than to neoliberals on the particulars in Iraq. Whereas neoliberals were restrained and attuned to costs in their endorsement of the war, liberal hawks were enthusiastic. It was a war of good versus evil. Whereas neoliberals imagined regime change in the image of emancipation, liberal hawks envisioned regime change as transformation. Nevertheless, both agreed on the fundamentals: liberal principles apply universally, and American power is indispensable to fulfilling universal principles. Thus beguiled by the axioms, liberal foreign policy elites and politicians barely contemplated how being invaded, conquered, occupied, and remade according to the dictates of cosmopolitan, secular, liberal values might be experienced by Iraqis, whose traditions and history were not liberal. Proving they sincerely believed in the universality and altruism of their values, both kinds of prowar liberals brushed aside the question of resistance. They knew what Iraqis wanted.

The hawkishness of Democrats with national ambitions, then, registered electoral calculations, but it also reflected the ideology of liberal political and foreign policy elites. In fact, the closer the particular Democrat was to the foreign policy establishment, the more likely he or she was to support the war. Most senior foreign policy advisors who had held prominent positions in the second Clinton administration backed the war, including Madeleine Albright, Sandy Berger, Richard Holbrooke, and Joseph Nye. These two patterns—political ambitions and proximity to foreign policy elites—converged most forcefully in the person of Hillary Clinton, who was both a front-runner for a future presidential nomination and immersed in the Democratic foreign policy establishment (having, not coincidently, been instrumental in getting Albright appointed as secretary of state in her husband's administration).[5] But membership carries costs. The elites that spoke through Clinton were the undoing of her presidential ambitions in 2008.

Liberal Hawks

Kenneth Pollack, an assistant on Bill Clinton's National Security Council, made the liberal, pragmatic, ostensibly nonideological argument for attacking Iraq in a best-selling book that he published during the run-up to the war. In *The Threatening Storm: The Case for Invading Iraq* Pollack vouched that Saddam still retained chemical and biological weapons, and declared, "It is only a matter of time before Saddam's regime is able to acquire nuclear weapons if left to its own devices."[6] Containment-plus-sanctions already was breaking down due to French, Chinese, and Russian duplicity.[7] Once Saddam acquired nuclear weapons, US policy would be exposed as untenable and the United States (and Israel) would be able to stop his aggression only by making nuclear threats of their own.

Deterrence works against sensible regimes, like the USSR during the Cold War (and, apparently, Mao Zedong during the Cultural Revolution), but Pollack's Saddam lacked the good sense to be deterred by the threat of annihilation. "Saddam Hussein is one of the most reckless, aggressive, violence-prone, risk-tolerant, and damage-tolerant leaders of modern history. While he may not be insane, he is often delusional in constructing fantastic conceptions of how his actions are likely to play out."[8] To drive the point home, Pollack three times compared Saddam to Adolf Hitler, and he discerned that "the threat that Saddam presents to the United States and to the world is just as real, and the one we have today is no less pressing than those we faced in 1941."[9] Alas, isolating Saddam offered no relief. If his end approached, Saddam was "highly likely to use whatever forces remain to him at the end to lash out in a final paroxysm toward Israel and possibly others."[10] With sanctions exhausted, deterrence unreliable, coexistence dangerous, and Israel in peril, regime change loomed as the best option, even though that might have precipitated the final paroxysm.

Pollack discussed regime change in two voices, one happy and the other worried. The happy voice accentuated the positive. With the United States restructuring the state and economy and reconciling Iraq's rival ethnic and religious groups, the Iraqi people would get pluralist democracy and a market economy; their neighbors would get a peaceful trading partner and a democratic model to emulate; and the United States would get prosperity and stability in a troubled region. In keeping with the axioms that convert American power interests into ideals and that universalize the ideals, Pollack had the United States doing what was best for it by enacting regime change in Iraq in the confidence that the United States also would be doing what was best for Iraqis (and the region and the world). Dissolving the choice between the right and the advantageous, between justice and self-interest, liberal hawks believed that the United States would do well by doing good.

Yet even as Pollack peddled the invasion, ominous undertones were audible. Pollack's approach "*starts* from the belief that the current Iraqi political and social framework cannot produce a government that is stable or legitimate."[11] Pollack's point of departure, in other words, was that the Iraqi state and society bred both instability and illegitimacy. It follows, silently, that the United States would have to remake both state *and* society if a stable and legitimate order was to be established. Because Pollack lets the admission slip only in passing, he seems oblivious to what his diagnosis implies. Pollack was calling on the United States to establish a new army and administer Iraq through the American military, the UN and kindred international NGOs, and local Iraqi notables.[12] That is, Pollack expected the United States to disband the army and de-Ba'athify the state (thus providing more evidence against the charge that Bremer invented the policies from thin air), and to provide security and execute decisions itself once it cleared the Iraqi army and Ba'ath Party from the scene. Translated, Pollack wanted the United States to claim for itself the attributes that Max Weber famously identifies as defining states.[13] By surfing over the deeper logic of his policy proposals, Pollack's best-seller lured liberals down the primrose path.

Pollack was neither insincere nor duplicitous. As a pragmatic, atheoretical policy-maker, he took it as self-evident that Iraqis were unprepared to govern or administer themselves. But Pollack did not stop there. When he declared that *society* as well as the state was responsible for Iraq's problems, for breeding illegitimacy and sowing instability, Pollack ratified the neoconservative image of regime change. Before Iraqis could be trusted to govern themselves, their society must be transformed. Without realizing what he was doing, then, Pollack steered the government he envisioned for Iraq into an adversarial relationship with the people it ostensibly was rehabilitating. Because Iraq's underlying problem was that its society was deformed, obviously its government could not be representative. Representing the deformed society would cause only more illegitimacy, more instability, and more deformations.

Pollack required Iraq's government and society to be transformed by force of American arms, yet he evinced little awareness of the risks he was incurring. Expecting order to hold and resistance to melt even though he was conferring control onto foreigners who were to remake Iraqi society according to American lights, Pollack exemplified the hold of the axioms. Pollack granted the United States effective control to enact its interests, and assumed that its interests amounted to ideals and that Iraqis would embrace the ideals. He expected, therefore, the United States to achieve regime change easily. "We *could,* and should, prevent all systematic violence. This means no reprisal killings, no repression, no ethnic or religious cleansing, no civil war, no bids for dictatorship. While this may sound daunting, it is likely to be the *least challenging* task we face and one that is *well within demonstrated U.S. capabilities*—as long as we have the troop strength to do the job."[14]

Like Friedman, Pollack had the United States doing the acting and Iraqis getting acted upon. Americans were subjects; Iraqis were rendered as objects. As Pollack put his conclusion in the peroration ennobling the invasion, "A U.S. invasion of Iraq . . . would give *us* an opportunity to turn Iraq from a malignant growth helping to poison the Middle East into an engine for change for the entire region. It would allow *us* to harness the human and material resources of what is probably the most richly endowed of all of the Arab states and try to make it a force that could help start to bring the Arab world out of the miasma into which it has sunk."[15] Amid the mixed metaphors, it is clear the United States was to get the "material resources" (Pollack's euphemism for oil). But Iraqi society and culture, as Pollack's cancer metaphor suggests, were to get the radical surgery that would cut the malignancy that otherwise would metastasize throughout the region. The axioms hid the import of his rhetoric, but Pollack's policies disclosed the scale of the project. Pollack wanted 300,000 troops to occupy Iraq, and even then Iraq would preoccupy United States foreign policy "for years to come."[16]

Pollack shows neoconservatives and liberal hawks both demanded war for regime change, both understood regime change as attacking Iraqi social institutions and cultural norms for the purpose of creating a better model for Arab societies, both equated the interests of Iraqis with those of the United States, and both were backed by senior officials.[17] Neoconservatives and liberal hawks also sensed, without realizing the significance of their intuition, that Iraqis would experience defeat differently, which is why Pollack expected a prolonged occupation and targeted Iraqi institutions for destruction. Finally, both neoconservatives and liberal hawks featured Saddam's WMDs in their advocacy, but both also regarded the war as justified independently of Saddam's WMDs. "Freeing the Iraqi people from Saddam Hussein's depredations would be justification enough for his overthrow if the American people were willing to pay the price of doing so."[18]

Pollack was a policy analyst, far removed in spirit from grand issues of philosophy. Yet his arguments stem from and depend on Immanuel Kant, who cast the mold for liberal theories of international relations in 1795. Writing at a time when republics were few and far between and were vulnerable to the kings, tsars, emperors, sultans, aristocrats, and oligarchs—call them autocrats—who dominated European affairs, Kant favored republics. But Kant's republics could not live safely, securely, or consonantly with the goodness of their people in a world that was populated by states that were subject to the interests, demands, and whims of wicked autocrats. No republic is an island. Surrounded by threats, republics must respond. The good are imperiled by the bad.

Thomas Hobbes famously anticipated Kant's problem, and Kant borrows from his diagnosis and prescription. For Hobbes, people living in the state of nature must respond in kind to whatever endangers them. But meeting violence with counterviolence is insufficient; eventually the aggressor will hit his mark. Consequently, Hobbes observes that threats of violence must be eliminated. When discussing individuals, Kant has them appealing to universal reason for guidance and protection. But his republics cannot follow the example of his individuals. In applying Hobbes's logic to states,

Kant's republics must fend for themselves when they are stranded in the state of nature. Kant's republics recognize universal standards, but autocracies are subjected to the particular interests of their rulers, not to categorical imperatives. Inevitably, Kant's republic must respond to the context the autocrats create.

Kant departs from Hobbes on one pivotal point. He explains the international conduct of states via their form of government. Republics act one way, and autocracies act another. Kant's people are peace loving and commercial by nature, and if they had their preferences would act beneficently toward other peoples (and dissolve the state of nature). They trade, cooperate, and help other people from friendship, brotherhood, and common interest. States that represent their citizens, therefore, are naturally peaceable and act peaceably with other republics. But autocracies, because they represent the selfish interests of their rulers, not only choose war over the general interest in peace and commerce. They also thrust Hobbes's choice onto republics. Either Kant's republics get their enemies or their enemies get them. With autocracies forcing republics to adopt preemptive behaviors, republics neither can realize their inherent goodness nor mind their own business. The "state of nature," Kant writes, is "a state of war. For even if it does not involve active hostilities, it involves a constant threat of their breaking out."[19]

Kant favors the rule of law, but law protects law-abiding states only if *all* states obey it. If law is not universal, republics live in the state of nature and must fend for themselves. What, then, were Kant's republics to do about autocracies, given that the existence of just one outlaw forces every state to raise its guard, ruining sociability for everyone? Kant answers that, because they cannot behave liberally in a world that is inhabited by illiberal states, republics either change the world or the world changes them. If republics do not eliminate the external threats that prevent them from realizing their commitments to peace, commerce, and law, they live in the state of constant war. And if republics live with war, they cannot become fully liberal. By extension, the existence of illiberalism—anywhere—aggresses on republics everywhere, threatening their security and stunting the expression of their people's goodness. Unless liberalism prevails everywhere, liberals may not be liberal anywhere.

Kant does not dwell on the corollary, but liberal hawks adopt it intuitively. Republics must universalize themselves. If they are to make the world safe for democracy, they must create a world composed only of democracies. Because liberals cannot coexist with illiberal governments, democracies are entitled—or, in Kant's Hobbesian moments, compelled—to eliminate the threats that prevent them from realizing their peace-loving, commercially minded liberal telos. Unless they universalize their principles, republics renounce their destiny. Defense requires offense; aggression becomes preemption. Regime change, therefore, becomes a matter of the survival of liberal ways, not a choice for strategic advantage.

In practice, of course, capitalist democracies were powerful when the United States initiated Gulf War II, and Saddam was weak. They faced no material threats to their hegemony from Iraq, still less to their survival. They already had pronounced the "end of history." Yet Pollack's hysterical warnings echo Kant's undertones. When he held that Saddam's very existence posed an intolerable danger to Israel, the Middle East, the United States, and peace, and that Saddam resembled Hitler and single-handedly rendered deterrence unworkable by dent of his reckless irrationality, Pollack was channeling Kant's logic. It did not matter whether Saddam actually held nuclear weapons. His regime, merely by existing, condemned democracies to the state of nature. Legalistically, liberal hawks tried to pin the threat on his WMDs or his ties to Al Qaeda, but Saddam's real crime was operating outside what Kant called "the legal civil state."[20] Fortuitously, America's right to live peacefully in a world that is hospitable to its liberality grants the positive right to abolish regimes that are illiberal. The justification for war, therefore, implied the obligation to liberalize Iraq.

Liberal Hawks and Regime Change

Most liberal hawks thought their differences with neoconservatives were substantial. As liberals and Democrats, they disdained Bush personally and mocked him intellectually. But as Pollack illustrated and as British prime minister Tony Blair stressed, the actual differences on Iraq were slight. Blair, who was said to be the Clintons' "soul mate," shared their third-way, new-Democrat (or "New Labour") politics.[21] He also subscribed to the doctrine of preemption. The *casus belli* for Blair, like for Bush, was the prospect of an alliance of Saddam and his WMDs with Al Qaeda. Both Saddam and Al Qaeda, according to Blair, "detest the freedom, democracy and tolerance that are the hallmarks of our way of life. . . . The possibility of the two coming together—of terrorist groups in possession of weapons of mass destruction or even of a so-called dirty radiological bomb—is now, in my judgement, a real and present danger to Britain and its national security."[22] Because the problem was that illiberals might acquire WMDs, the solution was regime change. In his memoirs Blair recalled, "[P]eople would say: is it regime change you are after, or WMD? The true answer is that . . . of course, the two are connected. . . . In a very profound sense it was in the nature of the Saddam regime that the ambitions for WMD were to be found, and the risks to be judged."[23]

Unlike his American counterparts, Blair owned up to the reality of his politics. He agreed with Vice President Dick Cheney, the archvillain of Blair's American allies,

that the U.S. was genuinely at war; that the war was one with terrorists and rogue states that supported them; that it stemmed from a guiding ideology that was a direct threat to America;

and that therefore the only way of defeating it was head-on, with maximum American strength, with the object of destroying the ideology and allowing democracy to flourish in its stead. [Cheney] would have worked through the whole lot, Iraq, Syria, Iran, dealing with all their surrogates in the course of it—Hezbollah, Hamas, etc. In other words, he thought the world had to be made anew, and that after 11 September, it had to be done by force and with urgency. . . .

Of course, this attitude terrified and repelled people. But . . . I did not think it was as fantastical as conventional wisdom opined. Our enemy has an ideology. It does threaten us. The ultimate answer is in the spread of democracy and freedom.[24]

Actually, Blair went Bush and Cheney one better. Bush steadfastly refused to identify Islam as the source of the threat to the West, but Blair bought Bernard Lewis's assessment whole-hog. "Precisely because the roots of this wider struggle were deep, precisely because it was a visceral life-or-death battle between modernisers and reactionaries, precisely because what was—and is—at stake was no less than the whole future of Islam—the nature of its faith, its narrative about itself, and its sense of its place in the twenty-first century—precisely because of all this, there was no way the forces opposed to modernization, and therefore to us, were going to relinquish their territory easily."[25]

Blair's reactionary Muslims hated the United States and Britain for being modern, secular, capitalist, and liberal, for who the Americans and British are. The United States and United Kingdom could live in peace if, and only if, "they" became like "us." Western security and liberal values required that Middle Eastern societies be liberalized, but local modernizers could not perform their mission. "I never quite understood what the term 'neocon' really meant. . . . But what it actually was, on analysis, was a view that evolution was impossible, that the region needed a fundamental reordering."[26]

Blair agreed. "I looked at the region and felt the chances of a steady evolution were not good."[27] The United States and the UK therefore had no choice. Iraq's illiberalism was a moral wrong, an injustice borne by the Iraqi people, and also was a dire threat to the security of Britain and the United States. Because liberals in Iraq and the region could not achieve the modernization that their freedom and Western security required, Americans and British were forced to perform the work themselves.

Blair signed on to the Bush doctrine in all of its essentials. He invoked the threat posed by Saddam's WMDs, tied the WMD threat to the regime that allegedly held the weapons, asserted that Saddam's hostility to the United States and Britain arose from his irrational ideology (and not, say, from colliding geopolitical interests), warned that Saddam might make common cause with Al Qaeda (which likewise was motivated by blind hatred of liberal values), hinted that the ideologically based threats to market democracies issued from other Islamic Middle Eastern countries (thus implying Iraq was only the first in the series of wars that Cheney thought must include Iran), and, finally, concluded that the threat in Iraq (and elsewhere) could be subdued only if Islam was made liberal via regime change. Like Bush, Blair expected Iraqis would welcome the invaders as liberators, even though the regime-changers intended to defeat the very forces that they said were thwarting Iraq's spontaneous evolution into modernity. Expecting these "reactionaries" to expire meekly, Blair never anticipated "the nightmare that unfolded."[28] If, however, reactionary Islam had the power to prevent Iraq from reforming, which is what forced the war, why would Blair have expected happy outcomes? Why did he not expect that the reactionaries that thwarted domestic reform also would resist foreign liberalizers?

The answer is the universality of Anglo-American interests and ideals. Blair told Congress in July 2003: "There is a myth that though we love freedom, others don't; that our attachment to freedom is a product of our culture; that freedom, democracy, human rights, the rule of law are American values, or Western values."[29] "[O]urs are not Western values. They are the universal values of the human spirit, and anywhere, any time ordinary people are given the chance to choose, the choice is the same: freedom, not tyranny; democracy, not dictatorship; the rule of law, not the rule of the secret police."[30] It follows that wanting the benefits of liberal values was tantamount to achieving them, and that realizing liberal values in the West was not the culmination of a long historical process that defeated important obstacles to a politics of consensus—and, therefore, that Muslims would become liberal as soon as they were exposed to liberal opportunities. Thus, when Britain and America were faced with mass resistance from 2004 to 2008, Blair reflexively looked to "outside influences, hell-bent on chaos and destruction. Both al-Qaeda and Iran knew what was at stake in Iraq."[31] Of course, in projecting failure in Iraq onto Iran, Blair also ratified the predicate for the other wars that Cheney wanted.

Liberal hawks venerated Blair. With impeccable progressive credentials, he cast the war eloquently, tempered Bush's unilateralism, and, by prevailing on the United States to seek Security Council approval for the war, affirmed the status of international law. But in announcing his agreement with the Bush administration's analysis and objectives forthrightly, he parted company with his American admirers. They insisted, as the influential liberal hawk Anne-Marie Slaughter illustrates, that they were fundamentally different from Bush and neoconservatives. A leading liberal scholar of international relations, dean of the Woodrow Wilson School at Princeton University (an especially prestigious post for liberal internationalists), and later a senior assistant to Secretary of State Hillary Clinton, Slaughter favored the war for standard liberal reasons. Saddam held WMDs, violated basic human rights, defied international law, and ignored Security Council resolutions. The points about international law and organization were particularly salient to

Slaughter. They are what differentiated her Wilsonianism from Bush's unilateralism.

As the magnitude of the fiasco was becoming clear, Slaughter wrote a book that absolved her of responsibility for having advocated the war and offered suggestions for warding off similar mishaps in the future. Her solution was not to throw the baby out with the bathwater. She did not reject future interventions on behalf of regime change (as she showed in calling for American intervention in Libya in 2011 and international intervention in Syria in 2012).[32] Instead, Slaughter diagnosed the causes of the war's failure more narrowly, blaming it on delusions of American exceptionalism and Bush's disrespectful nationalism. Where Pollack and Blair treated liberal hawks and neoconservatives as indistinguishable, Slaughter regarded it as mere happenstance that liberal internationalists and neoconservatives both favored the war. That coincidence revealed nothing about underlying similarities in the two traditions. Bush and the neoconservatives are exceptionalists, and Slaughter's liberal internationalism rejects exceptionalism categorically. Accordingly, she called on the United States to learn from the humiliation of Iraq the importance of respecting, and being seen to respect, international opinion and of cooperating with liberal friends in affirming universal values. Having thus insisted that the United States adopt a better code of international conduct, Slaughter then faithfully replicated the axioms.

Slaughter asserts the first axiom immediately. Entwining American interests and values in the preface, she yearns for the United States to understand that its values comprise America's deepest interests. "We should stand for our values, the values this country was created to achieve and that define us as a nation. Standing for those values is both an end and a means. It reflects who we are as a people; it also serves our long-term national interests."[33] As she weaves American values into American interests (and turns interests into values), Slaughter specifically rejects American exceptionalism.

American values are not exceptional. They are universal, the property of all humanity. It is unclear whether Slaughter regards the United States as the source, or as the custodian, of universal values; whether she has universal values applying to Americans or has American values applying universally; and whether she recognizes that, in erasing the distinction between American values and American interests, American values and universal values, and, indeed, America and the world, she is imposing exceptional obligations on the United States. What is clear is that, whether knowingly or unknowingly, Slaughter makes the United States into the avenging angel of liberalism.

Slaughter's America was conceived to achieve a universal purpose. Other states might monopolize the legitimate use of violence, allocate resources authoritatively, protect the lives, property, and security of their citizens, establish the conditions of capitalism, or accumulate as much power as possible. Instead, Slaughter's America has a higher purpose. Embodying universality, it is "founded on a set of universal values—self-evident truths—that come . . . from the fact of our common humanity."[34] As an idea, America must transcend territorial boundaries both to realize the universality of the idea that *is* America and to bring the idea to those who are not American. Yet Slaughter somehow dodges the logical deduction. If liberal values are to rule the world, then American power must carry them.

Averting her eyes from her imperialistic telos, Slaughter retreats into utopianism. She concludes *The Idea That Is America* with advice for a makeover. What matters is how Americans think of themselves. In accepting that their identity is an idea and the idea is universal, Americans must shed particularity. They must become universal.

Liberty, democracy, equality, justice, tolerance, humility, and faith—these are America's fixed stars. If we think of ourselves as a city on the hill, we suggest to the rest of the world that *we* are the beacon spreading light to other nations. But if we think less of ourselves and more of our ideals, we can join with other nations in seeing them shine above all of us. If we aspire continually to the idea that is America, rather than contenting ourselves with the reality, we must look to those stars to steer by. If we stay the course, they will lead us to a better and safer world.[35]

Slaughter summons America to bask in internationalism. Remembering that it is but one democracy among many equals, her America is cooperative and cosmopolitan, not unilateral and nationalist. Focusing on the universality of its ideals, and not on the particularity of its interests, America becomes the idea that is available to all humanity, and not the property of one particular people. The axioms, in other words, have done their work. America's interests are its ideals, as Slaughter wrote from the beginning, and its ideals are universal. American power has become the executor of the liberal idea and, invisibly, the liberal ideal has become the occasion for asserting American might. With the distinction between America and liberal ideas erased, American power becomes disembodied, altruistic, and universal. "Believing in America means believing in values that apply to all people everywhere."[36]

Of course, Slaughter does not see that in declaring the United States as the envoy of universal values, she would universalize American *power*. When she calls on Americans to steer by the stars, she thinks she is calling for them to shed their particular interests in communion with the universal, to look upward and beyond themselves. But Slaughter's "stars" are not stars. They are reflections of the universal values that originated in, and that constituted, America. America is the sun; Slaughter's "stars" are mere moons that reflect America's light. Thus, when America abides by Slaughter's universal values, it really honors the values that America was created to protect, uphold, and proselytize, and that are entangled in its interests. But Slaughter's sleight of hand succeeds because it fools liberals into rethinking themselves as universal, and not as particular and embodied. In concealing from themselves the realpolitik of their power, Slaughter sees the velvet glove that liberates. Iraqis got the fist.

Slaughter's poetry has the United States increasing its power without letting others—liberals especially—in on the secret. But, carelessly, she had let the cat out of the bag when she was advocating the war. As the war was beginning, Slaughter conceived an idea that would clear up the problem of attacking Iraq without having received prior approval from the Security Council. Slaughter backed the attack. Agreeing with Bush on America's right to pursue its "vital national security interests" regardless of the Security Council's inaction, she then added a codicil. The war was "illegal but legitimate." It was illegal because the Security Council, which she endows with the authority to legalize war, had not authorized it. But the war was legitimate because Saddam endangered American security and violated liberal norms, and because the United States may use self-help in self-defense. Hoping to raise the policy she favored into a precedent worthy of her faith, Slaughter called upon the United States to seek post facto Security Council approval as "a necessary component of the use of force."[37] If the United States were to receive the Security Council's authorization even after having started the war, the war would become legal as well as legitimate. After acting unilaterally, the United States would get multilateral sanction retroactively.

Not much was left of Slaughter's claim to principled internationalism once she asserted that the United States could self-legitimate the war, and that the United States did not need approval from the UN. For one thing, law is not law if obedience to it is optional. For another, authorizing the United States to go to war on its own say-so and then to seek UN approval at its convenience exposes international organizations as rubber stamps for the world's superpower. Slaughter's problem is not the familiar one that vexes adherents of international law. It is not that the UN lacked the power to enforce its law on the United States. Her problem is that America's cause was legitimate with or without the UN's authorization, which suggests that it was best for all concerned that the UN could not prevent the United States from acting unilaterally. Thus, the respect for international law that Slaughter has distinguishing liberal internationalism from unilateralist exceptionalism turns out, when tested, to exert no material influence on either the substance or the legitimacy of the US decision to go to war unilaterally. Exceptionalism motivates; internationalism soothes.

Slaughter's position on the Iraq war stripped internationalist views on American power to their essence. Merely requesting Security Council approval for what the United States was doing already, and would continue to do regardless of the UN's verdict, satisfied her standard of multilateralism. Nodding to the forms and appearances of international law eased the misgivings liberal hawks felt about the neoconservative company they were keeping, but liberal internationalist commitments required little of them otherwise. In fact, both Blair and Slaughter reproved Bush for letting his unilateralism get in the way of universalizing liberalism. The gestures of seeking Security Council approval, they promised, would abet the war effort. At bottom, their criticism was that liberal internationalists provided a more effective way of fighting Saddam.

Hillary Clinton

Hillary Clinton might have lost the 2008 Democratic presidential nomination even if in 2002 she had cast her vote in the Senate against authorizing the war, but it is hard to see how the eventual winner, Senator Barack Obama, would have defeated her. She would have retained the same money, organization, name recognition, constituencies, and family ties. Plus, she would have been in better graces with antiwar liberals, party activists, and Democratic primary voters and caucus-goers, who were more opposed to the war than Democratic voters in general. Finally, voting against the war when Bush was at the height of his popularity would have answered accusations that she was consumed by her ambition. As John Judis put the point in an autopsy of her 2008 campaign, Clinton lost to Obama largely because she "reinforced an impression that, on an issue as central as the war, she was willing to put politics before principle."[38] James Carville agreed that the vote was fatal for Clinton's presidential ambitions.[39] Her critics charged she would do anything to get elected; if she had voted against the war, her vote would have reminded voters of her courage, judgment, and independence. Clinton's vote for war was the oxygen to Obama's challenge.

Senator Clinton's vote usually is explained in terms of political calculation and expediency, as illustrated by Judis's formulation. Having to establish her national security credentials, both as a Democrat and as a woman, she voted for a war that she questioned privately. Clinton rejects this account. In fact, she denied she even voted for war. Having taken to heart the promises of President Bush and National Security Advisor Rice, she said she voted to give the administration leverage to force Saddam to admit weapons inspectors into Iraq. Actually the vote did authorize war, not just the threat of war, and Bush and Cheney had made their intentions to go to war clear in the months preceding the congressional vote in October 2002. But the flimsiness of her excuse does fuel suspicion that Clinton supported the war because she knew she would face questions about her national security credentials when she eventually ran for president. In fact, Clinton spoke that way herself in 2005: "If you can't persuade a majority of people that you're going to be strong and tough where we need to protect America and our [national] interests, you can't cross the [electoral] threshold."[40]

With her senior political advisor, Mark Penn, later bragging that her vote shored up her national security credentials, the case seems clinched.[41]

The problem with reducing Clinton's vote to expediency is not that it weighs Clinton's political calculations for supporting the war. As a politician contemplating a run for the presidency in the future, and a woman to boot, it would be inconceivable if she had not assessed the impact of her vote on her prospects. The real problem with featuring expediency as the explanation is that it neglects the record and sensibility of the Clinton administration in Iraq, the balance of opinion among Democratic foreign policy advisors, especially those associated with the Clintons, and the ideology of Democratic foreign policy and political elites. If Clinton supported the war because, as a woman who saw the presidency in her future, she had to prove her willingness to go to war, then why did John Kerry cast the same vote and offer the same explanation? Perhaps, as Shrum suggests, he voted as a fearful Democrat, even though he was a man and a war hero. In that case, the motivations were not specific to Clinton. But perhaps, as suggested by the foreign policy advisors who endorsed war and maintained close ties to her and her husband, Clinton's political incentives in voting for the war augmented her policy reasons. She voted for the war, in other words, because she favored it.

In the Senate speech explaining her vote, Clinton repeated Bush's national security arguments. It was "not in doubt" that Saddam was developing chemical and biological weapons, missiles, and a "nuclear program," or that he was giving "aid, comfort, and sanctuary to terrorists, including Al Qaeda members." These "undisputed" facts convinced Clinton that Iraq must be disarmed. Saddam had committed all manner of misdeeds and would continue committing them as long as he remained in power. Clinton also recalled that regime change in Iraq had been official American policy since 1998. But she did criticize Bush's unilateralism. Clinton urged the administration to seek Security Council authority for a new round of arms inspections, while also reserving America's right to attack Iraq if the Security Council refused to approve the war. Presenting the trip to the Security Council as a win-win proposition, she noted that American legitimacy would increase if the Security Council sanctioned the war. If it did not sanction the war, the United States would gain credit for having tried and could go to war anyway. "We can attack him with far more support and legitimacy than we would have otherwise."[42]

Clinton evaded the central issue before her—authorizing the war—by featuring the UN's approval as desirable but not essential. The congressional resolution that authorized the war did not require Bush to obtain, or even to seek, UN approval before attacking Iraq. It authorized the United States to use war to enact regime change because Saddam was pursuing WMDs in violation of the terms of his surrender in Gulf War I. Clinton (along with other prominent Democratic hawks) called on Bush to seek authorization for the use of military force from the Security Council. Ironically, Bush later did just that. At the behest of Tony Blair, he courted the Security Council in February and March 2003. But when the Security Council refused to approve, the United States derived little of the sympathy from world opinion that liberal hawks had promised would accrue as the reward for having tried.

Clinton, like other leading Democrats (Kerry and Gephardt, for two), skirted the issue in front of her. She accepted Bush's rendition of the "facts" (which closely resembled the version of her husband's administration), agreed they warranted war, and voted to authorize war. The substantive differences between the Clintons' wing of the Democratic Party and Bush amounted to a dispute over Bush's diplomatic preparations for war. Bush preferred to act unilaterally, whereas Democratic hawks thought seeking Security Council approval was more efficient than spurning it. Hillary Clinton wanted the UN's blessing partly to buttress its authority, but mostly to facilitate America's purposes. She spoke of the benefits international institutions confer, of the common values they propagate, and of the legitimacy their blessings bring. But disapproval from international institutions could not prevent the United States from doing what it wanted. Actually, international institutions enabled the United States. Clinton rested her advice to act through the Security Council on the presupposition that the Security Council was not a site of independent power. The Security Council either would promote America's agenda without interfering with it, or it would be ignored.

Clinton's position expressed the sense of the leading foreign policy advisors in the Democratic Party at the time—Albright and Richard Holbrooke primarily, and Sandy Berger to a lesser extent. Although the three differed in their analyses, enthusiasm, and objectives, they converged on points of immediate policy. Albright and Berger thought the United States should confront Saddam with the demand for unlimited inspections, should back its demand with the threat of war, and should back its threats with the Security Council's authority. The end was disarming Saddam; the means was threatening war. The flaw in Albright and Berger's strategy was that they were unconvinced that their means would achieve their ends. They were threatening war with the foreboding that threats would not produce inspections, let alone disarmament, and the United States would be left with a war that neither wanted. That is, Democratic foreign policy advisors endorsed war, and then undercut their arguments in favor of it—Albright in particular. The mismatch between the means Clinton urged and the ends she sought reflected the confusion in her husband's erstwhile foreign policy team.

Sandy Berger, Bill Clinton's national security advisor from 1997 to 2001 (and deputy advisor before that), affirmed that Saddam had chemical and biological weapons in hand. Worse, Saddam had established a program for developing nuclear weapons, which could not be allowed to reach fruition. Whereas many hawks used Saddam's alleged WMD violations as the pretext for the regime change that was a moral imperative regardless of his weapons, Berger acquiesced to regime change because he took disarmament as America's primary objective. Berger did not want war, and he avoided the subject of regime change. He recognized the costs and the risks, and foresaw a number of potential disasters, including the collapse of friendly governments in Jordan and Pakistan (which, by the way, actually had nuclear weapons). But Berger accepted the risks because he could not countenance the possibility of Saddam acquiring nuclear weapons. The danger, however, was not imminent. Having time to explore alternatives, Berger advised the United States to demand international inspections of Saddam's nuclear programs and to back its demands with the Security Council's authority. The threat of war, Berger hoped, would bring Saddam to his senses. Besides, if the United States had to resort to war anyway, the efforts that it had taken to round up international approval would "greatly [reduce] the risks of any future military action."[43]

Berger addressed fears that Saddam would get hold of nuclear weapons and affirmed the value of international institutions. But his strategy suffered two major drawbacks. First, it hinged on Saddam submitting. Saddam, however, had other enemies besides the United States, and he feared what Iran, Kurds, and Shi'as might do once they learned that he was disarmed. Second, Berger's bluff had to be backed. If Saddam called it, the United States must fight even though war might yield "a region that is less stable rather than more peaceful and democratic."[44] Thus, if Saddam failed to satisfy weapons inspectors, and Saddam had sound reasons for fearing what would happen when it became known that he had disarmed, Berger was providing the final argument for the war that he did not want. Once Bush had Security Council approval, he could invoke the Security Council's authority. Hoping to stall the momentum for war, Berger shoveled fuel into the engine.

The counterpoint to Sandy Berger was Richard Holbrooke, who was Bill Clinton's ambassador to the United Nations, the chief

American negotiator of the Dayton Peace Accords, presumptive candidate for secretary of state in the future Kerry and Hillary Clinton administrations, former investment banker, and longtime member of American International Group (AIG) board of directors. Berger, who was committed to disarmament and multilateralism, centered his policy on the authority of the UN and international law, and avoided talk of regime change. Holbrooke, on the other hand, was raring to go. He did chastise Bush, as was his obligation as a Democratic spokesman, but only for getting in the way of the march to war. By mishandling diplomacy, Bush forged a coalition between those opposed categorically to going to war and those opposed to going to war without having consulted Congress and the UN. Holbrooke criticized the administration's methods, not its goals.

Holbrooke repeated neoconservative talking points. Dispensing with niceties about WMDs, Holbrooke demanded regime change. "Saddam Hussein's activities continue to be unacceptable and, in my view, dangerous to the region and, indeed, to the world not only because he possesses the potential for weapons of mass destruction but *because of the very nature of his regime.* His willingness to be *cruel* internally is not unique in the world, but the combination of that and his willingness to export his problems makes him *a clear and present danger at all times.*"[45] Holbrooke followed the example of neoconservatives in joining the national security case and the moral case for regime change. Saddam's alleged weapons violations were mere pretext for Holbrooke's real objective. "[O]nce the goal of regime change is established, the United States should work to achieve it."[46] Given that, as Clinton noted, the goal had been established in 1998, Holbrooke's meaning was clear.

Holbrooke knew Iraq was unpredictable. Saddam's successor "might be almost as bad, or bad in a different way. Chaos could follow."[47] But Holbrooke did not obsess about the danger of chaos. Having been candid in declaring that the "goal of American policy in regard to Iraq is regime change," Holbrooke understood the

United States had to build a new regime after it deposed Saddam. The United States could not walk away from Iraq, as it had walked away from Afghanistan in 1989 and from Iraq after Gulf War I. Urging "reconstruction," the on-and-off investment banker implied globalization—regime change in the second sense—as the objective.

Madeleine Albright, Bill Clinton's former secretary of state, hit the familiar themes, but with clear reservations when she offered her counsel to the Senate. Bush should seek the UN's help in getting Iraq to accept more arms inspections. If the United States obtained a Security Council resolution, Saddam would be boxed into either allowing inspections or defying the UN. Although Albright expected Saddam to refuse inspections anyway, and although she thought war at that time was inadvisable, she nevertheless advised Congress to authorize war in hope of avoiding war. Of course, if Saddam rebuffed demands for new inspections, as Albright expected, the United States would have to make good on its threats.

Albright explained where war would lead. Once the United States went to war, the United States could be

> confronted with a no-win choice. One option might be a prolonged U.S. military occupation of the country that served as the cultural capital of Islam during that civilization's Golden Age. This would hand a new organizing tool to anti-American terrorists worldwide. The other option is to withdraw promptly and risk plunging the country into factionalism and civil war. It is naïve to think that a peaceful and democratic Iraq will automatically emerge from the ashes of our invasion. It is crazy to believe we can run postwar Iraq alone. And it is essential that the Administration think the consequences of all this through in advance, which it is not yet evident to me that they have done. One thing is certain. We may be able to win a war against Iraq without a broad coalition. But there is no way we can win the peace without help from many others.[48]

Albright's misgivings were palpable. Retired secretaries of state do not customarily read prepared statements to Senate committees that characterize the policies of their successors as "crazy." Yet having criticized Bush administration policies as ill conceived, provocative, and counterproductive, she endorsed them anyway. She chastised the administration's "irrational exuberance for this conflict" and "ostentatiously hegemonic language," and she recognized that Bush was not interested in disarming Saddam.[49] But because she categorically refused to tolerate the possibility that Saddam might acquire WMDs, she urged Congress to give Bush "the authority to use all means necessary to enforce Iraq's compliance with U.N. Security Council resolutions."[50]

Albright recommended that Congress authorize war to increase Bush's leverage over the Security Council and that the Security Council authorize war to increase American leverage over Saddam. But her strategic vision was marred by two conspicuous contradictions. First, she portrayed Saddam as a brutal, dishonest, evil despot who was seeking WMDs in pursuit of his nefarious and intolerable ambitions in the region. But if Saddam was concerned only with his own power and welfare and lacked decent respect for international opinion, why would he submit to demands from the UN? Why would Saddam spurn threats of war by the superpower, and then accede to the UN's moral suasion? Second, Albright recognized that Bush wanted war, and chastised him for it. She thought that he was committed to a reckless course of action. Yet in spite of his determination to do something stupid, Albright recommended enabling him on the off chance that Bush would act against his inclinations.

Albright's position did not make much sense, and not only because neither Bush nor Saddam was interested in a new round of inspections. Albright wielded the threat of a war that she did not want so that she could get inspections. But Albright did not expect to acquire inspections through threats and, even if she had gotten inspections, doubted they would have produced disarmament.[51] She encouraged Bush's threats in the expectation that Saddam would call their bluff, and thus obligate the United States to fight the war. But unlike Holbrooke, she did not want the war she was endorsing, because she feared it might empower radical Islamists or catapult Iraq into anarchy. Foreseeing failure, Albright then advocated it. She questioned Bush's timing but favored his project. "America must respond firmly to Saddam Hussein and it may be necessary to wage war to remove him."[52]

It is one thing to use war as an instrument for pursuing national interests. It is another to threaten war while expecting that the threats will lead to war and the war will lead to disaster, but such was the import of Albright's position. She bemoaned the administration's incompetence, doubted the war was advisable and necessary, and explained why it would produce either a surge of support for Al Qaeda or chaos, unless the United States hit the parlay and achieved both. Worse, she allowed that Saddam, the enemy the United States knew, was manageable and of secondary importance anyway. Then, unmoved by her assessment, Albright called upon Congress to authorize war against Iraq. She and her party's foreign policy establishment were convinced of Bush's incompetence, and yet they were undeterred by impending disaster.

Berger, Holbrooke, and Albright agreed that the United States should fluff up the American case for war by seeking UN approval and that the course of action they were advising was risky. All noted the dangers of enacting regime change and predicted a long, hard slog. They disagreed on important points. Berger and Albright hoped against hope that Security Council backing would intimidate Saddam into allowing more inspections. Holbrooke, on the other hand, was looking for war, and Albright agreed that the regime, not its WMDs, was the real problem. Berger disagreed. Vainly resisting the logic of his argument, he identified WMDs as the real objective. But he ended up favoring regime change as the means of achieving disarmament. Thus, the advice from Bill Clinton's circle of advisors, which had become the center of gravity in the Democratic foreign policy establishment, was either beside the point, reckless, incoherent, or self-subverting. Either these advisors were trapped because they were committed to their old policies, whatever their effects; they wanted, consciously or not, to punish Iraq for Saddam's sins; or they expected that ultimately order would be regenerated, in spite of their warnings. Although they said order was precarious, they counseled as if a hidden force—the trajectory of history, perhaps— would rescue them from the dangers they were courting. In any event, their advice was unequal to the strategic challenges before them. No wonder that Hillary Clinton voted one way and explained another.

Neoliberals and Technique

Hillary Clinton adopted her emphasis on international law and international organizations from liberal hawks, but her dutiful tone and pragmatism associated her with neoliberals. Riding the democratic capitalist wave of history, neoliberals are confident of ultimate success, which is why Clinton weighed the costs of the war but elided over the risks of failure. History is on their side and, as Francis Fukuyama had demonstrated, the twentieth century vindicated market capitalism. While all regime-changers said they favored instituting market capitalism, neoliberals prioritized breaking down barriers to marketization, bringing globalization, and reorganizing Iraq's political economy neoliberally.

President Reagan and British Prime Minister Margaret Thatcher instigated the neoliberal transformation in the early 1980s. Bill Clinton and Blair then extended the process in the 1990s. Like Reagan and Thatcher, they agreed on the primacy of markets, favored deregulation, especially of financial markets, and directed state policies to increasing economic growth. But Clinton and Blair were more administrative in temperament, professional in class orientation, and pragmatic in sensibility. As pragmatists, they emphasized technique, science, planning, and flexibility as priorities. Methods produce results; processes determine outcomes. Pragmatic neoliberals embrace expertise, demonstrate open-mindedness, apply technical knowledge, and scorn incompetence and dogmatism. Thus, in endorsing regime change, pragmatic neoliberals brought their characteristic concerns. They worried about opportunity costs, questioned the preparation and competence of the Bush administration, complained that it had not enlisted the Security Council, and warned that Bush was not planning for the war and its aftermath. Blaming failure on bad methods, bad planning, bad policies, and bad management, neoliberals called for more pragmatic policies in Iraq.

Joseph Nye stated the pragmatic case against Bush at the time the war was initiated. A leading thinker about international relations, inventor of the term "soft power," and undersecretary of defense in the Clinton administration, Nye expressed ambivalence. He disagreed with the timing of the war, but he accepted that "the Bush administration has made a strong moral argument for action."[53] Containment and sanctions had run their course, and Nye approved of the war's objectives. One of his opinion pieces was titled "The Right War at the Wrong Time."[54] The war was right because it was likely to produce "a better and more pluralist regime" (although not a full democracy) and because international opinion refused to countenance Saddam's WMDs. But the timing was wrong because Bush had botched the diplomatic preparations. His unilateralism had alienated world opinion.

Nye agreed with *what* the Bush administration was trying to do, but he objected to *how* it was doing it. If the United States was to succeed, it needed to win friends and augment its hard military and economic power with the international consent that comes from the massage of soft power. Bush's unilateralism, however, was insulting allies, threatening fence sitters, and turning both against the

United States even though many shared objectives with America. Neoconservative unilateralism "guarantees losing."[55] Sadly, multilateral legitimacy was readily available. Bush needed only to have requested UN approval.

> The United States should incline toward multilateralism whenever possible as a way to legitimize its power and to gain broad acceptance of its new strategy. Preemption that is legitimated by multilateral sanction is far less costly and sets a far less dangerous precedent than the United States asserting that it alone can act as judge, jury, and executioner. . . . To implement the new strategy successfully, therefore, the United States will need to pay more attention to soft power and multilateral cooperation than the new unilateralists would like.[56]

The point was for America to get its way, and honey catches more flies than vinegar. The pragmatic promise was that, as masters of technique, neoliberals knew how to achieve the objectives they share with neoconservatives. Paul Krugman, a critic of the war, echoed the point. "If you want to win a war, don't hire a movement conservative. Hire a liberal, or at least an Eisenhower-type Republican."[57]

Hillary Clinton shared Nye's sensibility about the war. Accepting tacitly the administration's ends, she accentuated questions of technique, strategy, and policy. Clinton expressed moral approval for the war, but she displayed none of the triumphalism and blood lust of neoconservatives. Fervor, swagger, and hysteria never entered her voice or manner, and she did not refer to Hitler or Stalin in advocating the war or defending her vote. Instead of seeing glory and heroism, she envisioned "a very difficult undertaking in very treacherous terrain."[58] She warned of the "considerable burden of rebuilding a secure and peaceful post-Saddam Iraq."[59] Regime change is hard work, but her formulation suggests that the costs would prove higher than the risks.

Clinton's pragmatism faced an obvious problem in Iraq. If good policies are those that achieve their ends efficiently, she needed to define the objective she wanted before she could assess the efficiency of the policies. Clinton did offer justifications aplenty for the war. She pointed to Saddam's WMDs, alleged ties to Al Qaeda, the many times he had defied UN resolutions, the dangerous precedent of letting him get away with violating international treaties and snubbing the UN and international law, and the danger he posed to peace and stability in the region. Israel mattered to her too. "The security and freedom of Israel," she explained a few years into the war, "must be decisive and remain at the core of any American approach to the Middle East."[60] Once the war got going Clinton discovered more "vital interests" in Iraq: stopping Al Qaeda, blocking Iran, defending the Kurds, and protecting friends in the neighborhood.[61] She noted from the beginning that regime change was established US policy and in 2005 made a passing reference to "the experiment in freedom and democracy."[62]

Although she did not clarify the actual objectives of the war, Clinton was adamant on one point. At every junction before and during the war, she repeated the need for preparations, policies, and strategies. Neoconservatives have will; pragmatic neoliberals have plans. She used the floor speech explaining her vote in favor of the war to sketch her plan for getting the diplomacy right. When the scale of the fiasco dawned on her, she updated her earlier cautions. She attributed American defeat to foolish policies. "The Administration and Defense Department's Iraq policy has been, by any reasonable measure, riddled with errors, misstatements and misjudgments. From the beginning of the Iraqi war, we were inadequately prepared for the aftermath of the invasion with too few troops and an inadequate plan to stabilize Iraq."[63] Exempting the fact of war from blame, she narrowed her criticism: "Our strategy in Iraq is failing."[64] Running for the Democratic presidential nomination in 2007–2008, Clinton spoke repeatedly of the "flawed and failed strategy in Iraq."[65] The common denominator in Clinton's criticisms, like those of the Elite Consensus, was that problems arose because particular policies failed, not because the war was misbegotten. If the problem was the strategy, then the problem was not the objective of regime change.

Clinton's position was that good plans perform better than bad plans. But it also was that the quality of American plans, not the enterprise of the war or the conditions in Iraq, is what decided between success and failure. With a good plan, success was ensured. Failure, therefore, proved planning was bad. If Bush had devised better strategies, by Clinton's logic, the war would have been vindicated. Although convenient in absolving her of culpability for voting for the fiasco, Clinton made the same point going into the war. In her cast of pragmatic neoliberalism, problems are managed through technical knowledge and expertise. The root problem, then, was not that Iraqi interests were inconsistent with American national interests, or that Iraqi cultural values clashed with gender-neutral liberal individualism, or that war for universalizing markets raised Iraqi fears that their oil was to be stolen. Brushing aside the substantive bases for Iraqi resistance to regime change, Clinton predicated her criticisms of Bush's defective implementation on the assumption that the ends were achievable.

Hillary Clinton mocks stargazers, rejects idealistic rapture, stares facts straight in the eye, and prides herself on her pragmatism and realism. Actually, she exemplifies the difference between two modes of politics that sometimes overlap in practice but that are distinct in principle. Realists see power lurking behind not just interests, but values and ideals too. They either are altruistic words that ennoble the self-interest that governs all human behavior, or they are dangerous, self-subverting indulgences. Either way, realists debunk the role of values and ideals. That, as E. H. Carr points out, is their defining failure. Because for realists politics is always and only the unceasing and unchanging competition for power, it has no ends.

But in restricting politics to the pursuit of power, and only power, realists deny the potency of the beliefs, convictions, and loves that, ironically, are essential components of power. Failing to understand that power requires purpose if it is to inspire and thrive, realists misunderstand the nature of their idol. The failure to understand power would compromise any politics. But it ruins realism as a positive politics, as shown by the failure of their prescient warnings to mobilize opposition to the war.[66]

Pragmatists are different. Their ends are so obvious, self-evident, and uncontestable that they often pass unspecified. "It is only when you take your ethics for granted," as Louis Hartz wrote, "that all problems emerge as problems of technique."[67] Because their ends are incontrovertible and self-evident, pragmatists can concentrate on means. But in focusing on means to the neglect of ends and in assuming that their ends were shared by Iraqis, pragmatists were bereft when Iraqis rejected what regime-changers thought were liberal ideals on the grounds that they were manifestations of American power. Not seeing the power politics that was embedded in their values or that was deployed in instituting such liberal values as markets, pragmatists were bewildered when these values—and, therefore, American power—were resisted.

Realists, because they see American power *as* power, predicted that Iraqis would resist American power.[68] It was for them both *power* and *American*. Power for realists does not become exceptional because Americans exercise it. Power remains power and, whatever the intentions of exceptionalists, power is destined to be balanced. But pragmatists, because they operate *within* structures of power that they do not see *as* power, do not understand themselves to be promoting particular economic or state interests. Steeped in the win-win market ideology of neoliberalism and believing that history culminates in them, pragmatists regard power as the means to their uncontroversial pragmatic ends. What matters are intentions and competences. Because instituting market society in Iraq would make Iraqis freer, happier, and richer, reasonable Iraqis—and neoliberals follow the discipline of economics in assuming rationality—would embrace that which would emancipate them from the shackles of Saddam's statist despotism.

Neoliberal pragmatists, therefore, minimized the risks of Iraqi opposition to the occupation. Liberal regime change was, and would be experienced as, emancipatory. The success of liberal capitalism, having been ordained by history, answered the question of ends. With goals resolved, technical questions assume paramount importance. Consequently, Hillary Clinton reflexively and necessarily attributed the fiasco in Iraq to Bush's manner of making decisions.

> The mistakes in Iraq are . . . the responsibility of our . . . Commander-in-Chief. From the decision to rush to war without allowing the weapons inspectors to finish their work or waiting for diplomacy to run its course. To the failure to send enough troops and provide proper equipment for them. To the denial of the existence of a rising insurgency and the failure to adjust the military strategy. To the continued support for a government unwilling to make the necessary political compromises. The command decisions were *rooted in politics and ideology, heedless of* sound strategy and *common sense.*[69]

Not recognizing her ideology *as* ideology, Clinton offered a dose of hardheaded common sense as the cure to Bush's ideology. But Clinton lost the forest in the trees. Focusing on confused means, she overlooked the larger unity among neoconservatives, liberal hawks, and neoliberals. All meant to universalize American power in the name of promoting liberal values.

The Limits of Pragmatism

Clinton entered the race for the Democratic presidential nomination in 2008 heavily favored, and her position on the war seemed to do what was required. It maintained continuity with her husband's policies, shielded her from charges of softness, distinguished her from the Bush administration, married her to Israel, advanced American national interests, and represented the views of her party's foreign policy establishment. It presented her as presidential. Yet her positioning failed because, ultimately, it was pragmatic without being realistic. Not understanding American power as power, Clinton was blindsided by Iraqi resistance, just like Bush and Blair. She understood that progressive change might be hard, but not that it would be rejected.

Liberal hawks and neoliberals turned the United States into the vehicle of capitalist liberation, took market capitalism—and, therefore, US power—as altruistic, and predicted that the war would produce win-win, positive-sum outcomes and advance freedom and universal interests.[70] They even agreed with neoconservatives about the source of the crisis in Iraq and the Middle East. Thus, parts of the neoliberal United Nations Development Program *Arab Human Development Report* on what ailed Arab economies and societies, which was written by Arab technocrats in 2002, read as if Bernard Lewis wrote them. Although the authors opposed the war, the *Report* complained about Arab deficits in "civil and political freedoms, the status of women in society and access to knowledge."[71] The *Report* blamed the rot on statist economies, not Islam, but the policy recommendations were similar. Neoconservatives called for conquering Iraq and then using the state to transform the culture. Neoliberal hawks agreed on the need to conquer Iraq and reorganize the state, but they were interested in marketizing Iraq, not in reforming Islam. Of course, marketizing society also marketizes values, and marketizing values also transforms culture. Neoliberals did not worry about Islam when they thought about the Middle East, but their indifference to religion reflects their conviction that markets instill incentives and disincentives that regulate behavior regardless of cultural norms. Neoliberals, in other words, did not need to worry about religion because markets neutralize the effect of religion on secular life.

Neoliberal and neoconservative policies toward Iraq were similar, but their objectives were different. Neoconservatives regarded neoliberals with contempt, denigrating them as commercial, unheroic, and unmanly, as more interested in maximizing marginal utility than in accomplishing national greatness. But neoconservatives, as they betrayed with their fear of existential annihilation, are not riding the wave of history. The great irony of the neoconservative war in Iraq was that winning would have promoted neoliberal ends. Thomas Friedman got that point. Neoliberals fretted that the war might take too long or cost too much in actual or in opportunity costs, and they had powerful reasons for deeming the war to be unnecessary, given that history and human psychology were on their side anyway. But their strongest reason for opposing the war—that it was redundant—testifies to neoliberal certainty. Taking for granted that at the end of the day the war would produce a market economy, a market society, and a global sensibility, neoliberals spoke little about ends precisely because they were self-evident. The future was theirs.

Clinton backed the war, then, because her ideology minimized the risks. If she had cast her vote only opportunistically, as she was accused of doing, and yet she had understood the import—and, therefore, the risks—of regime change, the self-same opportunism that supposedly explains her support would have had her voting against authorization. Clinton failed, in other words, conceptually and politically, not morally. But neoliberals, although thoroughly underestimating the import of the regime change, at least envisioned a destination for Iraq that was not implausible. They did not get the market society they wanted because, in weakening the Iraqi state by disbanding the army and de-Ba'athifying the administration, the United States weakened the agent that they needed to impose markets. Yet they were right, as Bremer illustrated in his orders that were to reorganize Iraq's economy, in thinking that the historical import of the war was to clear the way for market civilization, for finance capital and for globalization—for neoliberalism.

Liberal regime change, then, aimed at the most recalcitrant holdout in the most illiberal region of the world. It meant to crack the Arab nut. Seeking what the neoliberal international relations theorist John Ikenberry calls "an empire of capitalist democracy,"[72] neoliberals favored war in Iraq because they know the capitalist order is inevitable and yet that it still must be produced. The terms are obvious, but the reality is not given. Neoliberals meant to remake the state in the cradle of civilization, to release market forces, and to globalize Iraq, much as Bill Clinton hoped a month before the war. "It's going to take years to rebuild Iraq. If we do this, we want it to be a secular democracy. We want it to be a shared model for other Middle Eastern countries. We want to . . . shake the foundations of autocracy in the Middle East and promote more freedom and decency."[73]

6

American Exceptionalism Meets Iraqi History

Americans never had to worry about creating a
government. This gap in historical experience made
them peculiarly blind to the problems of creating
effective authority in modernizing countries.

Samuel P. Huntington

John Maynard Keynes famously observed the influence of long-
ago thinkers on the most hardheaded, anti-intellectual figures. Nose-
to-the-grindstone actors proceed on the basis of assumptions, which
they might not recognize themselves as making, about how the
world operates. These assumptions, ironically, derive not from the
practical experience that is the source of their pride, but from thinkers they demean and might not have read. "The ideas of economists
and political philosophers, both when they are right and when they
are wrong, are more powerful than is commonly understood. Indeed the world is ruled by little else." Then, as if foreseeing the intellectual origins of the demand for regime change in Iraq, Keynes
continues: "Practical men, who believe themselves to be quite ex-
empt from any intellectual influence, are usually the slaves of some
defunct economist [or political philosopher]."[1]

The advocates of regime change maintained that Saddam, by inserting fear and violence in place of affect and sentiment, had destroyed social cohesion. In fact, they highlighted this charge when

making the case for regime change. Breaking what remained of the state after Saddam's depredations made sense as policy, therefore, only on the shoulders of one of three assumptions: either the champions of regime change did not believe that social disintegration posed a serious danger to Iraq; they accepted the fact that disintegration had occurred but were unconcerned with—or favored—political disorder in Iraq; or, most likely, they underestimated the import of dismantling state power amid the social disintegration they declaimed. Although some neoconservative ideologues announced their disdain for Arab civilization and their desire to smash it, their practical, nonideological, policy-making collaborators in the political and foreign policy establishments, instead of recognizing the radicalism of regime change, thought they were following the well-traveled path of dominant world powers. Regime-changers called explicitly for ridding Iraq of the despot who personally controlled the state, sadistically pitted Iraqis against each other, preempted the development of civil society, and fractured the Iraqi sense of solidarity, unity, and common destiny. Thus regime-changers should have realized that, by the terms of their indictment, deposing Saddam must unleash political disorder. Yet lulled by liberal verities, regime-changers ignored the implications of their position.

Regime-changers, with the exception of a minority of neoconservatives, did not appreciate the meaning of what they had in mind. A few neoconservatives might have wanted to overturn all Islamic or Arab nationalist regimes in the Middle East, but most hawks expected more familiar outcomes. They were, as Keynes might have noted, wearing eyeglasses that they had lifted from dead political philosophers. The detail that reveals their debt is not that, after weighing the matter, regime-changers concluded they could break Iraq's state without breaking civic order too. The detail is that civilian policy-makers did not register the question; they barely asked what *principles* would order Iraq after state power was broken. They did ask how order was to be *maintained* during the interim between Saddam and the consolidation of the new regime. They thought about that, and they thought about whether Iraqis or Americans should rule after Saddam's demise. But taking for granted the givenness of liberal order, they reduced the threat of disorder to a mere *transitional* issue between the fall of the old order and the emergence of the new order.[2]

American policy-makers would say otherwise. The State Department is said to have prepared for the travails ahead by commissioning thirteen volumes of reports, ideas, and policies to prepare for regime change. Unfortunately, the story runs, Secretary of Defense Rumsfeld prevented them from being implemented. These reports, by the State Department's description, covered "public health and humanitarian needs, transparency and anti-corruption, oil and energy, defense policy and institutions, transitional justice, democratic principles and procedures, local government, civil society capacity building, education, free media, water, agriculture and environment and economy and infrastructure."[3] Picking up the point, the Elite Consensus blamed the Bush administration for ignoring these plans, largely for reasons of bureaucratic jealousy, and thus for catapulting Iraq into chaos.[4] Typically, Rumsfeld was more concerned with fending off the State Department's influence than with navigating Iraq's transition to lasting stability.

The problem with these objections—and, therefore, with using the State Department's reports to disprove the thesis that America's liberal tradition disposed pragmatic policy-makers to assume deep wellsprings of order in Iraq once Saddam's corrupting influence was excised—is that the reports did not amount to real plans for governing Iraq. They were issued by "working groups" of Iraqis, sometimes after two or three days of meeting, brainstorming, and horse-trading. The working groups often broke into task forces that wrote the specific reports and then submitted them to coordinating committees. But little actual planning could occur in brief meetings and subcommittees (and in the absence of an authoritative state). Often the reports were affirmations of principles, platitudes, and silliness.[5] One report on tax policy, for example, dismissed income tax as a Marxist idea.[6] The working groups conducted their work separately, and no authority integrated the various reports into a coherent package, figured out how to allocate resources among them, or specified which institutions could be assumed and which remained in doubt. Like wish lists, the working groups set forth policies that they called on the forthcoming state to honor. The reports also assumed away problems that would be caused by scarce resources, limited state capacity, and, most importantly, disagreements about the sovereignty of liberal principles. They ground their policies on the liberal foundations they merely assumed.

The report by the Democratic Principles and Procedures Working Group illustrates the aggressiveness of the assumptions that were made about the prospects for liberal order. The report called for a liberal constitution, a bill of rights, a democratic government, and respect for civil society and the separation of powers. It also expected de-Ba'athification and efficient administration. Although the report on democratic principles implicitly acknowledged some obstacles to instituting liberal democracy in Iraq, these were superseded by the two decisive assumptions it made. First, it prescribed that democratic Iraq would recognize standard liberal rights to equality under the law, due process, property, security from unreasonable search and seizure, and freedom of expression. It also prescribed rights for women and self-determination (although not necessarily statehood) for Iraq's minorities.[7] It did not say how these commitments would be achieved or maintained.

Second, the Working Group also expected—or encouraged the State Department's expectations—that liberal rights would order post-Saddam Iraq and that they would be ratified democratically. The plans assumed, first, that Iraqis would consent democratically to liberal rights and, second, that consent was sufficient to secure rights for Iraqis. That is, the plans for building liberal order in Iraq assumed the primacy of the very liberal values that needed to be built. The reports prove, in other words, not that the United States recognized that establishing the new order in Iraq would be difficult. Actually, they suggest the precise opposite. The reports included few actual policies; they were prepared by Iraqis, not Americans; and the plans, such as they were, assumed that Iraqis would embrace liberal values, that liberal values would order Iraq, and that, therefore, the hard work would be achieved before the government took office.

The Iraqi advisors took their cue from American regime-changers. Americans worried about maintaining order during the interval between Saddam's fall and the emergence of the new regime. They did not, however, dwell on deeper questions of what the new order would be, where it would come from, and who would support it and why. Americans assumed, not without reason, that most Iraqis would favor rights, equality under the law, and constitutional, accountable government. But Americans also assumed, more ambitiously, that consensual government was possible in Iraq in the absence of agreement on national identity, the role of religion, the supremacy of individualism, the status of secular values, and the primacy of markets in allocating resources. By assuming that liberal order was Iraq's destiny, regime-changers could assume also that Iraqi society would shed its old skin and grow a more suitable state, naturally. Breaking state power, therefore, was not understood to be tantamount to breaking civic order; and the terms of civic order, after being upset by regime change, would surface uncontroversially despite the breakdown of state power and authority. The antenna of regime-changers had been numbed by liberal political and economic thought.

Liberals distinguish themselves from rival traditions on several familiar scores. They pronounce inalienable rights, identify individuals (as opposed to families, ethnic groups, classes, or some other association) as the bedrock of society, declare equality under the law as a foundational principle, believe in progress and constitutional government, and they blend these commitments together with an abiding commitment to property rights. But liberals also introduced a theoretical innovation that is taken for granted. Prior political traditions in Europe were preoccupied with questions of political order. They focused on where political order comes from, what may be done to establish it, whether it is subject to standards of justice or whether, as the condition of the law and moral standards, it is unaccountable to them, and how order connects to God and church. What was original about liberals is that they deproblematized the source of civic order as a first-order political and theoretical issue, and not just because they focused on other concerns. Deproblematizing the origins of order was the predicate of the liberal project.

Contemporary Western liberals surf over the issue of political order for obvious reasons. Writing in societies with stable government, rule of law, high levels of legitimacy, and low levels of political violence, they take security for granted. But liberals also deemphasized order as a theoretical problem from their early days, long before liberal societies became stable, through two distinctive theoretical moves. First, liberals posited order as originating independently of and prior to states. The point is not that liberals reject order; they rest their whole edifice on it. But liberals had to assume the givenness of order if they were to escape its clutches and get the rights they craved. Their vulnerability was that if rights were seen to have issued from and to be granted by states, then rights would become answerable to the state that awarded them. The fundamental commitment of liberals, however, is to make states answerable to (liberal) rights, not vice versa.

Liberals, therefore, make their second distinctive theoretical move. They render political order as congruent with rights, and they construe the origins of political order accordingly. If, as the prior absolutist traditions in Europe had it, civic order is established by states declaring the principles that are to order the regime and then imposing them over recalcitrant subjects, liberal rights are not supreme and inviolable. Rights can be accorded sovereignty, as liberals want, only on condition that they produce order—that exercising them fulfills and completes, as opposed to compromises, the obligation of states to provide civic order. Liberals kill both birds with one stone. They must establish the existence of both rights and order as independent of states, and they achieve these dual purposes by *naturalizing* both.

By making rights natural, liberals remove them from the state's dominion; and by making order natural, liberals relegate states to enforcing, not promulgating, the principles of civic order that are deemed to be preexisting and given by nature. Having rendered rights as prior logically and temporally to states, liberals can require states to respect rights, not the other way around. Liberals, in other words, first shrink the question of creating rights to the lesser matter of merely securing them; and, second, shrink the question of establishing political order to merely enforcing it. This is why the Declaration of Independence could announce, "We hold these truths to be self-evident, that all men are created equal, that they are endowed by their Creator with certain unalienable Rights [and] that to secure these rights, Governments are instituted among Men, deriving their just powers from the consent of the governed." Having conceived of rights as mutually complementary and innately ordered, liberals make order the by-product of, not the alternative to, the free expression of natural rights. Rights become self-ordering.

Naturalizing order greased the case for war in Iraq. In theoretical regimes that have states imposing the *terms* of civic order, breaking state power is fraught with danger. In fact, it is likely to yield chaos as rival interests and ideologies fight over the rules of the game in the absence of rules that determine how the fighting is to be conducted. If, however, the risks of disorder are exempted from the calculation, which follows from assuming the terms of order even amid states that are in shambles, then the pros were not offset by the cons. Putting a thumb on the scale, hawkish images of regime change proceeded as if societies can regenerate states like iguanas regenerate new tails.

Liberals should have anticipated that breaking Iraq's state would unleash lawlessness anyway, inasmuch as they have states enforcing law and regime change was disarming the enforcers. But if states had been seen also as *producing* the principles of civic existence, as setting the terms for how Iraqis would decide the rules that determine how they would live together, then the risks of regime change would have been seen as rising exponentially. There would be no order to enforce and no institutions for establishing one. US policymakers, who prided themselves on their hardheaded practicality, underestimated the import of regime change, and not only because they were captives of Keynes's dead political philosophers. Their real problem is that they remembered the wrong ones. They should have heeded Thomas Hobbes. But steeped in liberal thought, their lodestar was John Locke. Imagining Locke's natural order, they brought Hobbes to Iraq.

Locke versus Hobbes

If liberals are committed to enshrining the supremacy of universal and innate rights, how can they allay fears that they are upsetting order? If rights and liberties are to be accorded primacy in organizing state, society, and economy, what must be assumed before they can play their assigned role? The answers are foreshadowed in the political theories of Hobbes and Locke. Beginning with different conceptions of the state of nature, they derive different kinds of states. Locke's state of nature produces liberal government (or, perhaps, his liberal commitments dictate his conception of nature). Hobbes, on the other hand, opens with dire assumptions about the state of nature and develops their logic remorselessly. Locke stacks the deck. Hobbes just rolls the dice.[8]

The state of nature for Hobbes was not an anthropological stage. It is both a thought experiment that he designed to highlight the salient features of the existing order and the historic reality in civil wars and international relations, which pit "every man against every man."[9] Locke's state of nature is a happier place. It lacks states too, but it has "a law of nature to govern it," which God decreed before men got around to creating states. Benign, Locke's law of nature forbids offensive violence and theft. "[N]o one ought to harm another in his life, health, liberty, or possessions: for men being all workmanship of one omnipotent, and infinitely wise maker."[10] Equally importantly, the law is known to all men because God implanted the reason that allows them to apprehend natural laws.[11] With the state of nature ruled by natural law, and men able to discern it by virtue of God-given reason, Locke's men know right from wrong, understand justice, and possess most elements of the good life.

The deficiency, and the reason why men abandon Locke's state of nature, is that it provides plentitude but not the security to enjoy it. Enforcement is patchy. Natural law is "plain and intelligible to all rational creatures," but men are "biased by their interests."[12] They know the law and might believe they are obeying it, but they favor themselves when they get into disputes with others. Locke's statelessness fails, then, not for lack of law but for lack of impartial judges and disinterested executors to apply law in particular instances. With every man judging his own case, life in Locke's state of nature becomes precarious, natural freedom becomes dangerous, and property becomes insecure. Locke's solution follows easily. Because they lack only government, his subjects delegate to the disinterested state their natural right to adjudicate in cases that involve themselves, which is the cause of "inconveniences" in the state of nature.[13] In exchange for giving up the right to enforce their rights, they get to keep the substance of the rights they possess already.

Locke can require his state to respect inalienable rights, to be liberal, because he disagrees with Hobbes about what organizes life in the absence of the sovereign state. They agree that men enter into states to escape life's uncertainties in nature, but disagree radically about the status and content of law there (as well as the security of life and limb). For Locke, order is immanent in nature. Order cannot be realized without states, but it is impressed on mind and society by God and is both known and beneficent. Even while Locke's men are fighting, they agree on the terms of the law, just not on how to apply it to resolve particular conflicts. Having thus reduced disorder in the state of nature to an enforcement problem, Locke assumes away questions about *how* people decide on their fundamental laws and *what* they decide. God resolved these questions before people contemplated establishing states.

Hobbes assumes less. His natural law confers the right to do almost anything. Therefore, every liberty threatens, and is threatened by, every other liberty. One person's right to kill and to take—which are not to be confused with murdering and stealing because the state of nature brooks no law to define killing as murder or taking as stealing—collides with every other person's selfsame right to kill and to take. Hobbes's state of nature does deliver equality, but it is the equality of the coffin and of the destitute. Not only is property unattainable in practice amid conditions of chaos, but it is a logical impossibility. Property is a legal relationship between the property and its owner, but Hobbes's state of nature—in marked contrast to Locke's—excludes law. Law is promulgated by states, but Hobbes's state of nature lacks lawmakers (and not just law enforcers). There is no law to enforce.

Locke can attribute the failure of the state of nature to shortcomings in enforcement only on condition that he assumes law and order to exist incipiently before the founding of states. In other words, Locke not only assumed the can opener; he invented it. Sneaking in order on the sly, Locke has God doing the heavy lifting. God creates rights, makes them compatible with each other, and endows man with the reason to behold natural law. Consequently, Locke's state does not need to establish the positive principles that curb human conflict and allow people to live in society harmoniously. In writing that the biased pursuit of self-interest is what spoils the opportunities of the state of nature, Locke identifies the problem as imperfect administration, not natural design. Natural design works ideally in principle, thus sparing his government the obligation to create definitions of freedom, equality, justice, and the terms by which citizens may live together peacefully. By postulating those blessings as present at the creation, Locke's natural rights do not need to be checked at the door as the price of entering the state and civil society. Already encoded in man and society, rights can be harmonized in practice by the disinterested, unbiased administration of law. The task of good governance is reduced to refereeing man's rights, not creating them.

Something, however, is askance in Locke's conception of the state of nature. He admits that it is consumed by deep and abiding conflicts as each man, judging his own affairs partially and unreasonably, stakes claims to properties that other men, with their own partiality and unreasonableness, judge as theirs. Locke's fights mostly concern who owns what. Locke, therefore, makes two inconsistent assumptions. First, he assumes that sufficient order prevails in the absence of states to facilitate society, to agree on definitions of property, and to encourage the accumulation of property, including the cultivation of land, in spite of the incessant disputes about who gets the fruit of whose labor. Second, Locke assumes enough disorder in nature to jeopardize the enjoyment of property and to motivate men to establish the states that protect the property that somehow has been assembled.

Hobbes conceives nature altogether differently. For Locke, the propulsion to form states is to secure benefits that were acquired prior to states. For Hobbes, it is to escape death. Unlike Locke,

Hobbes recognizes the right to total and absolute aggression: "every man has a right to everything; even to one another's body."[14] Justice is unknown. "To this war of every man against every man . . . nothing can be unjust. The notions of right and wrong, justice and injustice, have there no place."[15] Abandoned to his own devices amid mortal danger, "each man hath to use his own power, as he will himself, for the preservation of his own nature."[16] Hobbes, in other words, admits not just the conventional right to self-defense, as Locke would, but also the right to act on "anticipation."[17] In the absence of the sovereign state, anyone may strike anyone who might be construed as a potential threat—that is, everyone. Even the strongest is vulnerable to the weakest.[18] Launching preemptive attacks now might secure the attacker's safety later.

Hobbes's point is that in the absence of a sovereign state that affords protection, aggression and preemption are obligatory survival strategies that everyone must imitate. The only defense becomes a triumphant offense. The logic of statelessness is get or be gotten, and the law of nature compels survival. Even if violence merely looms as a potential and not as a present danger, the prospect of eventual violence triggers the logic of self-help, condemning all inhabitants to war with all other inhabitants. "[W]ar consisteth not in actual fighting, but in the known disposition thereto during all the time there is no assurance to the contrary."[19]

Hobbes, therefore, dismisses the possibility of accumulating property. He leaves no room "for industry, because the fruit thereof is uncertain," in nature.[20] Without sovereignty, there is no law; without law, there is no order; without the law to define and the order to accumulate property, there can be no property. Property for Hobbes not only is not a right in nature; it is impossible to accumulate. By assuming property rights in the state of nature, Locke assumes both the security that is required to assemble property and the authority that defines property rights. By Hobbes's logic, Locke has no right to either assumption. The insecurity of property is a practical inconvenience for Locke; it is a logical necessity for Hobbes.

The root difference between the Hobbesian and Lockean states of nature, then, is that Hobbes problematizes and Locke deproblematizes the origins of political order. Locke invites the people to delegate to government only those powers that are necessary for securing the full benefits of nature's bounty. Nature—not states or violence or politics—sets the terms of consensual order. In thus naturalizing political order, Locke depoliticizes it. His state merely completes the circle of nature. Hobbes, however, construes nature precisely as that which must be escaped. With natural law endowing men with the *right,* and not just the power, to seize and kill, Hobbes cannot have his sovereign enforcing the order that is immanent in natural law. It is nature that, in mandating offensive violence, introduces the war of all against all. Thus, where Locke's state only enforces the preexisting natural order, Hobbes's state must forge the content and status of law before order can be enforced. Hobbes's sovereign must perform the work that Locke leaves to God.

Luckily, Hobbes's nature provides the escape route from statelessness. The selfsame survival instinct that permits all manner of aggression also disposes those stranded in the state of nature to agree among themselves to surrender their right to all their liberties (except the right to survival) to a sovereign that remains unencumbered by the covenant. The sovereign, which may be a person or an organization, and only the sovereign, retains the right conferred by nature to use offensive violence, declare right and wrong, and make order however it sees fit. Sovereignty, then, is the power and authority to monopolize violence, to set the terms of political order and define standards, rights, and obligations in the state, and to punish transgressors. For Hobbes, in other words, justice is defined by and derives from power, not the other way around. Sovereign power, having made justice possible, is not answerable to its issue.

Locke disagrees. Deriving order from natural law, he writes of the obligation of states to *preserve* property rights. The "end of law is . . . to preserve and enlarge freedom."[21] Indeed, the conflicts over property that propel Locke's men to form states can arise only because natural law prevails already. With property and rights existing before states, Locke exempts states from having to establish the terms of order. With Locke's rights given and the hard work of defining and harmonizing the exercise of rights completed by God at the birth of man, states merely enforce preexisting rights and fulfill preexisting order. For Hobbes, order is whatever the sovereign says it is, and justice is defined accordingly. Justice follows from, rationalizes, respects, and cannot judge the political order. For Locke, justice and order are two sides of the coin minted by God.

What Makes States into States

Locke posits order as existing prior to the state and Hobbes has it issuing from the state. But what are "states," and what is at stake in how they are defined? Conveniently, social science agrees on an answer. In Max Weber's famous definition, the modern state is that which "(successfully) claims the *monopoly of the legitimate use of physical force* within a given territory." Elsewhere, Weber adds that modern "legal-rational" states require armies of rule-obeying and procedure-enforcing bureaucrats to administer the territory, and that states are "compulsory" associations and that they seek legitimacy. Born into states, citizens do not choose them. Territoriality, administration, compulsion, and legitimacy fill out and complete Weber's state. But it originates in violence.

Weber associates violence and states throughout his famous passage.

"Every state is founded on force," said Trotsky at Brest-Litovsk. That is indeed right. If no social institutions existed which knew the use of violence, then the concept of "state" would be eliminated. . . . Of course, force is certainly not the normal or the only means of the state—nobody says that—but force is a means specific to the state. . . . Today, however, we have to say that a state is a human community that (successfully) claims the *monopoly of the legitimate use of physical force* within a given territory. Note that "territory" is one of the characteristics of the state. Specifically, at the present time, the right to use physical force is ascribed to other institutions or to individuals only to the extent to which the state permits it.[22]

The ends of states vary, but the means of violence is both common and exclusive to states. All states, and only states, have recourse to violence, unless a particular state chooses to authorize the right of others to use violence. Organizations that may use violence legitimately are states, and those that may not are not states. Weber's states outgrow direct dependence on violence and contrive political or administrative means for resolving disagreements, but they can pass beyond violence only after mastering it first.

Weber's state is "the sole source of the 'right' to use violence,"[23] but two tests must be passed before the right to authorize violence is attained. First, violence must be monopolized as far as is feasible. If the state meets little or no violent resistance in the territory it claims as its own, then it holds the monopoly on *actual* violence. Weber's second test is slipperier. The state must monopolize *legitimate* violence too. Read democratically, Weber often is interpreted to mean that violence is legitimate when, and only when, the state using it originates in the consent of the governed. The legitimate state is the democratic state. Weber, however, does not issue this specification. He does not require the legitimate state to be democratic or to originate in consent. He does require, however, that the state follow *rules*. The state that follows rules, especially in its use of violence, is legitimate; the state that ignores or violates rules is illegitimate, and, therefore, is incomplete. Legitimacy completes the state, and the complete state is the one that, in following rules, rises above the impulses of its rulers. The consent of the people is not irrelevant, but it is not decisive either. Legitimacy becomes the dependent, not the independent, variable; it accrues to states that respect the laws, procedures, and norms they subscribe to. The state that is legitimate is the state whose violence is legal, rational, and rule abiding, and that monopolizes both actual and legitimate violence.

The monopolies on actual and legitimate violence distinguish the modern state from prior forms of states. Previously violence was disseminated throughout the realm; in feudal Europe, nobles, aristocrats, barons, and knights, in addition to kings and emperors, all had access to actual and legitimate violence. Access to violence, in fact, was integral to the status of all ranks; without violence, they were peasants. Weber's modern state ratifies the rules that count as right and lawful, holds sway over territory, and makes submission compulsory, just like Hobbes prescribes for his sovereign state. In fact, Weber borrows his first criteria from Hobbes in requiring that states monopolize violence and also borrows his second criteria in requiring that states monopolize legitimate—in addition to actual—violence. As Hobbes's state monopolizes actual violence by decreeing the sovereign as the sole source of offensive violence, and as it monopolizes legitimate violence by reserving to the sovereign the sole authority to pronounce what is just and unjust, legitimate and illegitimate, so Weber's state likewise monopolizes the violence that is right, just, and legitimate. But Weber differs from Hobbes on one pivotal score. Hobbes's sovereign may do whatever it pleases, defining what is justice one moment, redefining it the next, and ignoring the relationship between what it affirmed and what it did in the third moment. Hobbes's sovereign, still inhabiting the state of nature, is wholly unbridled in its absolute liberty. Weber's state, by contrast, is fundamentally constrained. It must honor the terms of its legitimacy.

Having defined the sovereign state in terms of monopolies on legitimate violence, Hobbes and Weber imply that extensive nonstate violence compromises the actual sovereignty of the legal state. The converse, however, does not hold. The absence of violence does not prove the existence of the sovereign, for reasons Hobbes explains (and Kant accepts). Violence is the worst manifestation, but is not the defining feature, of statelessness. If people live with the prospect that violence might erupt because no sovereign can prevent it, and if they must make preparations for fending for themselves because the state cannot fend off threats for them, which is what international relations theory calls "self-help," then people live with a version of statelessness in spite of the paraphernalia of legal states. The absence of violence counts as peace only if sovereign states prevent subjects from taking recourse to violence, and if the state's subjects surrender their preparations for self-help.

Of course, what Hobbes and Weber write is one thing and what illuminates politics in Iraq might be another. So what if, by their definition, states must monopolize both actual and legitimate violence to qualify as actual states, if the absence of violence does not conclusively prove the presence of the state, and if the state for Weber (but not for Hobbes) must satisfy the terms of its legitimation? The questions suggest a commonsense retort. Whatever the theoretical complexities, something approximating a state does exist in Iraq and has existed since 1921, even if Iraq's state never has satisfied the specifications of Hobbes and Weber. Those theorists were thinking in terms of geometrical images and ideal types, and it would be foolish to push either to the point of denying the practical stateness of Iraq's actual legal state. Nevertheless, Hobbes and Weber do raise two groups of questions that are critical for Iraqi history and contemporary politics. First, does the legal state exercise the monopoly on actual violence, has it ever established anything approaching the monopoly in its history as Iraq's legal state, and does it exercise effective administrative control of Iraqi territory? Second, is Iraq's legal state legitimate, and, indeed, has it ever been legitimate?

The two monopolies that define the state are never complete in practice, but the legal state must control the predominance of both actual and legitimate violence if it is to pass muster as a real state. Weber, notice, specified that the monopolies must be "successful" (although he softened the requirement by putting the word in parenthesis). Turning around the definition makes the specifications clearer. Even if a fully "successful" monopoly on both actual and legitimate violence is not required to qualify as a state, whatever comes closest to establishing these monopolies comes closest to qualifying as the state. The sense of Hobbes and Weber, and the reason for their relevance to Iraq's politics, is that Iraq's root problem was not national-religious conflict, the lack of social trust, weak institutions, or even quarrelsome politicians. These are important problems and worsen the circumstances of Iraqi life. But they are symptoms of the root absence of the two monopolies and administrative efficacy. Even when Saddam's brutality peaked, the state was weak. Without a sovereign, Iraq faced disorder; and amid disorder, Hobbes—not Locke—lurks.

Building Illegitimacy

Iraq was conceived in the marriage of liberal ideology, courtesy of Woodrow Wilson's internationalism, and time-honored, to-the-victor-go-the-spoils, imperialist realpolitick. In the midst of World War I, Britain and France negotiated the Sykes-Picot Agreement, which divided chunks of the Ottoman Empire between them. Britain took Palestine, Jordan, Baghdad, and Basra; France got Syria, Lebanon, and Mosul in the Kurdish regions of the north (which it soon swapped for a share of Britain's oil conglomerate, completing the boundaries of contemporary Iraq). But the outcome of World War I disrupted the familiar power politics. Britain and France could consummate their power grab because their side won the war, but it won only because the United States broke the battlefield deadlock between them and Germany. As his price, Woodrow Wilson demanded changes in the ideology, discourse, and, he said, the practice of international politics. When Wilson could not accomplish actual changes in imperialist practices, an accommodation evolved. Britain and France kept their new acquisitions, along with the rest of their empires; in exchange, they paid lip service to liberal duties.

The League balanced Wilson's idealism and imperial interests by wrapping the imperial interests in idealistic language. Under the "mandate" system, an idea conceived by the liberal South African and famed segregationist Jan Smuts, the winners (Britain and France) got territory in Asia and Africa from the losers (the Ottomans and Germany) on condition that the winners affirmed the principles of trusteeship.[24] The arrangement obligated the new rulers to accept their duty as civilized people to oversee the "well-being and development" of Middle Eastern and African peoples that were unprepared for the modern world. "The tutelage of such people should be entrusted to advanced nations." The moral responsibility would be burdensome, but it was "a sacred trust of civilisation."[25] Luckily, the interests of Iraqis in developing their capacity for self-government happened to coincide with the designs of the Sykes-Picot Agreement. The League's Covenant conferred sovereignty over Iraq onto Britain, and Britain promised to initiate Iraqis into the benefits and responsibilities of civilization.

Trusteeship provided legal justification for British control, but it exerted little influence on Britain's actual conduct. Anyway, British interests in Iraq were limited. Wanting mostly to secure trade, communication, and military routes to India, the jewel of the Empire, Iraq's significance to Britain was derivative. Iraq also was thought to hold petroleum, although the deposits were not proved until 1928. But the value of the hoped-for oil, like that of Iraq as a route to India, was primarily strategic. Naval power upheld the empire, and Britain had shifted from coal, which it had in abundance, to oil, which it lacked altogether, for fueling its fleet. With access to oil becoming an imperial imperative, and with British officials identifying Iran (and Iraq) as their preferred sources, Britain had additional reasons for centralizing aspects of Iraqi government—foreign policy and oil concessions—but not for concerning itself with Iraq's internal development otherwise. As long as Britain controlled Iraq's external affairs and secured access to petroleum, it was uninterested in realizing the League's happy promises.

Toby Dodge, who takes Britain's liberal professions seriously, nevertheless confirms that British interests were dominant. "British policymakers agreed that Britain could not put strategic and economic interests at risk by a premature loosening of control."[26] Adeed Dawisha makes a similar point. "The British had to construct a state in which government would be drawn from the country's own inhabitants, yet the British would retain enough political authority to check unacceptable policies and decisions by the indigenous government."[27] Peter Sluglett concurs that Britain's "own strategic and commercial aims were given first priority."[28] Britain wanted control, primacy, and vetoes; by implication, the League's promises amounted to little in practice, and just as well. If Britain had taken seriously its undertaking to govern Iraqis until they were prepared to govern themselves, and yet also was committed to safeguarding its imperial interests, Britain might have followed the incentives the League engendered. As long as Iraqis were unprepared to assume the burdens of self-government, British rule was justified. Thus, exactly contrary to its professions, the League rewarded Britain for keeping Iraqis undeveloped. Coincidentally, Smuts's defense of racial segregation in Africa produced the same effect.[29]

Britain briefly considered governing Iraq on the model of India, ruling it directly through British officials. But direct rule was expensive; Iraqis resisted it; and Iraqi resistance would increase costs to Britain, as was made clear in the 1920 Revolt. As Abbas Kadhim describes it, the Iraqi "population, except for a minority of the affluent, was united against a domineering British occupation." The Revolt brought together rival tribes and Sunnis and Shi'as, if only against Britain as the common enemy, before it was suppressed by Britain's monopoly on air power. "[B]oth Sunni and Shi'a Iraqis . . . found a common foe that united them, albeit temporarily, in the hope for autonomy and freedom." Although the Revolt was predominantly tribal in organization and rural in location, urban intellectuals framed it ideologically as a rebellion of the Iraqi people against foreign rule.[30] The nationalist interpretation might exaggerate the unity of Iraqis and the development of their national consciousness, but the Revolt did inflict substantial casualties on Britain, did cost the treasury large sums at a time when Britain had more urgent domestic priorities and international commitments, and did convince Britain to adopt a cheaper, three-pronged strategy for controlling Iraq.

First, Britain instituted indirect rule. Instead of governing Iraq directly, as in India, or according it commonwealth status, as with Canada, Australia, and South Africa, Britain decided on monarchic government for Iraq. Then Britain set about finding a king for Iraq who, on the one hand, would provoke minimal resistance from Iraqis and yet, on the other, would not inspire allegiances that were strong enough to allow him to challenge the primacy of British interests. Britain found its man in Prince Faisal, an ally from the Arab Revolt of 1916–1918 against the Ottoman Empire. Afterward Faisal served as king of Syria for five months before France, claiming its bounty from Sykes-Picot, deposed him. After consulting Iraqi elites, Britain chose Faisal to be king of Iraq because of his family's prominence, his nationalist credentials, and his reputation for religious tolerance, which made him less objectionable to Shi'as than the alternatives.[31] Plus, Britain calculated that his experience in Syria had taught him the consequences of displeasing imperial masters.[32]

Faisal's prime attraction for Britain was, however, his vulnerability. Because the British feared he might wiggle free from their control, Faisal's liabilities—that he hailed from what was to become Saudi Arabia, that he lacked local roots in what was becoming Iraq, that he was regarded "as an interloper" by many Iraqis, and that he had no independent power base in Iraq—were, as Judith Yaphe notes, "surely a plus in British eyes."[33] Dawisha observes that neither Shi'as in the south nor Kurds in the north wanted a "non-Iraqi Sunni sovereign."[34] Britain, therefore, had Faisal where it wanted him. He did not excite too much hostility due to his family, nationalist, and religious credentials, yet he faced threats from the Shi'i majority, the Kurdish minority, and the many Iraqis who were ill disposed to Britain and its Iraqi clients. Plus, Faisal had few administrative resources of his own. He governed through civil servants that were seconded from Britain to administer Iraq. Surrounded by suspicion and in no position to bite the hand that fed him, Faisal was trapped. Because weak, he was dependent; because dependent, he was compliant.

Second, Britain deemphasized the use of ground troops. It did not want to use its army in Iraq; the army was being decommissioned after World War I and was stretched by the problems of managing the empire. But Britain did not want the Iraqi state to establish an effective army of its own either. If Iraq developed an army with the size, weapons, discipline, officers, and effectiveness to impose order in Iraq, it would develop an army that also could threaten British control. Through the process of elimination, Britain decided in favor of depending on cheaper air power. Foreshadowing American air campaigns in 1991, 1998, and 2003, Britain's Colonial Office counted on the Royal Air Force (RAF) to bomb rebellious tribesmen into submission, as it had done in the 1920 Revolt.[35] But in preventing Iraq's new government from assembling military power, Britain also denied the Iraqi state the monopoly on violence, or anything approximating one.

Third, British strategy required Faisal to assemble enough support to spare Britain the costs of suppressing rebellions and of governing the unruly country itself, but not so much as to tempt him to seek actual independence. Britain struck the balance by rearranging land relationships. Previously tribes owned most land (and the Ottoman state owned some). Tradition and custom accorded sheiks, as heads of tribes, the right to lease land and to use the land they leased to reward friends and punish rivals. But tradition and custom also regulated how they got control of the land and what they could do with it. Inasmuch as custom was the source of their authority, sheiks violated it at their peril. Britain, however, suspected that Iraqi traditions obstructed its designs and inspired rebellions. Having decided to work through Faisal, Britain wanted him to win the allegiance of sheiks, which would give him a modicum of security and reduce his demands on British resources to maintain his position. But Britain also feared that Faisal and sheiks might ally against it. Britain and Faisal solved the problem through the simple device of transferring ownership of land from tribes to sheiks.[36] Converting tribesmen into tenants, according to Charles Tripp, provoked "resistance and rebellion among those who suddenly found themselves dispossessed or beholden to shaikhs to whom they felt no special attachment."[37]

Transferring land rights gave sheiks land, Faisal's government the support of sheiks, Faisal indemnification against an alliance of sheiks and tribes against him, and Britain indemnification against an alliance of Faisal, sheiks, and tribes against it. When sheiks violated custom by taking ownership of land, they embittered relations with their tribesmen, weakened the hold of tribal solidarities, diminished traditional authority, and became beholden to the new regime to protect their gains.[38] Now needing the backing of Britain to replace that of tradition, sheiks likewise were unlikely to bite the hand that fed them. Faisal and Britain then sweetened the deal. Friendly sheiks got to collect taxes, resolve disputes, and administer law, which allowed them to rebuild some of the support they had lost, reward their friends, and establish new sources of power for the monarchic-landlord-sheik regime.[39] Although Britain violated its promises about preparing Iraqis for self-government, it got effective control; Faisal got backing from sheiks; and sheiks and landowners got booty. Plus, if sheiks misbehaved, Britain and Faisal reserved the authority to replace them with more pliable instruments.[40]

Britain, in relying on the RAF, obstructing the growth of the Iraqi army, and seconding its officials to serve as "advisors" to Faisal's government, deprived the Iraqi state of the control over violence and administration that define modern states for Weber. Weber, however, does identify an alternative to the modern state that monopolizes legitimate violence and administers territory through bureaucracies. "Traditional" states value customs, defer to the authority of persons, and adapt to decentralized violence. Britain, however, subverted this route when it bought the loyalty of sheiks with the tribal lands.[41] Britain and Faisal hoped that tribesmen would do as they were told because age-old customs bound them to sheiks. But tradition, as Weber registers, not only binds the ruled to the rulers; it also binds rulers to rules. The ruled follow the rulers because the rulers follow traditions.

Consequently, Britain's strategy of co-opting sheiks subverted the authority of the very sheiks Britain meant to use. The swag that bought their compliance—land, the right to collect or not to collect taxes as the impulse struck, and the power to help friends and injure enemies in the name of administering justice—inevitably corroded the bonds of custom that tied sheik to tribesman.[42] Peasants, Dawisha reports, were "literally reduced to status of serfs," and

Tripp characterizes the state as "a powerful instrument for the acquisition of land, the preservation of privilege and the maintenance of a landscape ordered to suit particular networks of favour and interest."[43] Britain, according to Tripp, was "shaping the very tribal hierarchies and units that, it was claimed, constituted the 'natural' order of the society."[44] "The shallow foundations of the shaikh's authority became increasingly apparent."[45] By luring sheiks with land, Dodge explains, Britain and Faisal undercut the very relationships that were supposed to recruit tribesmen into backing their rule.[46] As long as Britain remained willing to deploy military force and the king and sheiks remained able to divide and conquer, the regime survived. But Britain's strategy of securing its supremacy on the cheap delegitimated traditions, discredited state power, and hollowed out social ties.

Britain left the Iraqi state to handle matters that were extraneous to its vital interests in foreign policy and oil. But if the government was to do Britain's bidding, it had to be kept beholden; and the greater the new state's power, the greater was its independence. Britain might not have intended to keep the state illegitimate, but its methods rendered the state illegitimate, and the state's illegitimacy was congenial to Britain's imperial interests. Britain recruited the king from abroad for the purpose of keeping him obedient, not of delegitimating his government, and it transferred ownership of the land from tribes to sheiks as bribery, not to make sheiks repugnant to the people they were to control. It also bundled three disconnected provinces from the Ottoman Empire into one country, in spite of the absence of a common history and the presence of sectarian divides, for the purpose of keeping the new state weak and indebted, not of making it impossible to legitimate. But whatever Britain's intentions, its methods set the terms for the evolution of the Iraqi state.

The Iraqi state was predatory. It had few resources at its disposal, did little with what it did have to build infrastructure or invest in human capital, and did not control access to oil. Wealth bought political influence (and was insecure without it), and, equally importantly, political influence brought wealth. But allocating wealth on the basis of influence, and vice versa, did not increase the wealth of the nation. Using the state to extract resources became the essence of politics, and the king, the sheiks, and their clients, who did the extracting, entered into an antagonistic relationship with society. The state coped by, among other devices, manipulating religious rivalries between Sunnis and Shi'as and national rivalries between Arabs and Kurds, thus etching communal conflict into the fabric of the new state. Religious, national, and class divisions were deep and bitter, and competition for oil revenues exacerbated them. Britain ordained the weak state, and the Iraqi state's weakness inexorably begat identity politics.

The Illegitimate Republic

Britain conferred "independence" on Iraq in 1932. But to safeguard its strategic and petroleum interests, Britain also insisted on retaining air bases and maintaining its advisors to the Iraqi government, which intensified "nationalist feelings" and spread "cynicism."[47] When Faisal died in 1933, the monarchy was weakened, and five years later it was weakened further when his successor's death placed a four-year-old on the throne. Nationalists, already angry at British influence and the snub to Iraqi sovereignty represented by the air bases and advisors, availed themselves of the uncertainty to attack the pro-British, pro-landlord regent who ruled in the name of the boy. When nationalists began flirting with Nazi Germany, Britain responded with a quick and decisive war in 1941. Britain's victory stabilized the monarchy for the time being, but at the cost of restoring the extremely unpopular regent and deepening nationalist hostility.

The people in the newly established country were tossed together in spite of their different histories, religions, and, in the case of

Kurds, civilizational identities. In that sense, Iraq was an "artificial" construction. But most states lack religious, ethnic, and national homogeneity at their inception. The signal failure of Britain and the monarchy was not so much that they did not unify Iraq's disparate identities and classes, which would have been excruciatingly difficult, as that they did not balance them in a way that established a stable equilibrium. The Hashemite regime was rejected by a broad coalition that included the middle classes, which were growing in tandem with the oil industry and the state; the rambunctious young working class, which also was growing from the oil industry and was receptive to the Iraqi Communist Party; and Shi'as, Kurds, and nationalist Sunnis. Sometimes the excluded interests and identities acted in concert. Yet in spite of the monarchy's weakness and illegitimacy, Iraq's dissatisfied classes, frustrated identity groups, and angry nationalists were too weak to overturn it. Nationalists, who arose mostly from the middle classes, egged on the military to seize power, spur economic development, modernize society, and restore Iraqi prestige—to achieve, in other words, what they could not do themselves. Nationalists thought their dreams were coming true with the July 14 Revolution in 1958. Army officers staged the coup d'état, deposed the monarchy, and, in the mayhem, most of the royal family and several senior politicians were killed.

It is revealing that a military coup is called a "revolution," but it was a turning point in Iraqi history. It dispersed the obsolete, British-sponsored, monarchic, landlord regime, and raised arguments about the meaning of socialism, ownership of Iraq's oil reserves, and whether Iraq's national identity should represent the Pan-Arabist feelings of Sunni middle classes or the non-Arabist preferences of Kurds and Shi'as. Several military governments ruled from 1958 until 1968, when the Ba'ath Party staged a coup, but none of them resolved Iraq's existential questions. They did institute overdue land reforms and lessen Iraq's vast illiteracy. But ruling by decree, the military had limited administrative capacities, and, besides, it was mired in factional in-fighting and disagreements about domestic policy, Pan-Arabism, the Kurdish question, and the role of the Iraqi Communist Party. Having become savior to the nation and agent of welcome reforms, the army also became the field for competing identities, interests, and classes. Political conflicts turned into conspiracies, and conspirators eliminated rivals.[48]

The successive military governments aspired to achieve national unity. But clashing personal ambitions, conflicting visions of the nation, class struggles, and the unavoidable fact that the country was not unified vexed all of them. The working class and the Iraqi Communist Party staged political strikes and mass protests in support of leftist and non-Arabist factions in the military, but they were too weak to claim power in their own name. Fighting in Kurdistan, which resisted Iraqi sovereignty, thrust questions of national identity to the forefront of politics. Meanwhile, politically active Shi'as complained about the Sunni hold on the civil services and what Eric Davis calls the "strident, romantic, and xenophobic" ideology of Pan-Arabist nationalism and its "vilification" of Iraqis who were not both Arab and Sunni.[49]

The state had been controlled by Sunnis since its inception and was organized along sectarian lines, although not indelibly.[50] The first military government, which was headed by Abd al-Karim Qasim from 1958 to 1963, challenged the parochialism of government officials and military officers. It favored a more inclusive, non-Arabist identity. But wanting inclusive identities was one thing and achieving them was another, and the military governments neither resolved nor successfully evaded questions of identity. Qasim's government broke into semi-political, semi-ideological, semi-national, and usually personal factions. Some officers, including Qasim, were close to Communists; some were Shi'a—including Qasim on his mother's side—or Kurd, and some were Sunni Pan-Arabs, as the military reflected Iraq's clashing national and sectarian identities (albeit with a decidedly Sunni Arab cast).

After a decade of inconclusive coups, reshuffles, and counter-coups, the Ba'ath Party, which was a small band of several hundred members, allied with Pan-Arabists in the military government and forced out their common enemies. Within a year the Ba'ath Party contrived to depose its allies in the military government and to establish the regime that held power from 1968 until the US invasion in 2003. The Ba'athist state differed from the military governments in its uncompromising Arab nationalism, tight organization, and more ruthless methods, and in the bounty that flowed into its coffers in the 1970s from unprecedented oil prices. With the new oil revenues, Ba'athists built apparatuses of state power—the army, police, ministries, and central control of the economy—and secured control through patronage as well as appeals to Pan-Arab nationalism and repression. Quelling American suspicions, the Ba'athist state also persecuted the Communist Party.

Saddamism

The Ba'ath Party's thirty-five-year reign was enforced by violence against Iraq's population and punctuated with wars against its neighbors. During the first decade of its rule, Saddam was a powerful figure in the government, but he was not dominant. Initially second in command to his patron (and cousin) Ahmad Hasan al-Bakr, he wrested power for himself in 1979. Promptly consolidating his position, Saddam purged senior echelons of the party, executed rivals, and a year later launched a fateful war with Iran. By the end of Ba'athist rule, Saddam's grandiose state was a caricature of the reality. Although bloated, intrusive, and violent, it also was chaotic at its core, thoroughly capricious, lawless, and illegitimate, and sovereign in name only.

Saddam's methods resembled those of totalitarians. As Kanan Makiya highlights, Saddam ruled through violence, torture, secret police, and pervasive fear. His state killed, denied rights, extinguished sites of independent power, and aimed to replace ties of affect and solidarity with the direct, unmediated power of the leader over his people, much as regime-changing hawks charged. Saddam established large, invasive, and brutal repressive structures; built a bloated army; used draconian methods; commandeered resources at will; and portrayed himself as the all-powerful leader of the all-powerful state. He held full and arbitrary discretion, prohibited pluralist representation of private interests in the state, and required all political participation to occur through organizations that his state sponsored. Yet Saddam's power was less than the sum of its parts. Pitting officials against each other, especially those with the potential of overthrowing him, Saddam paralyzed the very state that composed his power. Deliberately sowing suspicion inside bureaucracies and the military, Saddam prevented them from performing missions that required cooperation.[51]

Saddam employed the means of totalitarians, but he lacked their ends. Totalitarians are motivated by ideology and aim to control all domains of life in furtherance of their ideological commitments.[52] Saddam, however, lacked compelling ideological interests and was indifferent to aspects of human life that were unrelated to his power. He condoned nonparticipation in his political projects, providing no point was being made through it. In fact, passivity was his primary objective. If Saddam monopolized politics and controlled the state, he got the power to loot and feed the illusions of grandiosity that he wanted. Thus, instead of endeavoring to remake Iraq in accordance to his doctrine, Saddam built palaces, erected statues, staged parades, generated an obese cult of personality, and treated Ba'athist ideology opportunistically. A hodge-podge of Sunni Arab nationalism, confused Stalinism, and fascist zeal for the fatherland and its leader, Ba'athist ideology did not cause Saddam to adopt policies that were unwanted or to drop polices that were advisable otherwise. Ideology rationalized; it did not guide.

In ditching ideological ends for reasons of personal advantage, Saddam was Weber's "patrimonialist." By appropriating state resources as his "purely personal instruments," Saddam's state furthered his ambitions, pursued his feuds with domestic and foreign enemies, enriched himself, his family, his tribesmen, and his cronies, and, in concentrating powers in his person, preempted the development of citizens.[53] Citizens hold the right to make claims on and against their state, but the point of Saddamism was, precisely, to prevent Iraqis from making the leader accountable, from becoming citizens. In relentlessly engorging his appetites and ruthlessly dispersing centers of rival power, Saddam suffocated and extorted markets, nationalized businesses, both foreign-owned and domestic (to the particular disadvantage of Shi'i merchants), and hoarded the spoils for himself and his favorites.[54] But what funded these strategies and sustained Saddam's regime was, ultimately, the unprecedentedly high prices of oil in the 1970s. After nationalizing oil in 1972, the state owned the oil, and Saddam effectively owned the state.

Saddam, being intent on preventing economic power from translating into political power, threatened, harassed, and confiscated the property of the wealthy. For much the same reason, Saddam also thwarted the evolution of institutions in his power base. If the ministries, armies, and intelligence services that upheld his rule had developed methods, norms, and standards that were binding on those serving in them, they might have slipped beyond his personal control. Lest the instruments become independent of the master, Saddam aborted institutionalization through his usual means. He sowed distrust, broke down social ties, and instilled suspicion among officials and officers, turning them from teammates that served a common purpose into antagonists. Saddam, in other words, atomized officials inside his state (as well as Iraqis outside it). By deliberate design, Saddam brooked no interference with his whims, regardless of the collateral damage to his regime's power.

Saddam looted the state, but he also developed Iraqi society in the fashion of the 1960s- and 1970s-style modernizers. Keeping markets weak and using his powers over society and economy for his own purposes, Saddam spent oil revenues to rectify some of the social problems that had burdened Iraq from its foundation. As Phebe Marr put it, Saddam "provided widespread health, education, and social benefits that went well beyond those of any previous regime." He enacted land reform; made hospitals and education free, doubling the number of students in schools and including girls; established the basic infrastructure of development, like roads, electrification, and access to water; and reduced child mortality and increased life expectancy.[55] Saddam's motives were not altruistic. "These measures," Marr notes, "enabled the regime to allay discontent and establish greater control over society."[56]

Saddam also imposed tariffs, and behind their walls built and protected industries. His projects were thoroughly inefficient, however, and East Asian experience shows why. State-sponsored industrialization programs can succeed when professionally qualified and efficient technocrats make decisions in institutions that are autonomous. Within these institutions, rules are followed, norms are respected, an espirit de corps and a sense of duty are cultivated, and decision makers are insulated from political pressure, nepotism, and violence from their political masters.[57] Saddam's bureaucracies, on the other hand, were devised precisely to be servile. The Ba'ath Party enrolled state officials wholesale, conferred more privileges than duties on their members, rather like the Mafia, and preferred that they serve their leaders, not Iraqis. Ba'athist development, therefore, was wasteful, nepotistic, and corrupt. Nevertheless, soaring oil proceeds, which increased from $1 billion in 1972 to $33 billion in 1980, covered the costs of inefficiency in the first decade of Ba'athist rule.[58] Social spending spurted when oil prices were high, but reversed when prices declined and the costs of fighting Iran overwhelmed oil revenues.

Saddam instigated two major wars, and several substantial military campaigns in Kurdistan (and ongoing skirmishes with marsh Shi'as).[59] The war with Iran, which Saddam initiated against a three times more populous enemy, inflicted 100,000 deaths, 300,000 casualties, and, according to unusually precise estimates, $452 billion in material losses on Iraq.[60] The war in Kuwait was similarly disastrous, particularly its aftermath. As soon as Saddam surrendered, Shi'as rebelled across southern Iraq, executing state and party officials and jeopardizing Saddam's survival.[61] Bush I, prioritizing regional stability over regime change, allowed Saddam to deploy the powers of repression that remained to his regime to subdue the uprising. Then Saddam unleashed a wave of terror, killing enemies, suspected enemies, and whomever might get in his way or that of his executioners. About 150,000 Shi'as were killed in retribution. In addition, 180,000 Kurds had been killed when their insurrection was suppressed in 1988–1989, shortly before the invasion of Kuwait.[62]

The economic sanctions were more destructive than the wars. By conventional estimates, about 500,000 Iraqis—2 percent of the population—are thought to have died as a result of shortages in food and medicine.[63] The economic toll was extreme too. As Joy Gordon records, "In 1989 Iraq's GDP was $66.2 billion; by 1996 it was $10.8 billion. Per capita annual income went from $3,510 in 1989 to $450 in 1996."[64] Wealth evaporated, living standards plummeted, legal trade shriveled, black markets burgeoned, and, most damaging to American hopes for Iraq's postwar liberal prospects, middle-class professionals and technicians abandoned the country.[65]

Perversely, sanctions actually opened new opportunities for Saddam. Amid the scarcities they created, Saddam exploited his control of the distribution of food, medicine, and other essentials. His regime rewarded friends, punished enemies, and collected bribes. But none of this stabilized the regime. The vise of international sanctions and military pressure cut oil exports, prevented imports, and stripped the regime of the resources that had bought a modicum of support. It controlled, Ali Allawi writes, only "a few vital areas necessary for the immediate survival and continuation of the regime."[66] Without the oil revenues to buy friends and harm enemies, Saddam was reduced to relying on his tribesmen and manipulating tribal rivalries.

The Unsovereign State

The monarchy and Saddam's dictatorship were polar opposites on most scores. The monarchy was poorly armed, averse to modern nationalism, weak, compliant, and dependent on British military forces to survive and British advisors to govern, and it undermined the authority of the very traditions that it needed for legitimacy. Faisal, in the words of Tripp, "was sovereign of a state that was itself not sovereign."[67] Saddam accumulated vastly more military and economic power than the monarchy could have imagined, and was bombastic, nationalistic, militaristic, and intrusive. But Saddam's state did not develop monopolies on violence or effective administration, and it did not meet standards that confer legitimacy either. The monarchy and Saddam's dictatorship, therefore, were similarly deficient in the attributes that make for sovereign states. Neither the kings nor Saddam monopolized violence, organized administration efficiently, forged a shared national identity or, more feasibly, struck a rapprochement among different identities, or instilled legitimacy by respecting either tradition or legality. Twentieth-century Iraq, in other words, developed a state but not a sovereign one, and its unsovereign state passed four ongoing political crises onto post-Saddam Iraq.

First, Iraq's post-Saddam state did not follow an authoritarian, illiberal, and undemocratic, yet generally efficient, regime in the fashion of, say, South Korea in the 1980s, Taiwan in the 1980s–1990s, or apartheid South Africa in the 1990s. Like Taiwan and South Korea, Saddam's Iraq faced significant security threats. But instead of producing effective administrative institutions, Saddam loaded official bureaucracies with loyalists, distrusted professionalism, and stamped out rule-obeying officials in accordance to its patrimonialist logic. Exceptions were made. Saddam's economy required a strong oil industry and thus qualified petroleum engineers, and his development programs required effective schools, universities, and health care, and thus qualified professionals. In spheres where competence served the regime's needs without threatening its security, Saddam tolerated a modicum of autonomy. But for the most part the state was engineered precisely to frustrate cohesive, purposeful action. Saddam wanted bloated, meddlesome ministries to buttress his regime, but he also required them, paradoxically, to remain inefficient. If rules and norms had taken hold of institutions, they would have made his government more potent. But rule-obeying, rule-enforcing officials also would have blunted his powers.

Institutions, if they are to be real, bind, thwart, and entangle rulers. Saddam insisted, however, on the sovereignty of his impulse, and he shaped Iraq's bureaucracies accordingly. He oversaw the bloating of the state and the shriveling that later followed from sanctions. But whether the Iraqi state was growing or shrinking, Saddam made sure that it served as the adjunct to his will. Thus, when Saddam was defeated and the United States de-Ba'athified his regime, the bureaucracies had no capacity to act independently of the master. The vast majority of state officials—about 95 percent—kept their jobs in spite of de-Ba'athification.[68] But the United States, acting on the advice of Ahmed Chalabi, purged those officials who offered, or were suspected of offering, direction to the centralized, hierarchical state. Thus, the United States ordered the state purged, but it did not cleanse the old regime's habits of abuse. Maintaining Saddam's administrative structures and culture, the new regime still renounces institutional norms, still loots at the direction of its political masters, and still ignores the public welfare. Regime change, it turns out, did not undo Iraq's patrimonial ways.[69]

Eric Herring and Glen Rangwala, in writing about changes in Iraqi politics that were spurred by the American occupation, note some that occurred within Iraqi patrimonialism. Under Saddam, the state dominated patronage, awarding resources in exchange for the collaboration of its clients. The state was the puppeteer that pulled the strings; society was the puppet whose strings were pulled. Possessing the unconstrained power to seize whatever it pleased, Saddam's state was not accountable to social forces outside itself. But the war, the fall of Saddam, and the impact of the occupation stripped the state of its monopoly on patron-client relationships. That is, the evolving post-Saddam state became subject to patrons outside itself, forcing it to negotiate with, or acquiesce to, actors that are independent of it. Both locally and nationally, notables, sheiks, warlords, clerics, and Iranians penetrate the state, fragment its power, and turn it into prey to be plundered. The Iraqi state remains patrimonial, but it is balkanized internally.[70]

Second, Iraqis mostly identify with Iraq, and they have from the beginning. In 1920, clerics and sheiks overcame sectarian and tribal rivalries to rebel against imminent British rule. But the Revolt's success in drawing Sunnis, Shi'as, and rival tribes together in insurrection did not translate into lasting national unity, did not instigate lasting resistance to British rule, and did not articulate positive terms for an Iraqi identity that all, or even most, subjects in the newly founded country could share. Iraqis revolted against British imperialism, but they did not unite in support of an inclusive Iraqi identity. Again in the 1950s, politically active Iraqis—mainly Sunni nationalists, Shi'as, Kurds, middle-class modernizers, and the vanguard of the working class—fashioned a loose alliance against the pro-British, pseudotraditional, anti-nationalist Hashemite monarchy. The alliance was too weak to overthrow the monarchy, but almost all Iraqis hailed the 1958 military coup, expecting it to unify the nation and modernize the society. But reflecting widespread disagreements about what it meant to be Iraqi and what Iraqis wanted Iraq to become, the several military governments were factionalized by their disparate images of Iraq.[71] When the monarchy ruled, the disagreements within the country were overshadowed by common hostility to the old regime. But once the common enemy was swept away, the conflicts surfaced. Politically active Iraqis agreed on what they rejected, but not on what they wanted.

Following the pattern, conflicts between Shi'as and Sunnis revived with the fall of Saddam. This time, however, Shi'as won, and they turned the tables on Sunnis. Under the Ottomans, Hashemites, and Ba'athists, Shi'as advocated political identities that would include all Iraqis.[72] Sunnis, however, asserted exclusionary definitions of the nation. But when they got state power, Shi'as converted their sectarian identity into the new national identity for Iraq. Consequently, the "democratic" regime remains wracked by fierce and polarizing divisions about who Iraqis are, how they are to live together, and who gets to decide the rules of the game.

Third, in denying the authority of law or tradition over governance of the state, Saddam sacrificed the essence of sovereignty. Holding state, party, military, and security officials in fear for their lives and in thrall to his magnificence were effective strategies for maintaining Saddam in power. But they also interfered with purposes larger and smaller than killing, terrorizing, and taking. Saddam initiated two disastrous wars, and yet state officials and military officers did not dare question either venture. Lacking law to protect them from the punishment that is due cowards and traitors who preach defeatism, state officials and military officers acquiesced to Saddam's decisions to go to war, no matter what the consequences for Iraq. Law, as Weber recognizes, is what raises states above crass despotism. Without it, the state is uncoordinated, illegitimate, and unsovereign. It might have power, but it does not have authority. Law, however, was anathema to Saddam precisely because it inhibited his willfulness. Having shaped the state to respond to his will, Saddam set bureaucracies at cross-purposes with each other and stripped the state of constancy of purpose. Sovereign states achieve administrative efficacy, internal cohesion, institutions, and external legitimacy as compensation for accepting that rules govern their conduct. Saddam not only forfeited these advantages in pursuit of his autonomy of action. He also inscribed his methods in the state, where they survive him. The post-Saddam regime confers more security on its officials. Fewer live in palpable fear that their superiors might have them imprisoned, tortured, or executed. But officials still follow the path Saddam paved in rejecting law, coordination, and public interests.

Fourth, the Hashemites, military, and Ba'athists built and passed to their successors a state that is hollow. The signal achievement of sovereignty, as Hobbes recounts, is to end the preemptive attacks that occur amid statelessness. Because it monopolizes violence, the sovereign can prevent self-help and render it unnecessary. Conspicuously, Saddam produced precisely the opposite effect. By subjecting his officials to existential insecurity, he unloosed the rule of self-help *within* the Iraqi state. Having been bred to distrust, his officials connived against whoever threatened, or in the future might come to threaten, their lives, positions, or ambitions. In a fitting capstone to his regime, Saddam's generals could not coordinate a defense of the capital when American forces closed on Baghdad in 2003, having been forbidden to contact each other.[73] Alas, the rapacious conception of government that inspired Iraqi leaders and officials to treat the state resources as plunder was not born with Saddam and did not die with him. It accompanied the birth of modern Iraq and still subverts the new state's sovereignty, as parties continue to fill ministries with their loyalists and to pursue their particular agenda regardless of government policies.

Iraqi history, therefore, precluded the very harmony of interests, values, and rights that American regime-changing civilians assumed as their point of departure. Assuming that liberal order produces states, and not the other way around, regime-changers minimized the import of the project they set for themselves. They took the terms of order as known, uncontroversial, universally beneficial, readily applicable to Iraqis, and backed by the trajectory of history. Thus fortified, regime-changers were confident they could overcome weak institutions, lawless government, and adversarial national identities. As pragmatic, atheoretical liberals, American policy-makers predicated their dreams on the universality of their order. Iraq's realities were mere details.

7

The Semi-Sovereign Shi'i State

[Americans] attained democracy without the suffering
of a democratic revolution and . . . they are born equal
instead of becoming so.

Alexis de Tocqueville

The limits of American pragmatism were exposed after the United
States marched into Baghdad. Having absorbed exceptionalist
myths unthinkingly, atheoretical pragmatists paid little attention to
what really was exceptional about American history and to why it
mattered. Most societies grow in tandem with state power, which
provides them with the cone of security they need to develop.[1] By
contrast, society in America preceded, produced, and directed government (just as Locke had imagined when he wrote that in the
beginning all was America).[2] As Louis Hartz put the point in his
famous account of America's liberal consensus, schoolbook stories
of American history have the ring of truth. Self-reliant settlers did
self-organize into societies and their societies did delegate limited
and specified powers to government.[3]

Hartz's liberal consensus was not given naturally. It was brought
by settlers who drew on their experiences in England (where the
issues of rights and government were being engaged directly), required removing the indigenous population, presumed the absence
of external threats, and eventually necessitated the Civil War to
eliminate resistance to the national consensus of Lockean liberal-

ism. Americans, in other words, remember the primacy of society, but they forget how they produced their liberal consensus. Thus, in assuming that societies delegate powers to government, American exceptionalists took as common what was unusual; and in bleaching the struggles that produced the liberal consensus from their memories, they forgot the lessons of what was instructive about American history. Americans assumed both political order in the absence of states and liberal consensus in the absence of struggles to vanquish illiberal opposition.[4] This mixture of remembering and forgetting combined badly with American intervention in Iraq.

Regime-changers slated the Iraqi state for regime change in the belief that Iraqi society, after the fashion of their vision of America, would order and stabilize the country and that the truths embodied in the axioms about the universality of liberal values allowed them to dismantle the Iraqi regime without unleashing chaos. Regime-changers expected Iraqi society to hold together—maybe routinely, maybe rockily—even though the United States invaded the country, disbanded the army, de-Ba'athified the administration, and privatized the economy (a goal regime-changers were prevented from implementing by the chaos that enveloped Iraq after the United States stripped the legal state of most powers). But whether regime-changers assumed a short and quick or a long and laborious process, all except for the more astute neoconservatives thought they were freeing Iraqi society to realize the liberal rights that were buried inside it. Unexpectedly, they accomplished the opposite effect.[5] They freed the demons Saddam had bred from the shackles he had forged.

American regime-changers minimized the significance of Iraq's actual circumstances. They understood that Iraqi history was different from their own, but did not dwell on that detail. American policy-makers expected society to generate government and liberal values to apply in Iraqi circumstances, and these consequential truths to trump the particular handicaps of Iraqi society and government. It was this solipsism that allowed regime-changers to call for the war on the grounds that thirty years of Saddam's handiwork had brutalized Iraqis, next dismantle state apparatuses in the absence of agreement on the principles for governing Iraq, and, finally, watch bewildered as civic order disintegrated. The explanation for this failure, that breaking state power contributed to disorder, would seem self-evident. But it surprised exceptionalists, although not the national security bureaucracies, because they assumed, unthinkingly, that order issues from societies, which are free and spontaneous, and not from states, which are coercive. Viewing Iraq through the prism of their (selective) understanding of American experience, civilian regime-changers expected the inner liberals who were confined inside Iraqis by Saddam to begin emerging once he met his fate.

The United States did not abolish, or aspire to abolish, the legal state in Iraq, but it did neuter the features that converted the legal state into an actual state. Ministries survived but deteriorated into nests of conspirators, and a new army was patched together but amounted to little. According to Ali Allawi, the finance minister in the transitional government in 2005–2006, "Ministries had been gutted and could not produce effective spending plans and proposals."[6] The state's administration limped on anyway, shaking down yet not coordinating the centralized economy; but its security forces were overmatched by insurgents, warlords, criminal mafias, and, most of all, the militias that filled the security vacuum. As if Hobbes had been brought to life, gangs of armed men operated on the precept of attacking other gangs of armed men lest the others attack them first. Violence prevailed, distinctions between offense and defense evaporated, fear consumed life, and the state's ambition of monopolizing violence was reduced to pretense.

Iraq's violence was gruesome and pervasive; 118,865 civilians are reported to have been killed from 2003 to 2011.[7] Nevertheless, the violence did not descend into Hobbes's full-fledged, stateless state of nature. For Hobbes all loyalties and solidarities disintegrate in the state of nature, which forces people to operate individualistically, self-interestedly, and ruthlessly amid statelessness. Unencumbered by ties of affect, prisoners in his state of nature exploit each opportunity and every vulnerability. They gang up against the strongest actor, regardless of blood, religious, or any other tie, knock it down to size, and then the sides reshuffle to prevent the strongest among the winners from getting too big for the comfort of their erstwhile accomplices. As the fears of the weak cancel the ambitions of the strong, the balance of power rules, equilibrium becomes self-sustaining, victory is denied any actor, and the war proceeds incessantly.[8]

Hobbes looked to escape statelessness, where life is perilous and precarious, through his famous (yet rarely achieved) covenant. All actors but one foreswear the right to aggression, with that one becoming sovereign over others. Iraq, however, headed in a different direction. Its history had associated political allegiances with religious affiliations. Sunnis felt stronger attachment to the state than Shi'as did, but the correlations were imperfect. Many Sunnis were estranged from or were antagonistic to the state, whether because they were poor and illiterate in the days of the monarchy or because they hated Saddam and had no channels of political participation. Conversely, a small number of Shi'as belonged to the Ba'ath Party and rose in power. Ayad Allawi, who was appointed Iraq's interim prime minister by the United States in 2004, was a Shi'a and a Ba'athist before he broke with the party in the mid-1970s. On balance, however, Sunnis were more likely than Shi'as to regard the Iraqi state as, in some sense, theirs.

Sectarian allegiances were clarified and deepened by the experience of statelessness after the American invasion. Enveloped by lawlessness, Iraqis did not respond by burrowing into individualism and constantly trading old allies for new allies, as Hobbes would have it. Instead they clung tighter to those whom they trusted already. All Iraqis, including senior government officials, military officers, militia leaders, and widows and children, lived in danger and required protection. Hobbes, of course, had explained why fear, which is the defining emotion in statelessness, heightens distrust and isolation. Trust requires unbreachable commitments but statelessness, by abolishing the authorities that make and enforce covenants, dissolves loyalties. Commitments become one-sided and unenforceable, not mutual and binding. They are repudiated before they are reciprocated. Iraqis, however, averted the worst of Hobbes's corrosive logic. They responded to the insecurity of statelessness not by each turning on everyone in pursuit of immediate security, but by congregating in their religious communities. Instead of consuming all loyalties, statelessness strengthened and politicized bonds of religion.

Sunni insurgents tapped into the sense of dispossession, danger, and solidarity felt by most Sunnis, and their fear of the alliance between the Shi'i majority (and its government) and the United States government intensified their sense of common destiny. Sunnis did not agree on what to do or who was to lead them, and decisions were not taken democratically anyway. But statelessness mobilized the sectarian minority *as* a sectarian minority. Attacking Shi'as and Kurds while they were engaged in everyday activities through car bombs, suicide bombers, ambushes, and death squads, Sunni violence was openly sectarian. Therefore, it muted Hobbes's logic. For Hobbes, the weaker join together against the stronger, which prevents any side from winning. Sunni violence, however, countered the incentives of Shi'as to shift sides against the strongest elements in their coalition, motivated them to unify as a sectarian community, and, unexpectedly, raised a new principle of legitimacy over the state.

The outcome of Iraq's civil war accomplished something unprecedented in Iraqi history. The state was made accountable to a rule above the immediate power interests of its rulers—the cause of Shi'i hegemony. Obviously the cause was divisive. By elevating the power of Shi'as from a basic political reality into the (implicit) principle that sets the terms of Iraqi politics and defines rules for political membership, organization, and participation, Shi'i hegemony marginalizes the 40 percent or so of Iraqis who either are not Shi'a or do not derive political solidarities from religious communion. Obviously, too, the Shi'i state routinely betrays the welfare of ordinary Shi'as. Comprising one of the most corrupt governments in the world, Shi'i parties divvy up oil revenues, hoard as much as they can for themselves, and ignore the needs of ordinary Shi'as as well as Sunnis, Kurds, and sundry minorities.[9] Few goods and services trickle down to the Iraqi poor. The delivery of electricity, for example, remains unreliable a decade after Shi'as took control of government.[10] But in addition to being corrupt in practice, the new regime answers in principle to the Shi'i community and its leading clerics, and this distinguishes the contemporary Iraqi state from its predecessors. It also explains why Iraq escaped Hobbes's fate and why the foremost American military thinkers misapprehended the insurgency that regime-changing civilians had left them to handle.

COIN in Theory

When the occupation collapsed in 2004–2007, Washington panicked. The Iraqi state had no functioning police or intelligence agencies and the capital, reported Ricks, "resembled the pure Hobbesian state where all are at war against all others and any security is self-provided. Iraq appeared to be slipping steadily toward chaos."[11] By mid-2006 1,000 roadside bombs were exploding every week.[12] With the Bush administration scrambling to salvage the war in the face of what American intelligence identified as a cycle of "self-sustaining violence,"[13] the political and foreign policy elites that had endorsed the war in 2002–2003 worked to salvage the situation and their policy commitments.

The Iraqi Study Group (ISG), a blue-ribbon, bipartisan commission, was created by the Republican Congress in 2006 to exert pressure on the Bush administration.[14] The ISG not only advised withdrawing from Iraq, but its co-leader, former secretary of state James Baker, spoke as if it could set foreign policy. The ISG hoped "national reconciliation" would rescue Iraq, but it was not optimistic. Its driving fear was that state failure would create a political vacuum, and that the vacuum in Iraq would suck in neighbors that would seek either to take Iraqi territory and oil for themselves or prevent rivals from taking them first. Doubting that Iraqi politicians could get their house in order, the ISG recommended regional negotiations, and it proposed including Syria and Iran in them.[15]

Bush conceded in late 2006, after three years of denial, that the crisis in Iraq was dire and deteriorating, but he rejected the ISG's proposals. It was unacceptable to admit that the war was lost. Expecting Bush to add to his miseries by negotiating the terms of America's departure with Syria and Iran was to add insult to injury. Giving the ISG its comeuppance, Bush not only did not adopt its recommendations. He reversed them. Instead of withdrawing, Bush escalated, and not without reason. Because Iraq's legal state was on the verge of collapse, Iraqi society was nearing full-fledged, unlimited civil war, and immediate withdrawal might tip the oil patch into a regional war, Bush increased the number of American troops. More importantly, he appointed General David Petraeus, the army's leading expert on and advocate for counterinsurgency (COIN) warfare, to command American forces in Iraq.

Bush's escalation, known as the "Surge," excited considerable controversy in Washington when it was announced in January 2007, shortly after the ISG urged the United States to quit. Doves intensified calls for withdrawal, erstwhile Democratic hawks saw an opportunity to refurbish their newfound antiwar credentials by bashing the idea, and foreign policy elites worried that Bush was doubling down on a losing proposition. The point was to cut losses, they thought, not to increase them. Even congressional Republicans, who had lost control of both the House and the Senate in January 2007 due in substantial measure to the unpopularity of the war, were looking for ways to exit Iraq (which is why they established the ISG in the first place). The critics, who included all of the Democratic candidates for the presidency in 2008, were popular politically. But Petraeus, who recently had reviewed, revised, and rewritten American counterinsurgency doctrine in the *US Army and Marine Field Manual on Counterinsurgency,* mounted a case for escalation that was irrefutable in terms of the Elite Consensus.

Petraeus agreed with the EC that American strategies and tactics were misconceived in Iraq, that American techniques were inept, and that the military had gotten the how of the war wrong. That was his point. But instead of rejecting the war in Iraq, and similar wars in the future, Petraeus responded by improving American methods of warfare. If the United States was losing because the war and the occupation were being conducted incompetently, and if the mismatch between the tools at the disposal of the American military and the objective of consolidating the new regime caused the incompetence, then contriving new tools would reduce costs, increase benefits, and open options for victory in Iraq and elsewhere. Petraeus, in other words, refuted the EC by turning its pragmatic, neoliberal regard for technique and expertise *against* recommendations for withdrawal.[16] New and better methods, Petraeus argued, would convert failure into success.

When Petraeus implemented COIN warfare in early 2007, the Iraqi state was paralyzed, almost all Sunnis and the growing number of Shi'as who followed Muqtada al-Sadr resisted the occupation, militias ran rife, violence was rampant, American diplomats, generals, and intelligence analysts in Bagdad were conceding defeat, and American public opinion, which was essential to sustaining operations, had turned decisively against the war.[17] As the situation was deteriorating, Petraeus's predecessors had hoped against hope that they could train and rebuild Iraqi security forces and transfer security responsibilities to them. Petraeus, who had supervised the training of the Iraqi army in one of his two previous tours of duty, took a different track. He identified the strategic objective in the war as securing the physical safety of Iraqi civilians, and recognized that only the US military had the resources and capabilities to accomplish it.

Petraeus's counterinsurgency strategies were animated by the insight that people who are caught between insurgents and counterinsurgents favor neither side. Generally passive, most people go along with whoever can keep them safe. Insurgents, therefore, aim to discredit the legal state by destroying its monopoly on actual violence, crippling its capacity to perform routine tasks (such as delivering electricity), and prying territory from its control. Acting like Weberians in reverse, Petraeus's insurgents attack the legal state by attacking the attributes that constitute their target as an actual state. Aiming to de-state the legal state by preventing it from acting like a real state, insurgents win by spreading insecurity and disrupting administration. "Insurgents succeed," the *Field Manual* observes, "by sowing chaos and disorder anywhere; the government fails unless it maintains a degree of order everywhere."[18]

The failure of the legal state, however, does not ensure the success of the insurgents. On the model of the Chinese and Vietnamese revolutions, insurgents must acquire for themselves the attributes of stateness if they are to succeed. Petraeus's insurgents, in other words, begin by sowing disorder and insecurity, thus crowding out the legal state, but they win by providing the security and administration to the unaligned, apolitical majority of the population that constitutes them as the effective state. If insurgents paralyze the legal state's capacity to govern but cannot govern themselves, then neither side wins. Consequently Petraeus's COIN warfare is designed both to stymie the insurgents from performing the security and administrative duties of states and to bolster the legal state's stateness. Using "all instruments of national power to sustain the established or emerging government," COIN aims to achieve victory by consolidating the stateness of the legal state and by de-stating the insurgents.[19] In conventional warfare, the side that wins governs; in COIN, the side that governs wins.

Legitimacy for Petraeus is both the objective of COIN warfare and the measure of its success. In the first instance, "the long-term objective for all sides remains acceptance of the legitimacy of one side's claim to political power by the people of the state or region."[20] In the second, "victory is achieved when the populace consents to the government's legitimacy and stops actively and passively supporting the insurgency."[21] It is easy to interpret Petraeus's concern with legitimacy as typically liberal, but that is not his point. Legitimacy for the *Field Manual* is not what it is for liberals. For liberals, legitimate states are liberal because liberal states originate in consent. The *Field Manual* agrees that legitimate states receive consent, but it has consent performing a different function. Instead of constituting the liberal regime, consent ratifies that the state is performing stately duties. Reversing the liberal formula, the *Field Manual* derives legitimacy from security. "Legitimacy is accorded to the element that can provide security, as citizens seek to ally with groups that can guarantee their safety."[22]

Petraeus's *Field Manual,* in other words, adopts Weber's causality. By definition, states monopolize the legitimate use of violence. But states first get the monopoly on actual violence, and then they get the legitimacy. States do not get the monopoly because they already have legitimacy. They get the legitimacy because they gain the monopoly. Control of violence is the cause, and legitimacy is the effect. Because counterinsurgents act like states in concentrating violence in themselves, they are received like states. Legitimacy, popularity, and ties of affect follow in step. One side does not, in other words, become a state by becoming legitimate. It becomes a state by acting like a state, by monopolizing actual violence, developing administrative capacities, and controlling territory, and then the legitimacy that accrues to it by virtue of performing stately functions consummates its stateness.

Petraeus's causality reverses that which is hallowed in American political culture. Harkening to the Constitutional Convention that united the country, American political culture proceeds as if consenting to government is what creates government. In American liberalism, state legislatures sent representatives to the Constitutional Convention in 1787 for the purpose of convening with similarly selected representatives to delegate specific and limited powers to the federal government via the Constitution they were writing. Then the representatives sent the draft of the Constitution to the state legislatures for ratification, where it was amended through the Bill of Rights. In this view, democratic consent authorizes government; without consent, there is no government.

Petraeus identifies different origins for government. First, counterinsurgents establish security. Then, in the space they have cleared of insurgents, they build the legal state so that it can implement the routines of government. Finally, after being enthroned by COIN to behave like an actual state, the legal state reaps the legitimation that is accorded to the organization that monopolizes violence and administers territory. As condensed to the "clear, hold, and build" mantra, COIN operations:

- Create a secure physical and psychological environment.
- Establish firm government control of the populace and area.
- Gain the populace's support.[23]

Petraeus's COIN is designed to mirror insurgent warfare. As insurgents use war to make their new state, so counterinsurgents defeat them by building the state, and they build the state by defeating the insurgency. "War," as Charles Tilly formulated the point more generally, "made the state, and the state made war."[24] With the majority of Petraeus's population, which is unaligned, apolitical, and wants mostly to live as peacefully as possible, conferring legitimacy on whichever side delivers security and administers territory, COIN succeeds by converting the legal state into Weber's state. "The ultimate objective," declares the *Field Manual,* "is for military forces, police, and other security forces to establish effective control while attaining a monopoly on the legitimate use of violence within the society."[25]

Petraeus, therefore, would seem to be stuck in an inescapable quagmire. The legal state becomes a real state by providing security, and it wins the legitimacy that completes its stateness because it provides security. Yet it is counterinsurgents, not what Petraeus calls the "host government," that actually provide the security and conduct the administration. Inadvertently, Petraeus's counterinsurgents have become the state, thereby subverting his core mission in Iraq. With American public and elite opinion agreed in wanting to escape Iraq by the time he had been given command, Petraeus's assignment was to stand the Iraqi state upright, shrink American involvement in Iraq, and get Iraq out of the sight and the mind of Americans. If American COIN worked as designed, however, American disengagement would have caused Iraq's legal state—which had limited security and administrative powers—to crash and the country to sink into disorder. What, then, muted the logic of COIN and allowed the United States to withdraw and Iraq's legal state to acquire some of the substance of actual stateness?

COIN in Practice

The scope of violence in Iraq jumped about a year into the occupation and climbed steadily until August–September 2006, when it spiked. Then it declined abruptly and leveled for the year between September 2006 and September 2007, when it commenced a steep and lasting decline, until it began increasing again in 2013. In the month of August 2006, near the peak, 2,733 Iraqi civilians died in political violence; in August 2007, 1,598 died; and in August 2008, 226 died, one-twelfth the number two years earlier.[26] This decline provides the stuff for debates about the efficacy of American COIN warfare in Iraq.[27]

The debates engage military thinkers, analysts, and academics, but not political and foreign policy elites. The Surge and COIN served their needs too perfectly to look the gift horse in the mouth. By crediting COIN and the Surge with stabilizing Iraq, elites absolved themselves of blame for the misadventure in Iraq. If COIN succeeded where conventional methods had failed, then failures in Iraq were attributable to flawed methods; and if the sources of the failure were methodological, the problem was not the project of regime change. Elites, therefore, were culpable only of believing the president was competent to wage war, a mere misdemeanor. As Senator Joe Biden, later to become vice president, put the point: "I made a mistake. I underestimated the influence of Vice President Cheney, Secretary of Defense Rumsfeld, and the rest of the neocons; I *vastly* underestimated their disingenuousness and incompetence."[28]

Vindicating COIN brings a second benefit to elites. It preserves military intervention as a policy option. If the disintegration of civic order in Iraq under American occupation is imputed to the war for regime change, the prudential and normative cases against similar interventions mount. American intervention makes bad situations worse. But by pronouncing COIN warfare to have succeeded where conventional warfare failed, elites restore intervention as an alternative. Not coincidentally, the incoming Obama administration, facing a deteriorating situation in Afghanistan and not wanting to withdraw in defeat, sustained that failing war by promising to adopt COIN principles. Before long, Obama appointed Petraeus to run that war too.

The US military had deemphasized counterinsurgency war in the aftermath of the Vietnam War, and many officers were skeptical of its value in Iraq (and the claims on resources that counterinsurgents made).[29] But advocates and critics agreed on a couple of points. First, the reconstituted Iraqi military was undisciplined, unprofessional, and wholly inadequate to its security responsibilities. Iraq's legal state depended, therefore, on the American military to answer the Sunni insurgency, dislodge the Shi'i cleric Muqtada al-Sadr's growing control of Basra and Baghdad, and fend off foreign interventionists directly by deterring neighboring states and indirectly by filling the security vacuum that might lure some neighbors into invading Iraq. By performing these responsibilities, which were neither distinctively conventional nor distinctively counterinsurgent, the US military saved the Iraqi state. Without them, the legal state was heading toward collapse.

Second, the ongoing presence of American forces reduced the costs to Sunnis of (effectively) surrendering in the civil war that they initiated and then lost. With the US military guaranteeing the terms of the peace, the losers were spared from the full vengeance of the winners. Without the American presence, Sunnis would have been reduced to surviving at the sufferance of the victors, and Shi'as had many scores to settle. By offering Sunnis a modicum of security after their defeat, the American military discouraged Shi'i reprisals, reduced the costs of surrender, and therefore eased the balance of Sunni opinion into yielding to the inevitable. In the civil war in Syria that erupted in 2011, by contrast, both the Alawite minority and its allies and the Sunni majority continue fighting in part because they fear that surrender spells death. In Iraq, the US military gave Sunnis an alternative to persisting until the bitter end.

The *Field Manual* set forth the theory of COIN warfare, but the Surge confirmed the old adage about battle plans not surviving contact with the enemy. In Baghdad, counterinsurgents performed standard "clear, hold, and secure" operations against the Sunni insurgency. American forces attacked and defeated Sunni insurgents in one neighborhood, and then moved to the next. But contrary to expectations, the security they provided, or thought they were providing, was exposed as illusory. Instead of digging in and being killed, Sunni insurgents retreated to staging areas in Anbar province, the large Sunni area west of Baghdad that borders Syria, Jordan, and Saudi Arabia. When American units moved to the next theater, the insurgents then returned to the first. It became clear, therefore, that if the United States was to secure Baghdad, it had to defeat the insurgency in Anbar.[30]

Fortuitously for Americans, tensions were intensifying among the various elements of the informal coalition of religious groups, Ba'athists, former military officers, police and intelligence officials, local militias, and, most importantly, traditional sheiks and Al Qaeda Iraq (AQI) that comprised the Sunni insurgency. The most consequential contradiction pitted traditionalist tribal sheiks, who managed to maintain power and authority under Saddam, against AQI. When the Sunni insurgency commenced, sheiks had taken arms against the United States, the legal state, and Shi'as for the standard reasons. Fearing Sunnis were losing power and status, scorning Shi'as, resisting foreign conquest for reasons of national pride, and, perhaps, apprehending Hobbes's deep logic of statelessness, sheiks backed and led the Sunni insurgency.[31]

AQI, which was inspired but not directed by Bin Laden, was different. Composed largely of foreigners who had flowed to Iraq to conduct jihad, AQI penetrated regions in Anbar province that traditionally were controlled by Sunni sheiks, tried to take control of the insurgency, and, inevitably, clashed with sheiks over their authority, the meaning of Islam, and access to local women.[32] The sheiks wanted to restore their personal and communal power, avenge Shi'i attacks, and blunt Shi'i ambitions. But AQI's attacks on Shi'i civilians and religious symbols, most famously the al-Askari Mosque in 2006 and 2007, were calculated to provoke the three-to-one Shi'i majority. AQI expected that Shi'i retaliations would hit Sunnis indiscriminately and that vulnerable Sunnis would be forced into its arms. AQI's terror, in other words, was meant to create a demand for the services it was peddling. Sunnis would require security from Shi'i reprisals, and the AQI would provide it. Not surprisingly, sheiks—and other Sunnis—were repulsed by a strategy that effectively treated them as cannon fodder.

Petraeus exploited the rivalry between sheiks and AQI to shore up the legal state. AQI had made enemies galore—all Shi'as, Iran (whose influence was growing in Iraq), Kurds, the US military, the legal state and its sometimes brutal if inept security forces, and most of the Sunni establishment. By courting Sunni sheiks with displays of respect, caches of weapons, piles of cash, and promises of physical protection from AQI's attacks, Petraeus accomplished two aims simultaneously. He reduced the forces at the disposal of the enemy while enlisting as allies sheiks who retained local credibility and intimate knowledge of the interior of the Sunni insurgency. With AQI isolated and paralyzed, the United States could eliminate its leaders, reduce the violence it perpetrated and the retaliatory violence it provoked, increase security for most Iraqis, and thereby refurbish the legal state's credentials. Defeating AQI, by Petraeus's logic, interrupted the sequence of attack, reprisal, and counterreprisal that propelled the downward spiral of violence, and that destated the legal state.

Specialists in warfare debate the efficacy of COIN, the Surge, and Petraeus's alliance with Anbar sheiks ("The Sons of Iraq"). One of the most valuable contributions comes from Stephen Biddle, Jeffrey Friedman, and Jacob Shapiro in their article "Testing the Surge."[33] Asking why violence in Iraq diminished sharply in 2007, they answer that the interaction of two factors—the Surge, by which they mean the introduction of more troops and the adoption of COIN strategies, and the rise of the Sons of Iraq (SoI) in the "Anbar Awakening"—was decisive. Neither the Surge nor the SoI turned the tide alone. What salvaged the situation in Anbar—and, therefore, Baghdad—was the combination of the fresh strategy, the increased number of troops, and the alliance with sheiks who broke from the Sunni insurgency due to their hostility toward AQI.

The SoI were not the first defectors. Defections from the Sunni insurgency had occurred before the Anbar Awakening, but they had not amounted to much. In fact, many defectors were killed. The defections during the Anbar Awakening were different because the deployment of more troops enabled American forces to protect defectors, and because defectors "unveil[ed] the holdouts."[34] Now in possession of reliable intelligence, American counterinsurgents could identify and target their enemies accurately. Petraeus's success, then, depended on the Anbar Awakening, and the Awakening depended on the protection to defectors accorded by the Surge.

Biddle et alia counterpose their thesis to the "sectarian cleansing" thesis, which presents "spatial intermingling" of Sunnis and Shi'as as the reason for Iraq's violence and spatial segregation—that is, sectarian cleansing—as the reason for the decline in violence. As Biddle et alia summarize the rival hypothesis, Sunnis and Shi'as, because they lived in close proximity, feared attacks from each other, and therefore attacked before they were attacked. The "patchwork quilt of interpenetrated neighborhoods created a security dilemma in which each group was exposed to violence from the other. In this view, the war was chiefly a response to mutual threat, with each side fighting to evict rivals from areas that could then be made homogeneous and secure."[35] As Sunnis and Shi'as congregated among their own kind, according to this thesis, violence increased during the cleansing but diminished after the process was complete. Objecting to the sectarian cleansing thesis on the grounds that it does not fit data on the violence, Biddle et alia note that violence did not decline in Baghdad as Iraqis separated into homogeneous religious communities. "[W]hen neighborhoods unmixed, violence moved but did not diminish."[36] "Instead, Shiite militias used the newly secure cleansed zones as bases for onward movement into adjoining, homogeneously Sunni neighborhoods, where the fighting continued unabated."[37]

Biddle et alia defeat the sectarian cleansing thesis. Because violence continued at the same or higher rates after Baghdad segregated on the basis of religion, it follows that Iraq's violence was not motivated fundamentally by the pursuit of security through local homogeneity. But in concentrating on the year 2007, Biddle et alia do not develop the implications of their findings that extend beyond their time frame. Their findings suggest, more broadly, that Iraqi violence was sectarian, that a civil war was being waged, that security was the objective of the violence, and that cleansing particular neighborhoods was part of the larger project of asserting the hegemony of one community over the other. Accordingly, victorious Shi'as captured one neighborhood and then moved to the next, expanding their base and compelling Sunnis in the second neighborhood to leave—just as Biddle et alia describe Shi'as to have been doing. In fact, when Biddle et alia show that the Sunni insurgency used control over Anbar to threaten Shi'as throughout the country, they imply a more aggressive inference. Sunni control in some regions endangered Shi'as outside those regions.

If the combination of the Surge and the Anbar Awakening alone accounts for the decline in violence, the rates of violence should have revived when the Surge ended and the sheiks became disenchanted with the Maliki government (which repudiated promises of jobs and money for them and their tribesmen). What explains why Iraq's violence stayed low (at least until the civil war in Syria spilled into Iraq in 2013–2014) is that struggles for local control entailed struggle for national control too and the civil war was being decided concurrently with the Surge. Even before the Sons of Iraq helped the United States defeat AQI in Anbar, the loose coalition of the three-to-one Shi'i majority, Shi'i militias, and the new state's military and police forces was compelling Sunnis to abandon their insurgency. Consequently, violence dropped substantially in September–October 2006, several months *before* the Surge commenced. It was the Iraqi state and militias, acting hand-in-glove to displace, intimidate, and kill Sunnis, that forced Sunnis to submit to the Shi'i state (at least provisionally) and that explains why violence stayed low even though cash from the Americans to the SoI was cut off and the government marginalized and effectively disenfranchised

Sunnis, including Anbar sheiks. Shi'as, abetted by the Surge, won the civil war, and Sunnis tacitly (but not irreversibly) submitted.

COIN Succeeded in Practice Because It Failed in Theory

Shi'i victory rescued the United States from the logical culmination of Petraeus's theory. If counterinsurgents control violence and administer services, as the theory has them doing, talk of transferring sovereignty to the legal state made little sense. The transfer succeeded in Iraq because Shi'as won the civil war, and the Surge, by helping to eliminate threats to the Iraqi state, contributed to Shi'i victory. The Maliki government was in position to demand American withdrawal in 2011, and the United States was willing to accede to the demand, albeit reluctantly, because the state seemed viable; and the state seemed viable because COIN advocates undersold the achievements of the civil war and oversold those of COIN.

The US military was able to depart Iraq without undermining the Iraqi state because the circumstances the *Field Manual* expects in theory were fundamentally different from those that prevailed in Iraq. Conceiving of counterinsurgency war generally, the *Field Manual* assumes a depoliticized environment. In spite of the war that engulfs and endangers them, people in the *Field Manual* are disengaged from political conflicts, struggles, and passions. The whole strategy, in fact, rests on the assumption that the mass of the people has little affinity with, or hostility to, the sides in the insurgency. Uninterested and uninvolved, people are an indifferent blob inching toward whichever protector promises them a modicum of security. Their loyalties and identities neither tie them to one side nor repel them from the other. The reason security is the key to legitimacy is that few people see either side as theirs. The *Field Manual* does not have a "them" or an "us," just entrepreneurs of violence peddling security to consumers who are in the market for security because, in the manner of protection rackets, the entrepreneurs create the demand.[38]

The *Field Manual* got Iraqis half right and half wrong. They were frightened and insecure, but they also were highly motivated in choosing friends and enemies. Neither passive nor apathetic, Iraqis belonged to communities that were reinforced, mobilized, and remade by the statelessness that engulfed Iraq after the invasion. In creating the ubiquitous danger of death, statelessness put the premium on security. But where COIN theory predicts that people will respond to insecurity by withdrawing into their shells where they will await protectors, Iraqis struck their putative enemies. Iraqis were not the objects of the *Field Manual's* mind's eye; they were subjects engaged in a civil war. Acting on Hobbes's logic, they attacked their enemies—or those who might become their enemies—before their enemies, actual or prospective, could get them.

Consequently, circumstances in Iraq differed from those portrayed in the *Field Manual*. The purpose of the *Field Manual* is to explain how to win the sympathies of unencumbered individuals. But Iraqis were not unencumbered. Embedded in religious communities, most regarded their welfare as associated with that of their community, and preferred their side to the other. Aligned, they would not embrace whichever side could provide security in the hope that they could get on with their lives. Rooted in religious (or, for Kurds, national) communities, their conception of security was not individualistic. Consequently, COIN warfare was conducted amid identities that had been formed already, circumscribing its influence. Instead of shaping the political terrain by establishing security for the bulk of the population, counterinsurgents operated on a battlefield that was populated by sectarian responses to statelessness. Thus, the logic of COIN suggests that withdrawing American forces was tantamount to yanking the lynchpin of political order. But Shi'i victory in the civil war meant that the state did not owe its survival mostly to the counterinsurgents and that it might not fall without them. The Shi'i state was not the fragile, broken state with minimal popular support that COIN theory imagined.

The second reason why COIN was less important than its logic implied was that the theory makes inflated claims on the basis of favorable examples. Reflecting the influence of British counterinsurgency theory, the *Field Manual* emphasizes Britain's experience in Malaysia.[39] Given Britain's long and varied experiences across the Empire in conducting counterinsurgency warfare, it is revealing that the British feature this example. British imperialism typically allied with and worked through local *minorities* for the simple reason that the hostility of the majority sealed the minority's subservience to Britain. Malaysia is an atypical example of British counterinsurgency because Britain was allied with the majority group. COIN theorists, however, tell the story differently. In their version the Malaysian insurgency was a Maoist peasant revolution in the late 1940s and early 1950s, and Malaysia was rescued by agile and creative COIN warfare. Thus construed, the vital lesson is that COIN will succeed if only it is conducted intelligently. The critical variable, in other words, is not the particular situation in which COIN is deployed, but the professionalism of the counterinsurgents.[40]

Using Malaysia to test COIN methods, however, stacks the deck. British theorists acknowledge the ethnonational details of the Malaysian insurgency, but do not dwell on the fact that the insurgency, in asserting the power of the poor peasantry, also asserted the Chinese section of Malaysia's population. That is, the stakes for both counterinsurgents and insurgents involved ethnonational allegiances as well as landlord-peasant relations. Thus, in appealing to the Chinese minority of Malaysia's population, the insurgents also repelled the ethnonational majority.[41] By crediting its methods with the victory, therefore, British counterinsurgency theory downplays the ethnonational dynamics that isolated the insurgents. With counterinsurgents backing both the Malay majority and the state, they had the winds of identity at their backs.

Likewise, long-standing identities limited the appeal of the Sunni insurgency. Just like support for the insurgency in Malaysia was restricted to the minority, so too in Iraq. Petraeus was backing not only the legal state, but also the state that, by virtue of elections, expressed the identity of the Shi'i majority. Thus, just as interpreting Malaysia to prove the supremacy of COIN minimizes nationalism in explaining the counterinsurgent's victory, so emphasizing COIN in Iraq deemphasizes the civil war and its sectarian content. But when Iraq's legal state became the preserve of Shi'as, the miscue in theory of downgrading the influence of identities was corrected in practice.

The United States was able to escape the implications of substituting counterinsurgents for states because identities perform more functions than COIN theory acknowledges, because its test case exaggerates the value of counterinsurgency warfare, and because Petraeus, contra Weber, derives legitimacy entirely from security. For Weber, legitimacy accrues both from establishing security and from respecting standards, which is why states cannot self-legitimate (and why Weber is not Hobbes). Weber's state becomes legitimate by abiding by the principles that justify it. Petraeus was determined to prevent Iraq's civil war, yet ironically it was the civil war that produced de facto standards of legitimacy for the new regime, completed the Iraqi state for the first time since its inception in 1921 by promulgating the sovereign purposes that legitimate, and, unexpectedly, facilitated the departure of American forces. That does not mean that COIN was irrelevant. In attacking AQI and slowing the spiral of violence, COIN assisted Iraq's state materially (and, perhaps, indispensably). But what was decisive was the popular support the state garnered from the civil war through its identification with Shi'as. Shi'i victory, by settling the issue of sovereignty, winning support for the state, and positioning the state to move on to subdue Shi'i rivals (such as Sadr in 2007), let American counterinsurgents slip the trap they had set for themselves.

Hobbes's Limits

When Britain imported Faisal and tied his hands, it set the pattern for Iraq's political development. The monarchs lacked the monopoly on actual violence, legitimate violence, effective administration, and the control of territory that are hallmarks of modern states. Even Saddam, in spite of his notorious brutality, never secured a monopoly on legitimate, or even actual violence, in Kurdistan. Iraq's legal state from Faisal through Saddam also lacked the sovereign justifications that guide and give purpose to full states. Because it never was legitimate, Iraq's state never was sovereign. Britain subverted Faisal's aspirations to enact traditional authority, and Saddam ruled not by respecting higher authorities but by killing, imprisoning, and torturing enemies, manipulating tribal rivalries, playing sectarian politics, and exploiting the suffering that arose from economic sanctions.

Shi'as did not engage the civil war for the purpose of enshrining sovereign justifications for the Iraqi state. They responded to the Sunni insurgency, which aimed to recover the powers that Sunnis thought were rightfully theirs by attacking Shi'as (along with the United States, its coalition allies, and Kurds). Shi'as meant mostly to defend themselves, not to prosecute a civil war. But the Sunni insurgency, by attacking the majority population physically and symbolically *because* they were Shi'as, motivated Shi'as to respond *as* Shi'as. It also, by putting their security in danger, gave them reason to enact Hobbes's logic: The only secure defense was a victorious offense. Securing their persons and property required eliminating the threat that was directed at them collectively; eliminating the threat required them to unite; and unity required a cause to keep them together in the face of the centrifugal pressure that fragments the winning side in wars of all-against-all. The cause, which unified Shi'as in the civil war and endowed the state with purpose, was the hegemony of Shi'a symbols and identities.

Iraq's civil war often was compared to Hobbes's state of nature, where life is "solitary, poor, nasty, brutish, and short." But Iraq's civil war was not total, and ultimately it was not Hobbes's war-of-all-against-all either. In Hobbes, men are individually calculating, free-floating, and interested only in themselves. Even though Iraqis acted ruthlessly and self-interestedly, as Hobbes would expect of them, they did not conceive of their interests solely individualistically. Moored in their community, Iraqis located their welfare as individuals in that of their communities. Communal calculations, in other words, mediated Hobbes's individualistic logic. Thus, in mobilizing *as* Sunnis and targeting Shi'as *as* Shi'as, the Sunni insurgency converted the two religious communities into political communities too. It was not an unprecedented step. From the inception of the Iraqi state, most state officials were Sunni, and Sunnis identified more strongly with the regime. But although political identities were associated with religious commitments, they were not deducible from them. Many Sunnis opposed, and a smattering of Shi'as supported, the old regimes.

Shi'as are not monolithic. A large and diverse community, Shi'as are divided by class, tribe, region, access to oil, and imam. But the ties of solidarity that are born of religion were confirmed, in Patrick Cockburn's words, by their historic experience as a "faith of the dispossessed and opponents of the powers-that-be."[42] Shi'as had been marginalized in the Ottoman and monarchic periods, targeted as disloyal by Saddam, and estranged by Sunni versions of secular Arab nationalism. Religion influenced political orientations before the American invasion, but did not determine them, and religion did *not* ordain that sectarianism would constitute the sides in post-Saddam politics. Wolfowitz for one dismissed the significance of religion going into the war. Religious identities were likely to matter in the politics of post-Saddam Iraq, but what converted them into the hub of public life was the civil war. Statelessness caused the civil war, and the civil war turned religious solidarities into political solidarities.

Religious identities differ qualitatively from other kinds of identities, and Iraq's escape from the fate Hobbes foresees shows why. In the absence of sovereignty, as Hobbes recognizes, anything goes. Hobbes's sovereign individuals live in a world of other sovereign individuals, with no sovereign standing above them to monopolize violence, promulgate law, and pronounce standards and values. In the ensuing war-of-all-against-all, these sovereign individuals must prepare to fend off attacks from other sovereign individuals. When one individual takes measures to protect himself from another, he adds to the existential insecurity that already is felt by the other and motivates him to take measures to protect himself. Of course, the defensive measures of the second threaten the first, which accelerates the spiral of insecurity. In the absence of a single sovereign that extends over everyone, each sovereign individual takes defensive measures that are experienced as offensive by every other sovereign individual. If the first individual becomes too threatening, perhaps by gaining supremacy over another, a third might join with a fourth to balance the power of the first.

Realists magnify Hobbes's logic for the international stage. Positing as axiomatic that the greatest threat issues from the greatest power, they expect states, in their instinctive drive to survive, to join with other states to counter whatever state threatens them most directly.[43] As Hans Morgenthau puts the point, states "change sides, desert old alliances and form new ones" to balance the threat of the most powerful.[44] In this dance, loyalties, affections, and ties of solidarity count for naught. They must be ditched if states are to prevent the strongest from extinguishing the independence (or the existence) of all that are weaker.[45] Occasionally weaker states pursue the alternative strategy of allying with the strongest in the hope of gaining security. But that is risky. In "bandwagoning," the weaker reduces itself to surviving at the sufferance of the stronger, and anyway loyalty counts for little with realists. The choices of states are thrust on them from without, and the influence of solidarities is incidental.

As a matter of empirical fact, international society is not really anarchic. Sovereign states exist amid the system of global capitalism, which is replete with its own logic, resources, power, and transnational structures, and capitalism is not reducible to the property of any particular state. The paradox of realism is that its logic applies more purely to the internal politics of countries that are stateless, where militias, political parties, warlords, clerics, and the like compete for survival and advantage. With partners shuffled incessantly, identity counts for (almost) nothing and power considerations for (almost) everything in forming and dissolving alliances. In fact, realists downgrade ideological, ethnocultural, and religious solidarities to costly indulgences, diversions from the life-and-death business of securing survival. Facing elimination if they allow affect, sentiment, or bonds to interfere with the ruthless calculations of self-interest, actors do what is best for them in the here and now, regardless of past affinities. The alternative is extinction.

By realist logic, then, the side that is winning a civil war is prone to fall out as soon as victory is in sight. As Morgenthau writes, "Since in a balance-of-power system all nations live in constant fear lest their rivals deprive them, at the first opportune moment, of their power position, all nations have a vital interest in anticipating such a development and doing unto the others what they do not want the others to do unto them."[46] That is why the first characteristic of life in Hobbes's state of nature is "solitary," before "poor" and the rest.[47] It is also why Iraq did *not* degenerate into Hobbes's full-scale, no-holds-barred war of all-against-all, and it is why Iraq, contrary to the logic of realism (and COIN), produced an internal escape from Hobbes's equilibrium. The predicate of Hobbes's war-of-all-against-all—his very first criterion—did not obtain in Iraq. Life in Iraq's civil war was *not* solitary. In fact, statelessness and violence intensified the solidarity of religious communities. Iraqis remained divided by tribes, clerics, classes, and regions, as always. But threats from without herded them into their sects anyway.

Hobbes and kindred spirits, ironically, skate over important implications of the radical insecurity of daily life and pervasive violence. Craving security, people crave reliability too. With the state failing to furnish security and Iraqis having to provide it themselves, the principle of self-help ruled. But it operated within constraints. Security for reasons Hobbes explains was beyond the reach of individuals, families, and even tribes. People need trustworthy allies, but without sovereigns to guarantee covenants untrustworthy behavior is rewarded. Only the innocent trust, and innocence is punished by death. Yet, paradoxically, Hobbesian analysis of Iraq's civil war falters on this bedrock. Hobbes's radical individualism cannot allow Iraq to overcome the constant balancing of anarchic systems to produce a victor.

Hobbes offers two main ways out of the war-of-all. Either the inmates agree among themselves to surrender the right to offensive violence to a single sovereign that remains unimpeded in the use of violence, or a foreign conqueror subdues all. But if neither of these events occurs, Hobbes's war continues in perpetuity as balancers defect from the winning coalition, power balances power, and everyone is stranded in the unending war. Whenever one actor gets powerful enough to break the deadlock, the deck is reshuffled. Realist logic, then, assumes the free run of uninhibited ambition amid conditions of absolute distrust. Everyone is enemy to everyone because behavior is unconstrained, and promises are meaningless because they are unenforceable. Whoever receives promises must prepare to guarantee himself that the promises will be honored, and in taking necessary preparations the promise-receiver reproduces the regime of self-help.

Iraqis redirected Hobbes's logic from the beginning. Being solitary, his individuals depend on themselves alone. Iraqis, however, believe in Allah, and, equally importantly, believe their brethren believe in Allah too, which is why Hobbes's first criterion did not apply to Iraqis. For Hobbes, statelessness puts a premium on trust, but trust is unwarranted because no sovereign exists to uphold it. Iraqis, however, grounded their trust in commitments that were more secure than the shifting sands of self-interest. The familial and tribal ties of Iraqis likewise facilitate trust, and also are costly to betray. But even the largest tribes amount to a small fraction of the Iraqi population, and outside tribes and family blood does not tie. Common religions are different. Sects are large and, in raising treachery in pursuit of individual advantage into an affront to Allah, provide bonds that tie, particularly in the face of attacks from the rival sect. Therefore, Iraqis have, because they believe they have, the sovereign authority that guarantees covenants. Obviously countless promises were violated anyway, and sometimes the trusting died for their gullibility. But religious believers belonged to communities whose ties were believed to originate in, and to be enforced by, an omnipotent and omniscient Almighty. Thus, because of their unique reasons for trusting their coreligionists, Iraqi Shi'as and Sunnis could escape Hobbes's individualistic logic.

The religiosity of Iraqis blocked Iraq's civil war from becoming full-fledged Hobbesian statelessness. Pervasive insecurity put a premium on reliability, and reliability was enforced by shared religion. Consequently, individuals, militias, and community defense groups did not ally with and break from other units solely because of individual power advantages, without regard to solidarities. Their interests were steeped in and derived from their sect, and the combatants in the civil war almost always made alliances *within* their own religious community. Competition for resources and power was intense within both communities. But even when Sunnis fought Sunnis or Shi'as fought Shi'as, which was not uncommon, the combatants honored the religious divide. They did not seek allies outside their religious communities against rivals within their own. Religious communities were not monolithic, but the boundaries between them were inviolable. When push came to shove, threats that emanated from outside overcame the divisions and rivalries that arose internally in each of Iraq's three main communities.

Iraq's civil war originated in statelessness, and statelessness, by accentuating the value of security, converted religious solidarities into the basis of politics. Although hawks had dismissed the prospect of religious conflict on the grounds that Saddam's modernization had rendered religion as politically insignificant, their assessment was wrong. In addition to running counter to their general assessment of Saddam as worthless, it ignored the connection between sect and conception of the nation that arose with the foundation of Iraq and that Saddam intensified through his persecution of Shi'as and their clergy as his situation became more desperate. But it was the consequence of the civil war that rendered regime-changers wrong about the political role of religion in Iraq. In turning religious communities into political causes, the civil war propelled the cause that legitimates the new state for most Iraqis, and that delegitimates it for the rest.

Shi'i Hegemony

It is time to ask, "So what?" So what if Locke assumes order as natural, Hobbes and Weber define states in terms of monopolies on actual and legitimate violence, realists see disorder as self-sustaining, and Petraeus was rescued from the implications of his theory because the shotgun of the civil war married Sunnis and Shi'as to their communities? What does this have to do with regime change in Iraq? The answer is that Iraq defied American designs because the United States got its policy wrong; it got policy wrong because it got its basic assumptions wrong; and it got its assumptions wrong because the axioms pronounce that liberal ideals (and, therefore, American interests) are universal and because the dead political philosopher John Locke lulled American policy-makers into assuming that the terms of liberal order are natural. The United States took the conditions of consensual, nonviolent politics to be given, when in fact they were constructed through American history, often violently. The American Civil War, it might be remembered, *imposed* the hegemony of liberalism on the American South. In forgetting this history, Americans forgot what established the hegemony of liberal order.

Americans did not ignore political order as a practical issue. Specialists in state building and crisis management anticipated many problems. But those were details. The particulars had to be resolved, but liberal principles would guide them.[48] By assigning to the universality of liberal principles the work that Hobbes and Weber assign to states, policy-makers minimized the risk of enduring disorder. American policy-makers figured on appointing some familiar Iraqi politicians as "Iraqi faces," staging elections that their friends and associates would win, supervising the writing of a new, liberal constitution, making way for the elected government that would prove safe and reliable, and allowing fundamental questions about order to take care of themselves under a constitutional government that, after due negotiations, would free markets, respect liberal rights, and promote American strategic and economic interests. The process, some warned, might be difficult. But the destination was set because policy-makers were assuming, without knowing they were assuming, that liberal values would align spontaneously with the society that had survived Saddam's despotism. If, however, what remained of Iraq after Saddam's despotism, wars, sanctions, the flight and impoverishment of the middle classes, economic devastation, and the systematic suppression of civil society was not able to establish the terms of political order and resolve the most fundamental questions of Iraq's purpose and identity, then the United States was condemning Iraq to chaos.

The United States assumed either that Iraqis would agree on the first principles for government or that it would not matter if they disagreed about Iraq's boundaries, economic organization, national identity, the role of Islam, the status of ethnic and religious minorities, and the powers of the central government. Naively, American policy-makers proceeded as if the answers would emerge inexorably through give-and-take. Having assumed that reasonable people agree on the fundamental principles of civic order, American regime-changers did not understand the disorder that was consuming Iraq. Extemporizing, they looked first to patch together a state by including politicians from Iraq's warring communities; next, to contain civil violence by building Iraq's army and state capacities; and finally, to provide security through COIN warfare. Elections featured prominently in all of these plans because the occupiers equated elections with democracy and democracy with liberal rights.

Formally, Iraq's new political order affirms liberal rights. The constitution refers to full and equal citizenship in democratic Iraq, and it is democratic in the sense of representing the general sectarian identity of the majority. Actually, the state was empowered through the civil war, the civil war was won by the Shi'i majority, and the elected government completes the circle by recognizing Shi'i nationalism as its de facto sovereign principle. Shi'i nationalism offers the new regime important advantages. For one, it legitimates. Unlike previous governments, the parties that govern Iraq must win elections. Even if elections amount to religious censuses, in which almost all Shi'as and Sunnis vote for parties that are organized religiously, the winning parties still may claim the popular consent that was absent from all previous Iraqi governments.[49] Prime Minister Nouri Al-Maliki concentrates power, undermines constitutional promises, and governs through repression, intimidation, corruption, caprice, and patronage. But he holds office because elections empowered Shi'i political parties to install him, and because he recognizes their special place—and, therefore, that of the Shi'i people—in "democratic" Iraq.

Electoral success comes at a price. In depending on communal solidarities to sustain their political power, Shi'i parties must engender and reproduce the solidarities that uphold them. Mostly, Shi'i parties trade patronage for backing and add violence when they need it. But Shi'i parties also introduce a distinctive twist. Sunni politicians may occupy positions of formal authority in the state, but they acquire power over issues that matter to Shi'as only through the sufferance of Shi'as. By marginalizing Sunni parties, refusing to parlay as equals with their leaders, and even issuing an arrest warrant against the Sunni vice president, the Maliki government antagonizes Sunnis deliberately.[50] It inflames sectarianism, confirms Sunni hostility to the new regime, and thereby traps ordinary Sunnis and Shi'as into voting for those parties that purport to protect and represent them communally, whatever the other failings of "their" parties.

The rest feeds on itself. The optimal strategy for Sunnis is to seek alliances with Shi'as, which would expand Sunni influence and undermine the sectarian politics that disempowers them. But Shi'i parties follow the incentives for denying conciliatory Sunnis. Wanting to hoard power for themselves, they prefer not to share. More perversely, Shi'i parties motivate Sunnis to challenge the system of Shi'i hegemony, and then use Sunni responses, whether symbolic, political, or violent, to reinforce the solidarity of the three-to-one Shi'i majority and maintain the Shi'i parties in power. The strategy, of course, carries risks, as was illustrated in early 2014. The civil war in Syria was extended into Iraq as Al Qaeda–type Sunni jihadists captured Fallujah and Ramadi, declared an Islamic republic that traversed the border between Syria and Iraq, and, significantly, were tolerated by non-jihadist Sunnis who agreed with the jihadists in rejecting the state as illegitimate. Soon Maliki turned fruitlessly for help from the sheiks he had abandoned and repressed after the Sons of Iraq had done their work, thus underscoring that the Shi'i state lacked both monopolies on violence.[51]

The ongoing crises between Sunnis and Shi'as are Kurdistan's opportunity. Kurds wanted self-determination, whatever constitutional form it might take, from the inception of the Iraqi state, and the sectarian nationalism of the new regime reinforces their long-standing aspirations. Shi'i nationalism does not represent Kurds. But it does invite them to use their influence in the national government, which is considerable, to play Sunnis and Shi'as against each other to increase their power. Kurds already control autonomous military forces, administration, territory, and substantial oil deposits in the regions where they are concentrated. Plus they have taken to transporting "their" oil—the Baghdad government disputes ownership—through pipelines in Turkey, irrespective of the objections of the Baghdad government. With the Baghdad government unable to prevent Kurdistan from doing what it wants, even from negotiating as if it were a sovereign state with other sovereign states, Kurds likewise expose the Iraqi state as unsovereign.

In spite of the resistance it generates, Shi'i nationalism provides another important advantage to the state. By offering Shi'as symbolic benefits, giving them a sense of belonging, and, for the first time in Iraqi history, favoring *their* values and identity, the state wins support from Shi'as. A little patronage might trickle to the mass of Shi'as on the low rungs of the patronage ladder, but most receive emotional affirmation in lieu of material benefits. Conveniently, Shi'i parties, notables, sheiks, and clerics get a better deal. They take substantive benefits for themselves, and then they escape accountability to those Shi'as whose votes put them in government by sustaining Sunni threats to their regime. With the Shi'as and "their" state under siege, Shi'i critics are cast as giving aid and comfort to their common enemy.

Thus, the sectarian dynamic that originally marginalized the Sunni minority comes to disempower the Shi'i majority too. Excluding Sunnis from effective citizenship antagonizes them; antagonized Sunnis provide the base of support for militants that attack both the state and Shi'as; and attacked Shi'as are motivated to unite behind their leaders in defending their community, regardless of the unresponsiveness of the government to their demands for jobs and services. Sectarianism, therefore, relieves Shi'i parties of pressure to answer for their failure to improve the lot of the Shi'i poor, and it indemnifies them from the consequences of pervasive corruption, awful services, and abiding unemployment and economic inequality.[52]

The sectarian nationalism that grew in the civil war, then, ensnares the loyalties of Iraqis, organizes political participation, and shapes feelings of belonging and exclusion. Mostly, however, it offers a cut-rate strategy for perpetuating practices that have been entrenched from Iraq's earliest days. Iraqi politics still revolves around factions that loot the state and then distribute the booty among their families, friends, and followers. Shi'i parties fight with each other over the spoils, sometimes violently. They represent different constituencies, and they threaten each other's access to patronage, plunder, and power. Shi'i parties fight over portions, compete over influence, and obsess over pecking order. But they may fight among themselves only on condition that they respect one basic imperative: The predicate of pursuing their particular interests is that they uphold their collective interests in reserving effective power in the central state for Shi'i interests.

Iraq's new state, therefore, is familiar. The beneficiaries are different, but the new bosses learned rules from the old bosses. Patrimonialists still take oil revenues for themselves and their retinues, and they still turn ministries into personal, tribal, and party fiefdoms. But the rulers now are Shi'a, and their cause now is the sectarian nationalism that buys acquiescence, but not necessarily commitment, from the majority of the population and that estranges the rest.

Of course, the estrangement of minorities through sectarianism and the marginalization of most Shi'as through patrimonialist favoritism and corruption also raise the prospect of unending conflict, renewed civil war, and existential crisis. As demonstrated by prior regimes in Iraq, states that lack the attributes of sovereignty do not rest easily.

Conclusion

I think that Iraq is going to go down in history as the
greatest disaster in American foreign policy because we
have lost the element of the goodness of American
power and we have lost our moral authority.

Madeleine Albright

The United States launched Gulf War II with delusions of a quick
and easy military victory and of a lasting and inevitable political triumph. Although these lofty expectations were thwarted, the United
States did not leave empty-handed. It acquired a reliable ally in
Kurdistan, eliminated the nuisance of Saddam, and restored the
flow of Iraqi oil into world markets (which, admittedly, had been
interrupted by American-sponsored sanctions). But the United
States did not win oil or military bases for itself, friends for Israel
or Saudi Arabia, enhanced national power, or, most ambitiously, a
credible model for neoliberal globalization that it could display to
other Muslim societies.

The payoff for eight years, 4,500 dead Americans, and $3 tril-
lion, then, was small. Economically, the war solidified Iraq as the
unreformed, patrimonial, antimarket state that remains the bane of
neoliberals. Geopolitically, the war turned Iraq from the enemy of
Iran, which American elites have decided is their most formidable
enemy in the region (or the world), into Iran's close friend (and
filled in the Shi'i crescent). Before the war, Iran found allies in the

Assad regime in Syria and the Hezbollah party-militia in Lebanon. Now, to the deep distress of both Israel and Saudi Arabia, Iraq is a bridge connecting Iran to Syria. No wonder, then, that the war's backers shift full blame to Bush II personally. Inverting the great-man theory of history, the Elite Consensus retells the story of the war as the incompetent man soaring above his times and forcing a counterproductive war on reluctant elites.

The EC narrative, which was concocted when public favor was waning several years into the war, diverts attention from the approval of congressional Republicans, who voted almost unanimously for war; of the bulk of Republican elder statesmen (but, interestingly, not from former presidents Gerald Ford and Bush I); of the preponderance of elder statesmen and stateswomen in the Democratic Party; of about half the Democrats in Congress; and of pundits. The commitment of civilian elites—but not, ominously, of the national security bureaucracies that were charged with waging the war and consolidating the peace—bespoke the liberal creed's hold on political and foreign policy opinion. Movement conservatives, neoconservatives, neoliberal pragmatists, and liberal hawks agreed that Saddam's Iraq constituted a security threat, not only because of his alleged WMDs and his imagined Al Qaeda ties, but more fundamentally because he denied the ideals that express American interests. All of the traditions that called for regime change blended American power and values; all considered American values transportable; all equated threats to American values with threats to national security; and all assumed that American power was welcome in Iraq because it materialized liberal values. Bush mobilized these precepts in 2002–2003, but civilian elites promulgated and internalized them long before he arrived on the scene.

Regime-changers spoke in universals and employed categories, such as rights, that they imagined as timeless and placeless. Rights for them, being both inalienably human and fundamentally natural, are not contingent on history, culture, or context. All people, by virtue of their humanity, are endowed with them, but for regime-changers these rights also are fragile. Either they become universal, or they are at risk. With rights belonging everywhere, liberals must, as Kant understood, expand their domain perpetually or face elimination. Liberal societies need not be confronted with physical annihilation for the point to hold, although neoconservatives sounded that alarm. The mere existence of illiberal states might trigger Kant's logic. By rejecting international law, illiberals drag liberals into the world of self-help that nullifies liberal values and spur liberals to fulfill their telos of universality. Liberals must expand because their philosophy applies—or can be made to apply—everywhere, and because they cannot live liberally among illiberal others.

The United States meant to project national power and promote neoliberalism in Iraq. But in deciding to pursue these commitments through war and regime change, American elites fooled themselves about the downside risks of their ventures. They spoke explicitly about national security and market capitalism, but they also dispersed both aspirations into the ethos of liberal rights, universal freedom, and win-win, positive-sum outcomes. Material ambitions inspired regime change, but elites did not register the recklessness of the enterprise because they saw their interests not as interests but as values, as intrinsically moral and broadly beneficent. Bush II, his steadfast allies, and his allies-turned-critics converged half-consciously in converting standard American interests in accumulating power, increasing security, and imposing market economies into ideals that represented universal interests.

Conventionally, the practices and theories of international relations conceive of interests as the content of values. Thrasymachus enunciated the idea in Plato's *Republic*. In announcing that justice merely renames the interests of the stronger, that justice has no standing independently of power, and that power designates as morally good whatever benefits it, Thrasymachus anticipated the realist tradition in politics.[1] For such reductionists, right has no purchase beyond the interests of the strong. That which abets power is called right; that which harms power is called wrong. Because right and wrong do not affect the composition, conception, or pursuit of the underlying interests, values are illusory. Like moons, values emit no light of their own. But if values merely are interests, nothing more and nothing less, then the idealization of interests would make no substantive difference in how states behave. The United States would act on the basis of its interests, or its perceived interests, and that would be the end of the matter. Gulf War II shows, however, that the idealization of interests matters substantively. It affected whether regime change was attempted, why it was attempted, and what was attempted.

Idealizing national and neoliberal interests greased the desire for regime change in Iraq. While the war represented underlying interests, the gains that were anticipated had to be weighed against both real and opportunity costs. As the sole reigning superpower, the United States had opportunities to intervene in countless situations. If it *really* wanted to harm states that cooperate with terrorist states in developing WMDs, for example, the United States might have penalized Israel for cooperating with apartheid South Africa's nuclear programs.[2] If it *really* intended to protect innocents from predators, the United States might have done something about the 5,400,000 that died as direct or indirect results of the Second Congo War that renewed in 1998 (about the time when the United States announced regime change as its objective in Iraq). The United States passed on these and kindred options because its ideals stemmed from its interests, and because Israel was a close ally and Congo was deemed to be insignificant. The gains were low and the costs were high.

American elites chose war in Iraq because the two axioms inflated the incentives for war and deflated the disincentives. First the United States turned its interests into ideals, and then it universalized its ideals. Regime-changing elites, therefore, minimized costs, erased risks, and blinded themselves to the import of using American military power to enact regime change in the Muslim Middle

East. Although the illusions spun by entwining American interests with ideals and American ideals with universal principles favored intervention in many ways, the most momentous consequence passed unappreciated by true believers. In idealizing their interests, regime-changers assumed that liberal values would ground Iraq's new civic order and that they would spring naturally from American victory. Under the influence of the axioms, the *terms* of Iraq's post-Saddam civic order, which would have to bring together a traumatized, fractious society, were assumed. They became innate, obvious, incontrovertible, and binding, and thus skewed considerations about costs and risks of the war. Disconcerting questions were assumed away.

The United States failed to bring markets and liberal democracy to Iraq because American policy-makers assumed that, after deposing Saddam, elections would entrench democracy, democracy was equivalent to liberalism, and liberalism was the natural destination of history. Actually Saddam's demise precipitated civil war, which should have been predictable; the civil war produced a Shi'i government, which also was predictable; and the Shi'i government allied with Iran, which also was predictable inasmuch as Iran had sheltered Iraq's Shi'i parties during Saddam's reign. Neoliberal visions of a market society died in the crib because the United States, having naturalized order, deproblematized it. The United States would clear away the debris that obstructed the emergence of the liberal order and would reorganize the state (whose powers it was breaking), and then freedom would work its magic. In assuming liberal outcomes as normal, the United States first minimized the hard, lengthy, and complicated work of inculcating liberal values, of nurturing liberal institutions while suppressing illiberal traditions, and of hammering out the liberal consensus. Then the United States managed not to comprehend that Iraqis were encountering the reality of American military *power* through the experience of war and the humiliation of occupation, not emancipatory liberal values.

If the United States had understood itself to be asserting power against the Iraqi state, the problem of order would have loomed larger in both prewar planning and postwar execution. After breaking the old regime, the terms of Iraq's new regime would have had to be devised, agreed on, and imposed, and not merely enforced. But by assuming that order is embedded in liberal values and by assuming that American power disseminates liberal values, regime-changers took as given the principles of Iraq's new regime and banished questions about the social bases for liberal order in a society whose history was illiberal. The State Department's *Future of Iraq Project* illustrates the point neatly. The report on democratic governance, which was written by Iraqi exiles, assumed that liberal democracy was not controversial.[3] It also avoided questions about why liberal government would take root in, or emerge naturally from, a society that lacked a tradition of the rule of law, an independent middle class, a market economy, liberal social practices and values, or consensus about the common purposes that unite the people who live in Iraq. In spite of the violence of its history, Iraq's defining commitments remained unresolved.

The particulars of Iraqi history did not matter to American elites because, having assumed the can opener of agreement on liberal principles in the absence of the sovereign state, regime-changers expected to uncover Locke when they lifted the lid of Saddam off Iraq. Therefore, they misunderstood the import of their acts. The most striking detail about the project of regime change in Iraq was that, like a billiard player calling a shot, the United States announced that it would break state power, and then broke it. Breaking Iraq's state was not an unanticipated consequence of the war. It was the point of the war. Conceived as the oppressor of Iraqis, the state's hold had to be broken as the necessary condition for Iraqis to achieve their rights and neo-liberals to revamp the political economy. Yet the United States did not anticipate that peeling off state power, especially in the wake of Saddam's despotism, was tantamount to unleashing

Hobbes. American elites worried about transitional problems, but not about *how* Iraq was to be ordered. To them, the broad principles of civic order are natural and self-sustaining. That is why Bremer thought he could break the military and administrative capacities of the Iraqi state, order the state to implement neoliberal principles, and not detect the contradictions between these two fundamental commitments.

It is a long-standing rule in international relations that hegemons are status quo powers.[4] By institutionalizing international and regional orders, replete with hierarchies, norms, and sanctions, hegemons promote their purposes, uphold their powers, embody their values, embed their interests, and spare themselves the trouble of fighting about principles. Naturally, they strive to improve their position within the orders they devise and sustain. But hegemons seldom upend the orders they have established. They seek advantageous reforms, not revolutionary upheavals that upset the foundation of their hegemony. Yet the declared purpose of regime change in Iraq, as spelled out by Bush II, was precisely to overturn the domestic order in Iraq and, more strikingly, the American-sponsored regional order in the Middle East.[5] Hawks succeeded in breaking the established order, but they did not get the liberal, pro-American order they expected. Instead regime-changers strengthened the Shi'i arc that extended from Iran to Hezbollah in Lebanon via Syria. It now includes (providing the regime avoids jihad and civil war) Iraq.

The United States was in position to opt for regime change because the end of the Cold War removed external restraints and allowed the United States to push the idealization of its interests to the logical conclusion. By giving interests the form of universal values, policy-makers change the nature of the disagreements that are the stuff of international relations. When states that are deemed to be normal clash, the fact of conflict reveals little about the nature of the competitors. Their interests, or some of them, are in conflict, and states seek what is best for them. Conflicts, therefore, do not speak to the morality or the immorality of the conflicting states. If, however, values are seen to be at stake, the legitimacy of America's adversaries must come into question. States that are in conflict with the United States are not pursuing different interests. They are rejecting decent values and, therefore, are prone to be seen as *motivated* by malevolence.

When interests are clashing, today's enemy might become tomorrow's friend. But when *values* are seen to be clashing, stakes rise. Instead of being balanced, the adversary must be eliminated (or converted). Regime change follows logically from turning interests into ideals. The problem that was to be eliminated became Saddam's regime, not his WMDs. Hawks were uninterested in compromising because, as they emphasized, Saddam was evil, and evil is incorrigible. Thus, in the prewar debates neither hawks nor doves entertained the obvious explanation for why Saddam might have acquired, or wanted, WMDs. Having fought an eight-year war with Iran to a stalemate in the 1980s, Saddam had standard realpolitik motives for seeking to counter his enemy's three-to-one advantage in population.[6]

In dismissing rational motivations and attributing Saddam's (alleged) weapons to his irrationality, instability, and insatiability, American elites obligated themselves to attack. Offense became defense because evil aspires to universality. As the Cold War mandated a global response to the Soviet threat, so the specter of Islamic terrorism mandated the United States to globalize its power. In each case, genuine security interests were translated into imperatives to spread American power and values everywhere. Already aspiring to universalize their values, regime-changers cast their enemies as universal and, as a happy coincidence, licensed—or obligated—themselves to expand American power. By projecting their expansionist telos onto their targets, in other words, American universalists warrant themselves to expand their power preemptively, defensively, disinterestedly, and altruistically. By corollary, hawks equate traditional virtues in foreign policy—proportionality, limits, prudence, and measured self-interest—with appeasement.

Elites believed they were acting morally in Iraq. But in idealizing their interests, they not only ennobled the pursuit of power and advantage. More importantly, they abolished the moral foundation for evaluating the morality of American power. When interests are conceived conventionally, as material advantages in power, security, or wealth, they can be negotiated, adjusted, muddled, or compromised as circumstances warrant. Interests also can be evaluated in terms of other, more important, interests and of values that are distinct from interests. Values may judge whether the interest is right or wrong, just or unjust, and whether the importance of the interest supersedes moral concerns and whether the importance of the values outweighs the importance of the interest. But when ideals are interests that have been repackaged, displaced, and mystified, the distinction between them and interests vanishes. Instead of making interests moral, as regime-changers fancy themselves to be doing, the idealization of interests actually undermines the basis for issuing moral judgments. The interest becomes the ideal and the ideal, because it has absorbed the interest, cannot achieve the remove that is necessary to issue moral judgments. The point of the idealizing of interests thesis, then, is not to assert that ideals are wrong or inappropriate in foreign policy. It is to recognize that interests and ideals both play valid roles in deciding foreign policies, but that they are *different* and that erasing differences between them is dangerous. It leaves interests judging themselves.

Virtue becomes the reward of power when interests are idealized. By expanding its power to fend off evil, the United States gets to feel good about "smashing something" (in Thomas Friedman's felicitous phrase). For regime-changing hawks, America acts altruistically when it gathers more power and imposes new markets. But, and this was the consummate paradox of Gulf War II, regime-changing American exceptionalists ultimately subverted the very interests that were to have been served by idealizing them. The United States still pursued power, but it became burdened with the solipsistic delusions that American exceptionalism is universalizable and that liberal society was immanent in Iraq. Thus regime-changers turned an unexceptional conflict with a minor despot into an all-or-nothing, right-or-wrong affair. They distorted calculations of proportionality when they considered whether the conflict warranted war and stripped Iraq of the right to resist American power because it—like all of America's enemies—was rejecting rights and values, not countering power in the fashion of international relations. Then, in initiating war in the confidence that the "end of history" and the universality of America's liberal values would suffice to consolidate victory, regime-changers disregarded the history of Iraqis. Many Iraqis wanted rights, constitutional government, and political toleration. But wanting them and achieving them in the absence of traditions of individualism, secularism, capitalism, instrumental rationality, and hard-won consensus on national purposes and identities are two different things. Breaking the state was not tantamount to liberalizing Iraq.

Without rosy assumptions about the universal applicability of American values, the United States was embarking on a project to shift the trajectory of Iraqi politics, economy, society, and culture. Steeped in Locke, American elites thought that they could break the Iraqi state without rupturing order and that the new society was incipiently liberal. The United States, then, went to war—and failed to win the war—because regime-changers deluded themselves into believing they were the world and the world was the better for it.

Notes

Introduction

Epigraph: "Inaugural Address by George W. Bush," January 20, 2005, *New York Times*, http://www.nytimes.com/2005/01/20/politics/20BUSH-TEXT.html?_r=0.

1. Why Elect a Self-Defeating War?

Epigraph: Bob Woodward, *Bush at War* (New York: Simon & Schuster, 2002), 168.

1. For a discussion of the role US foreign policy plays in instituting the conditions for global capitalism, see Robert W. Cox, *Production, Power, and World Order: Social Forces in the Making of History* (New York: Columbia University Press, 1987), 211–267. For a discussion of the specifically neoliberal American objectives in Iraq, see Michael Schwartz, *War without End: The Iraq War in Context* (Chicago: Haymarket Books, 2008), 32–49; and Naomi Klein, *The Shock Doctrine: The Rise of Disaster Capitalism* (New York: Metropolitan Books, 2007), 411–430.

2. For casualties, see http://icasualties.org/Iraq/index.aspx. For budgetary costs, see Joseph E. Stiglitz and Linda J. Bilmes, *The Three Trillion Dollar War: The True Cost of the Iraq Conflict* (New York: W. W. Norton, 2008).

3. Bob Woodward, *Bush at War* (New York: Simon & Schuster, 2002), 109.

4. Richard A. Clarke, *Against All Enemies: Inside America's War on Terror* (New York: Free Press, 2004), 32.

5. Douglas J. Feith, *War and Decision: Inside the Pentagon at the Dawn of the War on Terrorism* (New York: HarperCollins, 2008), 15.

6. Maureen Dowd, "The Long, Lame Goodbye," January 18, 2009, http://www.nytimes.com/2010/06/16/opinion/16dowd.html?hp; Dowd, *Bushworld: Enter at Your Own Risk* (New York: G.P. Putnam's Sons, 2004), 18–24; and Jacob Weisberg, *The Bush Tragedy* (New York: Random House, 2008), 185.

7. Bush "writes that one of the motivating factors for sacking Saddam was that the Butcher of Baghdad tried to assassinate his dad." Maureen Dowd, "The Way They Were," *New York Times,* November 16, 2010, http://www.nytimes.com/2010/11/17/opinion/17dowd.html. The British government also worried about the possibility that the war for Bush II was "about avenging [his] Dad," although Alastair Campbell, the source of the claim, does not make clear what the son was seeking to avenge. Alastair Campbell, *The Blair Years: Extracts from the Alastair Campbell Diaries* (New York: Alfred A. Knopf, 2007), 634. Michael Isikoff and David Corn, in *Hubris: The Inside Story of Spin, Scandal, and the Selling of the Iraq War* (New York: Crown, 2006), 116, report some of the problems with this widely told account.

8. Bob Woodward, *Plan of Attack* (New York: Simon & Schuster, 2004), 421.

9. See, for example, Michael Kelly, "Look Who's Playing Politics," *Washington Post,* September 25, 2002. Andrew Sullivan, "The Opportunist," *Salon,* September 24, 2002, http://www.salon.com/2002/09/24/gore_79/. Adam Nagourney, "For Remarks on Iraq, Gore Gets Praise and Scorn," *New York Times,* September 25, 2002, http://www.nytimes.com/2002/09/25/politics/25GORE.html.

10. Coincidently, Frank Harvey offers a full explanation of the war through the counterfactual method. Harvey argues against the thesis that Bush and neoconservatives were uniquely responsible and identifies strong continuities in elite opinion toward Saddam from the Clinton to the Bush administration. He focuses particularly on issues of inspections and weapons of mass destruction. He does not, however, focus on regime change or broader American and neoliberal interests. Frank P. Harvey, *Explaining the Iraq War: Counterfac-*

tual Theory, Logic and Evidence (Cambridge: Cambridge University Press, 2012).

11. Leslie H. Gelb with Jeanne-Paloma Zelmati, "Mission Unaccomplished," *Democracy: A Journal of Ideas,* no. 13 (Summer 2009), 24.
12. Joy Gordon, *Invisible War: The United States and the Iraq Sanctions* (Cambridge, MA: Harvard University Press, 2010), 1.
13. Ibid., 3, 87 and Human Rights Watch, "War in Iraq: Not a Humanitarian Intervention," January 26, 2004, http://www.hrw.org/news /2004/01/25/war-iraq-not-humanitarian-intervention.
14. Samuel Berger, "Address by National Security Advisor Samuel Berger," Stanford University, December 8, 1998, http://clinton4.nara .gov/WH/EOP/NSC/html/speeches/stanford.html.
15. Madeleine Albright, *Madam Secretary: A Memoir* (New York: Miramax, 2003), 365. Saddam took the point, concluding in the 1990s that the US "would pursue regime change regardless of Iraqi compliance with UN inspectors' demands." Kevin M. Woods, David D. Palkki, and Mark E. Stout, eds., *The Saddam Tapes: The Inner Workings of a Tyrant's Regime, 1978–2001* (Cambridge: Cambridge University Press, 2011), 326.
16. General Hugh Shelton, *Without Hesitation: The Odyssey of an American Warrior* (New York: St. Martin's Press, 2010), 2. From the principals that Shelton lists as attending the meeting, the process of elimination suggests the speaker might have been Albright, although Shelton does not name her. He creates a sliver of ambiguity about the identity of the speakers by leaving unnamed "a few other senior administration officials." But he makes it clear that the officials he does name, with the exception of Albright, did not issue the recommendation. In any event, a cabinet minister suggested at an NSC meeting that the United States instigate a pretext that would allow it to attack Iraq.
17. Ali A. Allawi, *The Occupation of Iraq: Winning the War, Losing the Peace* (New Haven, CT: Yale University Press, 2007), 127–128.
18. Daniel Byman, "After the Storm: U.S. Policy toward Iraq since 1991," *Political Science Quarterly* (Winter 2000/2001): 502.
19. Ibid.
20. Martin Indyk, *Innocent Abroad: An Intimate Account of American Peace Diplomacy in the Middle East* (New York: Simon and Schuster, 2009), 30–43. Indyk, who was author of the strategy of

dual containment, was close to Israel. He served as an official for the American Israel Public Affairs Committee (AIPAC) and was a founder of the Washington Institute for Near East Policy, which AIPAC sponsored. Clinton subsequently appointed him ambassador to Israel. Indyk also was tempted by some of the nutty conspiracy theories involving Saddam. He acknowledged, for example, that he wanted to believe Laurie Mylorie's claim about Saddam's involvement in the first bombing of the World Trade Center in 1993. Isikoff and Corn, *Hubris,* 73.

21. F. Gregory Gause III, "The Illogic of Dual Containment," *Foreign Affairs,* March/April 1994, 59.

22. Daniel Byman, Kenneth Pollack, and Gideon Rose, "The Rollback Fantasy," *Foreign Affairs,* January/February 1999, 24–41; and Daniel Byman, Kenneth Pollack, and Matthew Waxman, "Coercing Saddam Hussein: Lessons from the Past," *Survival* 40 (Autumn 1998) for a more helpful assessment.

23. Ron Suskind, *The Price of Loyalty: George W. Bush, the White House, and the Education of Paul O'Neill* (New York: Simon and Schuster, 2004), 72–75.

24. Republicans gained control of the Senate in the 2000 elections but lost it in May 2001 when Jim Jeffords of Vermont left the Republican Party, which gave Democrats a 51–49 majority. Previously, the 50–50 deadlock had left Vice President Cheney as tiebreaker.

25. Bill Keller, "The I-Can't-Believe-I'm-a-Hawk Club," *New York Times,* February 8, 2003, http://www.nytimes.com/2003/02/08/opinion/the-i-can-t-believe-i-m-a-hawk-club.html?pagewanted=all&src=pm.

26. Isikoff and Corn, *Hubris,* 125.

27. Tony Blair, *A Journey: My Political Life* (New York: Knopf, 2010), 411.

28. Isikoff and Corn, *Hubris,* 29.

29. Bob Woodward, "Greenspan: Ouster of Hussein Crucial for Oil Security," *Washington Post,* September 17, 2007, http://www.washingtonpost.com/wp-dyn/content/article/2007/09/16/AR2007091601287.html.

30. Kevin Phillips, *American Theocracy: The Peril and Politics of Radical Religion, Oil, and Borrowed Money in the 21st Century* (New York: Viking, 2006), 69; and no author, "All Bush Wants Is Iraqi Oil, Says Mandela," January 30, 2003, *The Independent,* Cape

Town, South Africa, http://www.commondreams.org/headlines.shtml?/headlines03/0130-05.htm.

31. George Will, "A Mideast Specter: Modernity," *Washington Post,* August 15, 2002, http://search.proquest.com/docview/409309274/1?accountid=15054; and David Frum and Richard Perle, *An End to Evil: How to Win the War on Terror* (New York: Ballantine Books, 2004), 83.

32. Suskind, *The Price of Loyalty,* 96.

33. Paul Bignell, "Secret Memos Expose Links between Oil Firms and the Invasion of Iraq," *The Independent,* April 19, 2011, http://www.independent.co.uk/news/uk/politics/secret-memos-expose-link-between-oil-firms-and-invasion-of-iraq-2269610.html.

34. Paul Bremer, "Operation Iraqi Prosperity: Success Depends on the Birth of a Vibrant Private Sector," *Wall Street Journal,* June 20, 2003.

35. Michael T. Klare, *Resource Wars: The New Landscape of Global Conflict* (New York: Henry Holt and Co., 2001), 15, 23, 54–55.

36. Daniel Yergin, *The Prize: The Epic Quest for Oil, Money and Power* (New York: Free Press, 2003), 585, 646, 651–652, 658, 685.

37. John J. Mearsheimer and Stephen M. Walt, *The Israel Lobby and U.S. Foreign Policy* (New York: Farrar, Straus and Giroux, 2007), 142–143.

38. Daniel Yergin, "A Crude View of the Crisis in Iraq," *Washington Post,* December 8, 2002.

39. The CIA World Factbook estimates that in 2012 Iraq produced 2,987,000 barrels per day. World production, according to the CIA, was 89,250,000 million barrels per day. https://www.cia.gov/library/publications/the-world-factbook/rankorder/2241rank.html and https://www.cia.gov/library/publications/the-world-factbook/geos/iz.html.

40. Yergin, "A Crude View." Italics added.

41. For the Bush administration's statement on energy policy, see http://georgewbush-whitehouse.archives.gov/energy/National-Energy-Policy.pdf.

42. Dick Cheney, "Full Text of Dick Cheney's Speech," *Guardian,* August 27, 2002, http://www.theguardian.com/world/2002/aug/27/usa.iraq.

43. Timothy Mitchell, *Carbon Democracy: Political Power in the Age of Oil* (London: Versco, 2011), 147.

44. Ibid., 221.

45. Ibid., 44.

46. Mearsheimer and Walt, *The Israel Lobby,* 256.

47. Ibid., 230, 238.

48. John J. Mearsheimer and Stephen M. Walt, "An Unnecessary War," *Foreign Policy,* January–February 2003.

49. Dana Milbank, "The Audacity of Chutzpah," *Washington Post,* March 18, 2008, http://search.proquest.com/docview/410232521 /accountid=15054.

50. For a sample of the criticisms leveled at Mearsheimer and Walt, some of which question their motives and some of which suggest that they are compromised by the acclaim they receive from anti-Semites, see: Jeffrey Goldberg, "Fact-Checking Stephen Walt," *Atlantic,* December 8, 2010, http://www.theatlantic.com/international/archive/2010/12 /fact-checking-stephen-walt/67648/; Jeffrey Goldberg, "John Mearsheimer Endorses a Hitler Apologist and Holocaust Revisionist," *Atlantic,* September 23, 2011, http://www.theatlantic.com/national /archive/2011/09/john-mearsheimer-endorses-a-hitler-apologist-and -holocaust-revisionist/245518/; David Rothkoph, "Why Freeman Himself Was Wrong about What His Defeat Signified. . . ," *Foreign Policy,* March 12, 2009, http://rothkopf.foreignpolicy.com/posts/2009 /03/12/why_freeman_himself_was_wrong_about_what_his_defeat _signified; James Taranto, "Duke 1, Harvard 0," republished from the *Wall Street Journal,* March 28, 2006, http://www.icjs-online.org/index .php?eid=1164&ICJS=2394&article=858; Eliot A. Cohen, "Yes, It's Anti-Semitic," *Washington Post,* April 5, 2006, http://search.proquest .com/docview/410095190/1?accountid=15054.

51. John J. Mearsheimer, *The Tragedy of Great Power Politics* (New York: W. W. Norton, 2001), 12, 21.

52. Mearsheimer and Walt, *The Israel Lobby,* 231.

53. Mearsheimer, *Great Power Politics,* 11, 18.

54. The standard works on democratic peace theory include Bruce Russett and John Oneal, *Triangulating Peace: Democracy, Interdependence, and International Organization* (New York: W. W. Norton, 2001); Michael E. Brown, Sean M. Lynn-Jones, and Steven E. Brown, eds., *Debating the Democratic Peace* (Cambridge, MA: MIT Press, 1996).

55. Mearsheimer and Walt, *The Israel Lobby,* 231.

56. George W. Bush, "Transcript: George Bush's Speech on Iraq," *Guardian,* October 7, 2002, http://www.theguardian.com/world /2002/oct/07/usa.iraq.

57. George W. Bush, "War Message," March 19, 2003, http://www
    .presidentialrhetoric.com/speeches/03.19.03.html.
58. Dick Cheney, "Full Text of Dick Cheney's Speech," *Guardian,* August
    27, 2002, http://www.theguardian.com/world/2002/aug/27/usa.iraq.
59. National Security Council, "The National Security Strategy," Septem-
    ber, 2002, http://georgewbush-whitehouse.archives.gov/nsc/nss/2002
    /nss3.html. The ideas put forth in this document also will be referred
    to as the "Bush" doctrine and the "doctrine of pre-emption." The
    document also will be attributed to Bush personally, because it was
    issued under the presidential seal, and to the National Security Council.
60. Feith, *War and Decision,* 6.
61. Ibid., 51.
62. Byman, "After the Storm," 503.
63. Condoleezza Rice, "Interview with Condoleezza Rice," September 8,
    2002, http://transcripts.cnn.com/TRANSCRIPTS/0209/08/le.00.html.
64. National Security Council, "The National Security Strategy."
65. Ibid. Tony Blair made a similar defense of the war in 2010. "[W]e
    cannot afford the possibility that nations, particularly nations that
    are brutal, rogue states, states that take an attitude that is wholly
    contrary to our way of life, you cannot afford such states to be
    allowed to develop or proliferate WMD" (32). "[M]y assessment of
    the security threat was intimately connected with the nature of the
    regime" (65). 29 January 2010, https://docs.google.com/document/d
    /1QpQSN8vZhlbaN4xDPVfepRbfGHdQECAC8wDrUU--SKk
    /preview?pli=1.
66. Feith, *War and Decision,* 215.
67. On the distinction between preventative and preemptive war, see
    David Armstrong, Theo Farrell, and Hélène Lambert, *International
    Law and International Relations,* 2nd ed. (Cambridge: Cambridge
    University Press, 2012), 136–139.
68. George W. Bush, "President Bush Outlines Iraqi Threat: Remarks by
    the President on Iraq," Cincinnati, Ohio, October 7, 2002, http://
    georgewbush-whitehouse.archives.gov/news/releases/2002/10
    /20021007-8.html.
69. George W. Bush, June 1, 2002, http://georgewbush-whitehouse
    .archives.gov/nsc/nss/2002/nss1.html.
70. Bill Clinton, *My Life* (New York: Alfred A. Knopf, 2004), 935;
    "Clinton: I Warned Bush about bin Laden Threat," *World Net Daily,*
    October 16, 2003, http://www.wnd.com/2003/10/21299/; Ron

Suskind, *The One Percent Doctrine: Deep Inside America's Pursuit of Its Enemies since 9/11* (New York: Simon and Schuster Paperbacks, 2007), 1–2.

71. Hans Blix, *Disarming Iraq* (New York: Pantheon Books, 2004), 255–264; and Scott Ritter, *Iraq Confidential: The Untold Story of the Intelligence Conspiracy to Undermine the UN and Overthrow Saddam Hussein* (New York: Nation Books, 2005).

72. Kenneth N. Waltz, *Theory of International Politics* (Reading, MA: Addison-Wesley, 1979), 102–128; and Mearsheimer, *Great Power Politics,* 1–28.

2. Bring 'Em On

Epigraph: Michael Isikoff and David Corn, *Hubris: The Inside Story of Spin, Scandal, and the Selling of the Iraq War* (New York: Crown, 2006), 117.

1. Waltz, *Theory of International Politics,* 102–128.

2. Isikoff and Corn, *Hubris,* 1.

3. G. John Ikenberry, *Liberal Leviathan: The Origins, Crisis, and Transformation of the American World Order* (Princeton, NJ: Princeton University Press, 2011), 2.

4. Wendy Brown, *Undoing the Demos: Neoliberalism's Stealth Revolution* (New York: Zone Books, forthcoming in 2015). Naomi Klein (*The Shock Doctrine,* 411–430) and Michael Schwartz *(War without End),* along with Brown, are among the few writers who recognize the war's neoliberal objectives.

5. Ten years after the war began, the *New Republic,* which epitomized liberal hawks during the years prior to the war, collected the views of a number of liberal hawks. For a sample of their views, see "Arguing Iraq—Ten Years Later: A Symposium," March 20, 2003, http://www.newrepublic.com/article/112701/iraq-war-10th-anniversary-symposium.

6. Paul Wolfowitz, *Supplemental Appropriations for Fiscal Year 2003: Hearing before the Committee on Appropriations,* 108th Congress, 1st sess., March 27, 2003, 56, http://congressional.proquest.com/congressional/result/pqpresultpage.gispdfhitspanel.pdflink/http%3A$2f$2fprod.cosmos.dc4.bowker-dmz.com$2fapp-bin$2fgis-hearing$2f4$2f5$2f2$2f3$2fhrg-2003-sap-0021_from_1_to_104.pdf/entitlementkeys=1234%7Capp-gis%7Chearing%7Chrg-2003-sap-0021.

7. For examples of military reservations about the war, see: James Webb, Ronald Reagan's secretary of the navy, http://www.jameswebb .com/articles/wapo-occupyiraq30years.html. General Hugh Shelton believed Saddam might have had WMDs, but posed no "strategic threat to the United States—that contention was always utter bullshit and every one of them knew it, or should have known it." General (Ret.) Hugh Shelton with Ronald Levinson and Malcolm McConnell, *Without Hesitation: The Odyssey of an American Warrior* (New York: St. Martin's Press, 2010), 485. Thomas E. Ricks, *Fiasco: The American Military Adventure in Iraq* (New York: Penguin Press, 2006), 40; Ricks, *The Gamble: General David Petraeus and the American Military Adventure in Iraq, 2006–08* (New York: Penguin Press, 2009); and Linda Robinson, *Tell Me How This Ends: General David Petraeus and the Search for a Way out of Iraq* (New York: Public Affairs, 2008), 83. See Ricks, *Fiasco,* 50–51, for the criticisms made by Anthony Zinni, the former commandant of the Marine Corps.

8. Samuel P. Huntington, *The Soldier and the State: The Theory and Politics of Civil-Military Relations* (Cambridge, MA: Belknap Press of Harvard University Press, 1957) is the classic statement of the difference between military and liberal values.

9. Francis Fukuyama, *The End of History and the Last Man* (New York: Free Press, 2006).

10. It was a staple of nineteenth- and early twentieth-century social theory that liberal societies grow from distinct social conditions. Three mainstays of this theoretical position—Alexis de Tocqueville, Karl Marx, and Max Weber—viewed liberalism differently and made different arguments about its evolution. But all agreed that liberalism arose through long, complicated, and specific historical processes, and that they involved economic, political, social, and religious developments. See, for example, Alexis de Tocqueville, *Democracy in America,* ed. J.P. Mayer, trans. George Lawrence (New York: HarperPerennial, 1988); Tocqueville, *The Ancien Régime and the French Revolution*, trans. and ed. Gerald Bevin, with an introduction by Hugh Brogan (London: Penguin Books, 2008); Karl Marx, *The Eighteenth Brumaire of Louis Bonaparte* (New York: International Publishers, 1972); and Max Weber, *The*

Protestant Ethic and the Spirit of Capitalism (New York: Scribners, 1958).

11. National Security Council, "The National Security Strategy," September 2002, http://georgewbush-whitehouse.archives.gov/nsc/nss/2002/index.html, sec. 1.

12. George W. Bush, "Second Inaugural Address," January 20, 2005, http://voicesofdemocracy.umd.edu/bush-second-inaugural-speech-text.

13. Ibid.

14. See Seymour Martin Lipset, "Some Social Requisites of Democracy: Economic Development and Political Legitimacy," *American Political Science Review* 53, no. 1 (March 1959): 69–105, http://links.jstor.org/sici?sici=0003-0554%2819590 3%2953%3A1%3C69%3ASSRODE%3E2.0.CO%3B2-D. See also Fareed Zakaria, *The Future of Freedom: Illiberal Democracy at Home and Abroad* (New York: W. W. Norton, 2007), 45–73.

15. "The National Security Strategy," sec. 6, p. 1.

16. Edward Hallett Carr, *The Twenty Years' Crisis, 1919–1939: An Introduction to the Study of International Relations* (New York: Harper and Row, 1964), 41–62.

17. Bush, "Second Inaugural Address." Barack Obama made the same point in justifying the bombing of Libya in 2011. "For generations, we have done the hard work of protecting our own people, as well as millions around the globe. We have done so because we know that our own future is safer and brighter, if more of mankind can live with the bright light of freedom and dignity." "Obama Remarks on Libya," March 28, 2011, http://www.nytimes.com/2011/03/29/us/politics/29prexy-text.html.

18. Tony Blair, Prime Minister's Speech at the George Bush Senior Presidential Library, transcript of speech in *The Guardian,* April 7, 2002, http://www.theguardian.com/politics/2002/apr/08/foreign-policy.iraq.

19. Condoleezza Rice, "Promoting the National Interest," *Foreign Affairs,* January/February 2000, 49.

20. National Security Council, "The National Security Strategy," sec. 2, p. 1.

21. The topic of American exceptionalism is discussed by, among others, Tocqueville, *Democracy in America;* Louis Hartz, *The Liberal Tradition in America* (Orlando: Harcourt, 1991); Seymour Martin

Lipset, *American Exceptionalism: A Double-Edged Sword* (New York: W. W. Norton, 1997); Samuel P. Huntington, *Who Are We? The Challenges to America's National Identity* (New York: Simon and Schuster, 2004).

22. William Kristol and Robert Kagan, introduction to *Present Dangers: Crisis and Opportunity in American Foreign and Defense Policy*, ed. William Kristol and Robert Kagan (San Francisco: Encounter Books, 2000), 23. Anne-Marie Slaughter, a staunch liberal multilateralist, makes the same point, as is discussed in Chapter 5. See Anne-Marie Slaughter, *The Idea That Is America: Keeping Faith with Our Values in a Dangerous World* (New York: Basic Books, 2007).

23. Samuel P. Huntington, *Who Are We?*, 17.

24. Ibid., 104.

25. Ibid., 131.

26. Ibid., 212. Italics added.

27. "The significance of the 'nation' is usually anchored in the superiority . . . of the cultural values that are to be preserved and developed only through the cultivation of the peculiarity of the group." Max Weber, *Economy and Society*, vol. 2, ed. Guenther Roth and Claus Wittich (Berkeley: University of California Press, 1978), 925.

28. Carr, *The Twenty Years' Crisis*, 41–62.

29. National Security Council, "The National Security Strategy," intro., p. 1.

30. Ibid.

31. As quoted in Lloyd C. Gardner, *The Long Road to Baghdad: A History of U.S. Foreign Policy from the 1970s to the Present* (New York: New Press, 2008), 30.

32. As quoted in Bradley Graham, *By His Own Rules: The Ambitions, Successes, and Ultimate Failures of Donald Rumsfeld* (New York: Public Affairs, 2009), 385.

33. Harvey C. Mansfield, *Manliness* (New Haven, CT: Yale University Press, 2006), 97–98; William Kristol and Robert Kagan, "Toward a Neo-Reaganite Foreign Policy," *Foreign Affairs*, July/August 1996, 20; Elliot Cohen, as quoted in Michael Lind, *The American Way of Strategy: U.S. Foreign Policy and the American Way of Life* (Oxford: Oxford University Press, 2008), 152.

34. "Thomas Friedman Sums up the Iraq War," YouTube video, 2:24 from Charlie Rose PBS interview, May 29, 2003, http://www.youtube.com/watch?v=ZwFaSpca_3Q.

35. Max Boot, "Reality Check: This Is War," in *The Right War? The Conservative Debate on Iraq,* ed. Gary Rosen (New York: Cambridge University Press, 2005), 95.

36. Paul Wolfowitz, "Transcript of an Interview with Sam Tannenhaus," *Vanity Fair,*" May 9, 2003, http://www.defense.gov/transcripts/transcript.aspx?transcriptid=2594.

37. George Tenet, *At the Center of the Storm: My Years at the CIA* (New York: HarperCollins, 2007), 321, 310.

38. "The Secret Downing Street Memo," *The Times and Sunday Times,* May 1, 2005, http://downingstreetmemo.com/docs/memotext.pdf.

39. Shelton, *Without Hesitation,* 445, 479.

40. George Bush and Brent Scowcroft, *A World Transformed* (New York: Alfred A. Knopf, 1998), 399–400, 472. Scowcroft, Bush's national security advisor, is explicit in stating his preference for a military coup and not a popular revolution. Bush says he would have accepted either a popular revolt or a coup, although his actual policy suggests otherwise (489).

41. Libertarians such as Congressman Ron Paul and the CATO Institute are exceptions to this pattern. For a libertarian critique of neoconservatism, see Stefan Halper and Jonathan Clarke, *America Alone: The Neo-Conservatives and the Global Order* (Cambridge: Cambridge University Press, 2005).

42. It is an axiom of classic realist theories of international relations that hegemonic powers are status quo powers and reject attempts to revise the order. See Henry A. Kissinger, *A World Restored: Metternich, Castlereagh and the Problems of Peace, 1812–22* (Boston: Houghton Mifflin, 1973).

43. Authorization for the Use of Military Force Against Iraq Resolution of 2002, http://www.gpo.gov/fdsys/pkg/PLAW-107publ243/html/PLAW-107publ243.htm.

44. Donald P. Wright and Timothy R. Reese, *The United States Army in Operation Iraqi Freedom, May 2003–January 2005: On Point II; Transition to the New Campaign* (Fort Leavenworth, KS: Combat Studies Institute Press, 2008), 87.

45. Bill Clinton, "Statement by the President," October 31, 1998, http://www.freerepublic.com/focus/f-news/1440028/posts.

46. Bush, "Second Inaugural Address." Italics added.

47. Wright and Reese, *On Point II*, 93.
48. Donald Rumsfeld, *Known and Unknown: A Memoir* (New York: Sentinel, 2011), 498.
49. Ibid., 511.
50. Ibid., 717.
51. Michael R. Gordon, "The Conflict in Iraq: Road to War; The Strategy to Secure Iraq Did Not Foresee a 2nd War," *New York Times*, October 19, 2004.
52. Tony Blair, Testimony to Parliamentary Iraq War Inquiry, January 29, 2010, 172, https://docs.google.com/View?id=dfc8fkhx_134frn25fb. Tony Blair sometimes was reluctant to identify regime change as his motive for joining the Coalition, perhaps because Jack Straw, his foreign minister, thought the objective of regime change was "self-evidently unlawful." "Straw Says Iraq 'Most Difficult Decision' of His Life," 21 January 2010, http://news.bbc.co.uk/2/hi/8471511.stm.
53. David E. Sanger, "4 Years on, the Gap Between Iraq Policy and Practice is Wide," *New York Times*, April 12, 2007.
54. Tenet, *Center of the Storm*, 394–395. George W. Bush, *Decision Points* (New York: Crown, 2010), 254.
55. Wright and Reese, *On Point II*, 14.
56. Feith, *War and Decision*, 200.
57. Shelton, *Without Hesitation*, 475.
58. Feith, *War and Decision*, 200.
59. "Speech by National Security Advisor Samuel Berger," Stanford University, December 8, 1998, http://clinton4.nara.gov/WH/EOP/NSC/html/speeches/stanford.html.
60. The Iraqi Liberation Act of 1998, 105th Congress Public Law 338, U.S. Government Printing Office," http://www.gpo.gov/fdsys/pkg/PLAW-105publ338/html/PLAW-105publ338.htm.
61. Tony Blair, "Remarks by President Bush and Prime Minister Blair on Iraq War, Camp David, Maryland, March 27, 2003," in *We Will Prevail: President George W. Bush on War, Terrorism, and Freedom*, ed. National Review (New York: Continuum, 2003), 244.
62. Tony Blair, *A Journey*, 372.
63. Bush, *Decision Points*, 191.

64. Norman Podhoretz, "World War IV," in *The Right War? The Conservative Debate on Iraq,* ed. Gary Rosen (New York: Cambridge University Press, 2005), 157.

65. George W. Bush, "Speech at the National Endowment for Democracy," October 6, 2005, http://www.presidentialrhetoric.com/speeches /10.06.05.html.

66. David Frum and Richard Perle, *An End to Evil: How to Win the War on Terror* (New York: Ballantine Books, 2004), 40–41. Italics added.

67. Ibid., 40.

68. Ibid., 35.

69. Ibid., 139.

70. Ibid., 41.

71. Woodward, *Plan of Attack,* 150.

72. Wright and Reese, *On Point II,* 19.

73. Robert Draper, *Dead Certain: The Presidency of George W. Bush* (New York: Free Press, 2007), 189.

74. Wright and Reese, *On Point II,* 74.

3. What Went Wrong

Epigraph: John Maynard Keynes, *General Theory of Employment, Interest and Money* (Cambridge: Macmillan / Cambridge University Press, 1973), 158.

1. Larry Diamond, *Squandered Victory: The American Occupation and the Bungled Effort to Bring Democracy to Iraq* (New York: Henry Holt, 2005).

2. Ricks, *Fiasco,* 3–4. Ricks diverges from the rest of the Washington consensus in attributing responsibility to "a series of systemic failures in the American system" (4).

3. James Fallows, *Blind into Baghdad: America's War in Iraq* (New York: Vintage Books, 2006), 222.

4. Diamond, *Squandered Victory,* 14–15.

5. Zakaria, *The Future of Freedom,* 264.

6. Tenet, *Center of the Storm,* 446.

7. Ricks, *Fiasco,* 146.

8. Michael R. Gordon and General Bernard E. Trainor, *Cobra II: The Inside Story of the Invasion and Occupation of Iraq* (New York: Pantheon Books, 2006), xxxii.

9. John Edwards, on *Meet the Press*, NBC, February 4, 2007, http://www.msnbc.msn.com/id/16903253/.

10. Ricks, *Fiasco*, 115, see also 110, 127. George Packer, *The Assassins' Gate: America in Iraq* (New York: Farrar, Straus and Giroux, 2005), 298.

11. Ricks, *Fiasco*, 111.

12. Gordon and Trainor, *Cobra II*, 503.

13. Ricks, *Fiasco*, 79.

14. Gordon and Trainor, *Cobra II*, 498.

15. Peter W. Galbraith, *The End of Iraq: How American Incompetence Created a War without End* (New York: Simon and Schuster, 2006), 8.

16. Gordon and Trainor, *Cobra II*, 54.

17. Ibid., 71.

18. Alastair Campbell quoted in Will Woodward, "Campbell: Cabinet's Severe Doubts on Iraq: Former Spin Doctor's Diaries Reveal Tensions in Build-Up to Invasion," *Guardian*, July 8, 2007, http://www.theguardian.com/politics/2007/jul/09/iraq.iraq.

19. Galbraith, *The End of Iraq*, 95.

20. Ibid., 90.

21. Tenet, *Center of the Storm*, 308.

22. Diamond, *Squandered Victory*, 292.

23. Ricks, *Fiasco*, 392.

24. Geoff Hoon quoted in Patrick Wintour, "Hoon Admits Fatal Errors in Planning for Postwar Iraq," *Guardian*, May 1, 2007, http://www.theguardian.com/politics/2007/may/02/iraq.iraq.

25. Wright and Reese, *On Point II*, 183.

26. Mitt Romney in "Transcript: The Third GOP Debate," *New York Times*, Republican Party Presidential Candidates Debate, June 5, 2007, http://www.nytimes.com/2007/06/05/us/politics/05cnd-transcript.html?ex=1186372800&en=d97920bdae50bc6d&ei=5070 t.

27. Bob Woodward, *State of Denial: Bush at War, Part III* (New York: Simon and Schuster, 2006), 302.

28. Diamond, *Squandered Victory*, 98, 288.

29. L. Paul Bremer with Malcolm McConnell, *My Year in Iraq: The Struggle to Build a Future of Hope* (New York: Simon and Schuster, 2006), 106.

30. James A. Marks in Michael R. Gordon, "The Conflict in Iraq: Road to War; The Strategy to Secure Iraq Did Not Foresee a 2nd War,"

New York Times, October 19, 2004, http://query.nytimes.com/gst
/fullpage.html?res=9B07E2DD133AF93AA25753C1A9629C8B63
&pagewanted=4.

31. Packer, *The Assassins' Gate*, 245; Robert Kagan, "Send More
Troops," *New Republic*, November 27, 2006; Ricks, *Fiasco*, 381.

32. Josh Marshall, *Talking Points Memo*, "Stanley Kurtz's Excuse,"
November 30, 2006, http://talkingpointsmemo.com/profile/josh-m
/2032.html.

33. Thomas Friedman, "Tolerable or Awful: The Roads Left in Iraq,"
New York Times, November 8, 2006, http://www.nytimes.com/2006
/11/08/opinion/08friedman.html.

34. Wright and Reese, *On Point II*, 573.

35. Ricks, *Fiasco*, 42, 129.

36. Graham, *By His Own Rules*, 1, 11–12.

37. Diamond, *Squandered Victory*, 282; Graham, *By His Own Rules*,
455–456.

38. Ricks, *Fiasco*, 128.

39. John McCain in Roger Simon, "McCain Bashes Cheney over Iraq
Policy," *Politico*, January 22, 2007, http://www.politico.com/news
/stories/0107/2390.html.

40. Lady Morgan in Andrew Grice, "Blair: 'Hand on Heart, I Did What
I Thought Was Right,'" *New Zealand Herald*, May 11, 2007, http://
www.nzherald.co.nz/world/news/article.cfm?c_id=2&objec
tid=10439115.

41. Kenneth Adelman in David Rose, "Neo Culpa," *Vanity Fair*, November 3, 2006, http://www.vanityfair.com/politics/features/2006/12
/neocons200612.

42. Diamond, *Squandered Victory*, 285–286.

43. See William Branigin, "Three Retired Officers Demand Rumsfeld's
Resignation," *Washington Post*, September 25, 2006; for an example of
retired generals testifying in the Senate, http://www.washingtonpost
.com/wp-dyn/content/article/2006/09/25/AR2006092500731.html.

44. Packer, *The Assassins' Gate*, 245.

45. Gordon and Trainor, *Cobra II*, 8.

46. Ibid., 4.

47. Ibid., 103.

48. Donald Rumsfeld quoted in Ron Suskind, *The One Percent Doctrine:
Deep Inside America's Pursuit of Its Enemies since 9/11* (New York:
Simon and Schuster, 2006), 77.

49. Diamond, *Squandered Victory,* 300.
50. Bremer, *My Year in Iraq,* 4; see also Rajiv Chandrasekaran, *Imperial Life in the Emerald City: Inside Iraq's Green Zone* (New York: Alfred A. Knopf, 2006), 65.
51. Chandrasekaran, *Imperial Life,* 65.
52. Bremer, *My Year in Iraq,* 39–40.
53. Ibid., 93.
54. Miranda Sissons and Adulrazzaq Al-Saiedi, "A Bitter Legacy: Lessons of De-Baathification in Iraq," International Center for Transitional Justice, March 2013, 8, 22, http://ictj.org/sites/default/files/ICTJ-Report-Iraq-De-Baathification-2013-ENG.pdf.
55. Gordon and Trainor, *Cobra II,* 105.
56. Ahmed S. Hashim, *Insurgency and Counter-Insurgency in Iraq* (Ithaca, NY: Cornell University Press, 2006), 92–99.
57. Wintour, "Hoon Admits Fatal Errors."
58. Zakaria, *The Future of Freedom,* 264–265.
59. Packer, *The Assassins' Gate,* 18–20.
60. Ricks, *Fiasco,* 22.
61. Jacob Weisberg, *The Bush Tragedy* (New York: Random House, 2008), 168; Graham, *By His Own Rules,* 214; Peter Beinart, *The Good Fight: Why Liberals—and Only Liberals—Can Win the War on Terror and Make America Great Again* (New York: HarperCollins, 2006), 115, 129.
62. Fallows, *Blind into Baghdad,* 229.
63. Hashim, *Insurgency and Counter-Insurgency,* 279.
64. Ricks, *Fiasco,* 87.
65. Francis Fukuyama, *America at the Crossroads: Democracy, Power, and the Neoconservative Legacy* (New Haven, CT: Yale University Press, 2006), 116.
66. Charles Krauthammer, "Who's to Blame for the Killing," *Washington Post,* February 2, 2007, http://search.proquest.com/docview/410123601?accountid=15054.
67. Hillary Clinton in "The Democrats' Second 2008 Presidential Debate," *New York Times,* June 3, 2007, http://www.nytimes.com/2007/06/03/us/politics/03demsdebate_transcript.html?pagewanted=1.
68. Charles Krauthammer, "Why Iraq Is Crumbling," *Washington Post,* November 17, 2006, http://www.washingtonpost.com/wp-dyn/content/article/2006/11/16/AR2006111601359.html.

69. Thomas Friedman, "Tolerable or Awful: The Roads Left in Iraq," *New York Times,* November 8, 2006.

70. David Kilcullen, *The Accidental Guerrilla: Fighting Small Wars in the Midst of a Big One* (Oxford: Oxford University Press, 2009), 117.

71. See Linda Robinson, *Tell Me How This Ends: General David Petraeus and the Search for a Way Out of Iraq* (New York: Public Affairs, 2008), 293–300.

72. Frank Rich, "A Profile in Cowardice," *New York Times,* July 8, 2007. http://select.nytimes.com/2007/07/08/opinion/08rich.html?hp.

73. Weisberg, *The Bush Tragedy,* 29.

74. Maureen Dowd, "Bye, Mubarak," *New York Times,* February 1, 2011, http://www.nytimes.com/2011/02/02/opinion/02dowd.html.

75. Robert Kagan, "Lowering Our Sights," *Washington Post,* May 2, 2004, http://search.proquest.com/docview/409655357?accountid=15054.

76. Richard Perle in Rose, "Neo Culpa."

77. William Kristol in Peter Baker and Michael Abramowitz, "Opposition to Iraq Plan Leaves Bush Isolated," *Washington Post,* January 14, 2007, http://www.washingtonpost.com/wp-dyn/content/article/2007/01/13/AR2007011300561.html.

78. Rahm Emanuel in Thomas B. Edsall, "Democrats Bungle War Talking Points," *Huffington Post,* June 4, 2007, http://www.huffingtonpost.com/2007/06/04/democrats-bungle-war-talk_n_50690.html.

79. Joe Biden in Walter Shapiro, "Joe Biden Lets It All Hang Out," *Salon,* July 6, 2007, http://www.salon.com/news/feature/2007/07/06/biden/.

80. Hillary Clinton in "Democrats' Second 2008 Presidential Debates."

81. Hillary Clinton in Patrick Healy, "Clinton Calls on Bush to 'Extricate' U.S. from Iraq," *New York Times*, January 28, 2007.

82. Packer, *The Assassins' Gate,* 326.

83. Galbraith, *The End of Iraq,* 9.

84. Packer, *The Assassins' Gate,* 325.

85. Rich, "A Profile in Cowardice."

86. George W. Bush in David Savage and Solomon Moore, "Bush Sees Errors, Stands by Invasion," *Los Angeles Times,* January 14, 2007, http://articles.latimes.com/2007/jan/14/world/fg-iraq14.

87. Maureen Dowd, "Can The One Have Fun?," *New York Times,* June 9, 2009, http://www.nytimes.com/2009/06/10/opinion/10dowd.html.

88. Wendy Brown, "Review Symposium: Review of the New U.S. Army/ Marine Corps Counterinsurgency Field Manual," *Perspectives on Politics,* 2008, 6, 354–357, http://www.jstor.org/stable/20446701.

89. Douglas Feith, *War and Decision,* 199.

90. Ibid., 431.

91. Ibid., 366–367; General Tommy Franks, *American Soldier* (New York: ReganBooks, 2005), 525–526.

92. Bremer, *My Year in Iraq,* 40.

93. Wright and Reese, *On Point II,* 100, 105–107.

94. Bremer, *My Year in Iraq,* 53–55.

95. George W. Bush, *Decision Points,* 259–260.

96. Donald Rumsfeld, *Known and Unknown,* 499.

97. G. John Ikenberry, "Introduction: Woodrow Wilson, the Bush Administration, and the Future of Liberal Internationalism," in G. John Ikenberry, Thomas J. Knock, Ann-Marie Slaughter, and Tony Smith, *The Crisis of American Foreign Policy: Wilsonianism in the Twenty-first Century* (Princeton NJ: Princeton University Press, 2009), 9. Thomas J. Knock makes the same point in the same volume, "Playing for a Hundred Years Hence," 35.

98. George W. Bush, "Text of Bush Speech to the U.N." September 12, 2002, http://www.cbsnews.com/stories/2002/09/12/national/main 521781.shtml.

99. George W. Bush, "President Bush Outlines Iraqi Threat: Remarks by the President on Iraq," Cincinnati Museum Center—Cincinnati Union Terminal Cincinnati, Ohio, October 7, 2002, http://www-personal .umich.edu/~graceyor/govdocs/text/pres1002.txt.

100. Bill Clinton, "Attack on Iraq; Clinton's Statement: We Are Delivering a Powerful Message to Saddam," *New York Times,* December 17, 1998, http://www.nytimes.com/1998/12/17/world/attack-iraq-clinton -s-statement-we-are-delivering-powerful-message-saddam.html ?pagewanted=all&src=pm.

101. Wright and Reese, *On Point II,* 14.

102. Packer, *The Assassins' Gate,* 227.

103. Galbraith, *The End of Iraq,* 8.

104. Tenet, *Center of the Storm,* 448.

105. Gordon and Trainor, *Cobra II,* 503.

106. Ricks, *Fiasco*, 48, 99. Italics in original.
107. Bob Woodward, *Obama's Wars* (New York: Simon and Schuster, 2010), esp. 251, 277–280, 290–293, 302–303, 314, 332–333.

4. What Were Neoconservatives Thinking?

Epigraph: Lewis Carroll, *Alice's Adventures in Wonderland and Through the Looking-Glass* (New York: New American Library, 1960), 186.

1. William Kristol and Robert Kagan, "Toward a Neo-Reaganite Foreign Policy," *Foreign Affairs,* July/August 1996, 20, 23, http://www.jstor.org/stable/20047656.
2. Ibid., 23.
3. Ibid., 20.
4. Ibid., 27. Italics added.
5. Ibid., 19.
6. Neoconservatives differ internally on some of these points. Robert Kagan, for example, defended the democratically elected government in Egypt and opposed the 2013 military coup in spite of the Islamic government's illiberal values and Israel's preferences for the military government. "Time to Break Out of a Rut in Egypt," *Washington Post,* July 5, 2013, http://articles.washingtonpost.com/2013-07-05/opinions/40391756_1_mohamed-morsi-egypt-dictatorships.
7. Fukuyama, *End of History,* 42.
8. Fukuyama opposed war with Iraq and was criticized by his erstwhile friends. See also his interpretation of neoconservatism. Fukuyama, *America at the Crossroads,* 12–65.
9. Donald Kagan and Frederick W. Kagan, *While America Sleeps: Self-Delusion, Military Weakness, and the Threat to Peace Today* (New York: St. Martin's Griffin, 2000), 1.
10. William Kristol and Robert Kagan, "Introduction: National Interest and Global Responsibility," in *Present Dangers: Crisis and Opportunity in American Defense Policy,* ed. Robert Kagan and William Kristol (San Francisco: Encounter Books, 2000), 24.
11. Weisberg, *The Bush Tragedy,* 202–205; Mearsheimer and Walt, *The Israel Lobby,* 129; Beinart, *The Good Fight,* 129.
12. As quoted in Beinart, 157.

13. Donald Rumsfeld in "DoD News Briefing," March 20, 2003, http://www.defense.gov/Transcripts/Transcript.aspx?TranscriptID=2072.

14. Allan Bloom, *The Republic of Plato*, 2nd ed., trans. Allan Bloom (New York: Basic Books, 1991), n. 1, 439–440.

15. Leo Strauss, *Natural Right and History* (Chicago: University of Chicago Press, 1965), 136–137.

16. Leo Strauss, *The City and Man* (Chicago: University of Chicago Press, 1978), 48.

17. Ibid., 47.

18. David Wurmser, *Tyranny's Ally: America's Failure to Defeat Saddam Hussein* (Washington DC: AEI Press, 1999), xiv, 3, 6, 9.

19. Ibid., 72.

20. Ibid.

21. Ibid., 73.

22. Ibid., 74.

23. Ibid.

24. Ibid., 79.

25. Ibid., 87.

26. Ibid., 66.

27. Bernard Lewis, *What Went Wrong? The Clash Between Islam and Modernity in the Middle East* (New York: HarperPerennial, 2003), 152.

28. Ibid., 3, 159–160.

29. Bernard Lewis, *The Crisis of Islam: Holy War and Unholy Terror* (New York: Random House Trade, 2004), 76.

30. Edward W. Said, *Orientalism* (New York: Vintage Books, 1994).

31. Lewis, *What Went Wrong*, 153.

32. Ibid., 79–81.

33. Ibid., 101.

34. Lewis, *The Crisis of Islam*, 7.

35. Lewis, *What Went Wrong?*, 100.

36. Lewis, *The Crisis of Islam*, 138.

37. Lewis, *What Went Wrong*, 159.

38. Woodward, *State of Denial*, 83–84; Fred Barnes, *Rebel-in-Chief: Inside the Bold and Controversial Presidency of George W. Bush* (New York: Crown Forum, 2006), 106.

39. Lewis, *The Crisis of Islam*, 26.

40. Ibid., 28.

41. Ibid., 163–164.

42. Ibid., 163.

43. Ibid., 24.

44. Bernard Lewis, *The Emergence of Modern Turkey*, 3rd ed. (New York: Oxford University Press, 2002), 480–487; Bernard Lewis, *The Multiple Identities of the Middle East* (New York: Schocken, 1998), 132–137; Lewis, *The Crisis of Islam*, 168–169.

45. Lewis, *The Crisis of Islam*, 25.

46. Lewis, *What Went Wrong?*, 165.

47. Bernard Lewis, "The Roots of Muslim Rage: Why So Many Muslims Deeply Resent the West, and Why Their Bitterness Will Not Be Easily Mollified," *Atlantic*, 266 n. 3 (Sept. 1990), http://www.theatlantic .com/magazine/archive/1990/09/the-roots-of-muslim-rage/304643 /?single_page=true.

48. Thomas L. Friedman, "Yes, But What?" in *Longitudes and Attitudes: The World in the Age of Terrorism* (New York: Anchor Books, 2003), 48, *New York Times*, October 5, 2001, http://www.nytimes .com/2001/10/05/opinion/foreign-affairs-yes-but-what.html.

49. Friedman, "World War III," in *Longitudes and Attitudes*, 33, *New York Times*, September 13, 2001, http://www.nytimes.com/2001/09 /13/opinion/foreign-affairs-world-war-iii.html; see also "A Memo from Osama," in *Longitudes and Attitudes*, 28, *New York Times*, June 26, 2001, http://www.nytimes.com/2001/06/26/opinion /foreign-affairs-a-memo-from-osama.html; "Talk Later," in *Longitudes and Attitudes*, 44, *New York Times*, September 28, 2001, http://www.nytimes.com/2001/09/28/opinion/foreign-affairs-talk -later.html.

50. Friedman, "World War III."

51. Neoconservative advocates for the war often equated the war on terror with a world war, although most neoconservatives counted the Cold War as World War III and the war on terror as World War IV. See Eliot A. Cohen, "What's in a Name: World War IV, Let's Call This Conflict What It Is," *WSJ Opinion Journal*, November 20, 2001, https://groups.google.com/forum/#!msg/soc.history.medieval /GgMgiPoYEPs/DK9ejKTO8fwJ; Norman Podhoretz, "World War IV: How it Started, What It Means, and Why We Have to Win," *Commentary*, September 2004, http://www.commentarymagazine

.com/article/world-war-iv-how-it-started-what-it-means-and-why-we
-have-to-win/.

52. Friedman, "World War III."

53. Friedman, "Thinking about Iraq (1)," in *Longitudes and Attitudes,*
272, *New York Times,* January 22, 2003, http://www.nytimes.com
/2003/01/22/opinion/thinking-about-iraq-i.html.

54. Friedman, "The Real War" in *Longitudes and Attitudes,* 79, *New
York Times,* November 27, 2001, http://www.nytimes.com/2001/11
/27/opinion/foreign-affairs-the-real-war.html.

55. Friedman, "In Pakistan, It's Jihad," *Longitudes and Attitudes,* 70,
New York Times, November 13, 2001, http://www.nytimes.com
/2001/11/13/opinion/13FRIE.html.

56. Friedman, "Because We Could," *New York Times,* June 4, 2003,
http://www.nytimes.com/2003/06/04/opinion/because-we-could
.html.

57. Friedman, "Thinking about Iraq (1)," 273.

58. Friedman, "Fighting the Big One," *New York Times,* August 24,
2003, http://www.nytimes.com/2003/08/24/opinion/fighting-the-big
-one.html.

59. Friedman, "You Gotta Have Friends," in *Longitudes and Attitudes,*
226–227, *New York Times,* September 29, 2002, http://www.nytimes
.com/2002/09/29/opinion/you-gotta-have-friends.html. Italics added.

60. Friedman, "Starting from Scratch," *New York Times,* August 27,
2003, http://www.nytimes.com/2003/08/27/opinion/starting-from
-scratch.html.

61. Friedman, "War of Ideas: Part 3," *New York Times,* January 15,
2004, http://www.nytimes.com/2004/01/15/opinion/war-of-ideas
-part-3.html.

62. Friedman, "Iraq Upside Down," *Longitudes and Attitudes,* 221, *New
York Times,* September 18, 2002, http://www.nytimes.com/2002/09
/18/opinion/iraq-upside-down.html. Italics added.

63. Friedman, "Crazier than Thou," in *Longitudes and Attitudes,* 123,
New York Times, February 13, 2002, http://www.nytimes.com/2002
/02/13/opinion/crazier-than-thou.html.

64. Thomas Friedman in "Liberal Hawks Reconsider the Iraq War: Final
Words," *Slate,* Paul Berman, Thomas Friedman, Christopher
Hitchens, Fred Kaplan, George Packer, Kenneth M. Pollack, Jacob
Weisberg, and Fareed Zakaria, January 12, 2004, http://www.slate

.com/articles/news_and_politics/politics/features/2004/liberal_hawks
_reconsider_the_iraq_war/four_reasons_to_invade_Iraq.html.

65. Kanan Makiya, *Republic of Fear: The Politics of Modern Iraq*
(Berkeley: University of California Press, 1998), xi–xii.

66. This is what Alexis de Tocqueville meant by despotism. *The Ancien
Régime and the French Revolution*, 12–14, and *Democracy in
America*, 690–695.

67. Makiya, *Republic of Fear,* xi.

68. For analyses of Stalinism, see Isaac Deutscher, *Stalin: A Political
Biography* (Oxford: Oxford University Press, 1967); Roy Medvedev,
Let History Judge: The Origins and Consequences of Stalinism (New
York: Columbia University Press, 1989).

69. Marion Farouk-Sluglett and Peter Sluglett, *Iraq since 1958: From
Revolution to Dictatorship* (London: I. B. Tauris, 2003).

70. Fallows, *Blind into Baghdad*, 58.

71. For the classic statement of conservative fear of chaos, see Edmund
Burke, *Reflections on the Revolution in France* (Oxford: Oxford
University Press, 1999). See also Samuel P. Huntington, *Political
Order in Changing Societies* (New Haven, CT: Yale University Press,
1968); Kissinger, *A World Restored.*

72. William Kristol, "The Wrong Strategy," *Washington Post,* October
30, 2001, http://search.proquest.com/docview/409146829?accoun
tid=15054.

73. John Podhoretz, "Too Nice to Win?," *New York Post,* July 25,
2006, http://nypost.com/2006/07/25/too-nice-to-win-israels
-dilemma/.

74. For a comprehensive history of the rise of movement conservatives,
see Rick Perlstein, *Before the Storm: Barry Goldwater and the
Unmaking of the American Consensus* (New York: Hill and Wang,
2001).

75. Republican Party Platform, 1964, http://www.presidency.ucsb.edu
/ws/?pid=25840.

76. John Lewis Gaddis, *Strategies of Containment: A Critical Appraisal
of Postwar American National Security Policy,* revised and expanded
edition (New York: Oxford University Press, 2005).

77. George Kennan, "Long Telegram," 1946, http://www2.gwu.edu
/~nsarchiv/coldwar/documents/episode-1/kennan.htm.

78. George Kennan, "The Sources of Soviet Conduct," in *American Diplomacy*, expanded ed. (Chicago: University of Chicago Press, 1984), 111.
79. Ibid., 127–128.
80. Barry Goldwater, *Conscience of a Conservative* (Shepardsville, KY: Victor Publishing, 1960), 88.
81. Ibid.
82. Ibid., 118.
83. Ibid., 122. Italics in original.
84. Ronald Reagan, "A Time for Choosing," October 27, 1964, http:// www.nationalcenter.org/ReaganChoosing1964.html; Perlstein, *Before the Storm*, discusses the evolution of the speech, 499–500, 509–511.
85. Walter LaFeber, *Inevitable Revolutions: The United States in Central America,* expanded ed. (New York: W. W. Norton, 1984), 271–302.
86. Gaddis, *Strategies of Containment*, 362–379.
87. Sean Wilentz, *The Age of Reagan: A History, 1974–2008* (New York: Harper Perennial, 2009), 151–175, 245–263; Lou Cannon, *President Reagan: The Role of a Lifetime* (New York: Simon and Schuster, 1991), 302–308, 739–791.
88. Harvey Mansfield, *Manliness* (New Haven, CT: Yale University Press, 2006), 164.
89. Ibid., 50, 21, 16.
90. Ibid., 233.
91. Ibid., 226.
92. Ibid., 16.
93. Ibid., 233.
94. Ibid., 218.
95. Ibid., 207.
96. Ibid., 65.
97. Ibid., 49.
98. Ibid., 218.
99. Ibid., 230.
100. Ibid., 232.
101. Ibid., 236.
102. Ibid., 21
103. Ibid., x, 230.

104. William Kristol, "Dyspepsia on the Right," *New York Times,* February 4, 2008, http://www.nytimes.com/2008/02/04/opinion /04kristol.html?_r=0.

5. Democratic Hawks

Epigraph: Edward Hallett Carr, *The Twenty Years Crisis, 1919–1939* (New York: Harper Torchbook, Harper and Row, 1964), 79.

1. Robert Shrum, *No Excuses: Concessions of a Serial Campaigner* (New York: Simon and Schuster, 2007), 387–388.
2. Ibid., 466.
3. This is the thrust of the advice offered to Democrats by Stanley Greenberg and James Carville. Stanley B. Greenberg, James Carville, and Bob Shrum, "RE: Iraq," Democracy Corps Memo, October 3, 2002, accessed via archive.org, https://web.archive.org/web /20030316153651/http://democracycorps.com/reports/analyses/Iraq .pdf.
4. Hans J. Morgenthau, *Politics among Nations: The Struggle for Power and Peace,* 5th ed. (New York: Alfred A. Knopf, 1978), 8–9.
5. Albright, *Madam Secretary,* 279–280.
6. Kenneth M. Pollack, *The Threatening Storm: The Case for Invading Iraq* (New York: Random House, 2002), 174.
7. Ibid., 412.
8. Ibid., 271–272.
9. Ibid., 423. Pollack also associates Saddam with Hitler on pp. xv–xvi and 254. Wolfowitz also equates Saddam with Nazis. See Thomas E. Ricks, *Fiasco* (New York: Penguin Press, 2006), 386.
10. Pollack, *The Threatening Storm,* 178.
11. Ibid., 392. Italics added.
12. Ibid., 406.
13. Max Weber, "Politics as a Vocation," in *From Max Weber: Essays in Sociology,* ed. H.H. Gerth and C. Wright Mills (New York: Oxford University Press, 1969), 78.
14. Pollack, *The Threatening Storm,* 403. Italics added.
15. Ibid., 422. Italics added.
16. Ibid., 417.

17. Ibid., 66.

18. Ibid., 281.

19. Immanuel Kant, "Perpetual Peace: A Philosophic Sketch," in *Political Writings,* ed. H.S. Reiss (Cambridge: Cambridge University Press, 2008), 98.

20. Ibid., 98n.

21. Tony Blair in Simon Hooper, "Blair: Bush World View Had 'Immense Simplicity,'" *CNN,* September 1, 2010, http://www.cnn.com/2010 /POLITICS/09/01/blair.memoirs.bush.clinton/index.html.

22. Blair, *A Journey,* 435, also see 386.

23. Ibid., 385.

24. Ibid., 407.

25. Ibid., 388.

26. Ibid., 387.

27. Ibid.

28. Ibid., 372.

29. Tony Blair "Blair's Address to a Joint Session of Congress," transcript in the *New York Times,* July 17, 2003, http://www.nytimes.com /2003/07/17/international/worldspecial/17WEB-BTEX.html ?pagewanted=all.

30. Ibid.

31. Blair, *A Journey,* 389. See also 380, 462, 474.

32. Anne-Marie Slaughter, "Fiddling while Libya Burns," *New York Times,* March 13, 2011, http://www.nytimes.com/2011/03/14 /opinion/14slaughter.html and "How to Halt the Butchery in Syria," *New York Times,* February 23, 2012, http://www.nytimes.com/2012 /02/24/opinion/how-to-halt-the-butchery-in-syria.html.

33. Anne-Marie Slaughter, *The Idea That Is America: Keeping Faith with Our Values in a Dangerous World* (New York: Basic Books, 2007), xi.

34. Ibid., 1.

35. Ibid., 232–233. Italics in original.

36. Ibid., 9.

37. Ann-Marie Slaughter, "Good Reasons for Going Around the UN," *New York Times,* March 18, 2003, http://www.nytimes.com/2003/03 /18/opinion/good-reasons-for-going-around-the-un.html.

38. John B. Judis, "The Autopsy Report," *New Republic,* May 21, 2008, http://www.newrepublic.com/article/politics/the-autopsy-report.

Naturally the Obama campaign pushed the charge; see Ryan Lizza, "Let's Be Friends," *New Yorker,* September 10, 2012, http://www.newyorker.com/reporting/2012/09/10/120910fa_fact_lizza?currentPage=all.

39. Dan Balz and Haynes Johnson, *The Battle for America: The Story of an Extraordinary Election* (New York: Penguin Books, 2009), 101.

40. Thomas M. DeFrank, "Party Gotta Fight Back, Sez Hillary," *New York Daily News,* April 12, 2005, http://www.nydailynews.com/archives/news/party-gotta-fight-back-sez-hillary-article-1.585453#ixzz2qiF9sgEK.

41. See, for example, Michael Crowley, "What Undid Hillary Clinton," *Los Angles Times,* June 8, 2008: "Most fatefully, Clinton backed the Senate's 2002 Iraq war resolution. At the time, Washington wisdom held that no future Democratic presidential candidate could afford to oppose using force against Saddam Hussein. Top Democratic strategists—especially Clinton's pollster and strategy guru, Mark Penn—argued vehemently after 9/11 that Democrats had to appear 'strong' on national security or be steamrolled by jingoistic Republicans," http://www.latimes.com/news/opinion/la-op-crowley8-2008jun08,0,4704891.story. The *New Republic* made a fuller and more nuanced point in Michael Crowley, "Hillary's War: The Real Reason She Won't Apologize," April 02, 2007, http://www.newrepublic.com/article/hillary-clinton-september-11-iraq-war.

42. Hillary Clinton, "Floor Speech of Senator Hillary Rodham Clinton," *Congressional Record: Proceedings and Debates of the 107th Congress, Second Session*, Vol. 148, No. 133, October 10, 2002, S10288-10290, http://www.gpo.gov/fdsys/pkg/CREC-2002-10-10/pdf/CREC-2002-10-10-pt1-PgS10233-7.pdf.

43. Sandy Berger at the Hearing of the Senate Armed Service Committee, *U.S. Senator Carl Levin Holds Hearing on U.S. Policy toward Iraq, Day 2: Hearing before the Committee on Armed Services,* Senate. September 25, 2002, 3, italics added, http://congressional.proquest.com/congressional/docview/t65.d40.b84d804200005a11?accountid=14824.

44. Ibid., 4.

45. Richard Holbrooke in Judy Aita, "Holbrooke: Iraq Will Be a Major UN Issue for Bush Administration," January 11, 2001,

http://www.usembassy.it/file2001_01/alia/a1011102.htm. Italics added.

46. Richard Holbrooke at the Hearing of the Senate Foreign Relations Committee, *Next Steps in Iraq*, September 25, 2002, 6, http://congressional.proquest.com/congressional/docview/t29.d30.hrg -2002-for-0023?accountid=15054.

47. Ibid., 8.

48. Madeleine K. Albright, Hearing of Senate Foreign Relations Committee, September 26, 2002, 54, http://congressional.proquest .com/congressional/docview/t29.d30.hrg-2002-for-0023?accoun tid=15054.

49. Ibid., 57.

50. Ibid., 56.

51. Ibid., 53.

52. Ibid., 57.

53. Joseph S. Nye, "Before War," *Washington Post,* March 14, 2003, http://search.proquest.com/docview/409475953?accountid=15054.

54. Joseph S. Nye, "The Right War at the Wrong Time," *Boston Globe,* March 24, 2003.

55. Joseph S. Nye, "U.S. Power and Strategy after Iraq," *Foreign Affairs,* July 2003, 66, http://search.proquest.com/docview/214307513 ?accountid=14824.

56. Ibid., 69–70.

57. Paul Krugman, *The Conscience of a Liberal* (New York: W. W. Norton, 2007), 205.

58. Hillary Clinton in *Statements of Senator Clinton on Iraq and the Wartime Supplemental,* Project Vote Smart, March 24, 2003, http://votesmart.org/public-statement/5951/statements-of-senator-clinton -on-iraq-and-the-wartime-supplemental#.UlmKtWTwKes.

59. Hillary Clinton, "Authorization of the Use of United States Armed Forces against Iraq," 148, *Congressional Record* S 10233, Senate, October 10, 2002, *Statement of Senator Clinton,* Congress-Session:107-2 Reference Volume: Vol. 148 No. 133 Pg. S10233 HTTP://congressional.proquest.com/congressional/docview/t17.d18 .c45d429a09000163?accountid=15054.

60. Hillary Clinton in Daily Princetonian Staff, "Full Text of Hillary Rodham Clinton's Address," *Daily Princetonian,* January 18, 2006,

http://dailyprincetonian.com/news/2006/01/full-text-of-hillary
-rodham-clintons-address/.

61. "Transcript of Interview with Senator Clinton," *New York Times,*
March 14, 2007, http://www.nytimes.com/2007/03/14/washington
/15clintontext.html?pagewanted=all&_r=0.

62. Hillary Clinton in *Meet the Press,* "Transcript for February 20,"
NBC News, February 23, 2005, http://www.nbcnews.com/id
/7003226/ns/meet_the_press/t/transcript-feb/#.UlmhbmTwKes.

63. Hillary Clinton in Jake Tapper, "In Oregon, Clinton Makes False
Claim about Her Iraq Record vs. Obama's," *ABC News,* April 6,
2008, http://abcnews.go.com/blogs/politics/2008/04/in-oregon-clint/.

64. Hillary Clinton in CQ Staff, Congressional Quarterly, "Dems
Respond with Vitriol to Bush's Defense," *New York Times,* July 12,
2007, http://www.nytimes.com/cq/2007/07/12/cq_3070.html
?pagewanted=print.

65. Hillary Clinton in Rebecca Sinderbrand, "Clinton Criticizes Senate
on Iraq Funding Vote," *CNN,* December 19, 2007, http://political
ticker.blogs.cnn.com/2007/12/19/clinton-criticizes-senate-on-iraq
-funding-vote/.

66. Carr, *The Twenty Years Crisis,* 89–94.

67. Louis Hartz, *The Liberal Tradition in America: An Interpretation of
American Political Thought since the Revolution* (Orlando, FL:
Harcourt, 1991), 10.

68. See, for example, the advertisement placed in the *New York Times*
by prominent realists specializing in international relations on
September 26, 2002, http://www.bear-left.com/archive/2002
/0926oped.html.

69. Hillary Clinton in "Clinton's Iraq Speech at GWU," *Real Clear
Politics,* March 17, 2008, italics added, http://www.realclearpolitics.
com/articles/2008/03/clintons_iraq_speech_at_gwu.html.

70. On the role neoliberals and liberal internationalists assign to the
US government in creating the international conditions for the
order they favor, see G. John Ikenberry, *Liberal Leviathan* (Princeton,
NJ: Princeton University Press, 2011).

71. United Nations Development Programme, *Arab Human Development Report 2002: Creating Opportunities for Future Generations,*
United Nations Publications, 2002, 31, http://www.arab-hdr.org
/publications/other/ahdr/ahdr2002e.pdf.

72. G. John Ikenberry, *Liberal Order and Imperial Ambitions* (Malden, MA: Polity Press, 2006), 8.

73. Bill Clinton, as quoted in Michael Crowley, "Hillary's War."

6. American Exceptionalism Meets Iraqi History

Epigraph: Samuel P. Huntington, *Political Order in Changing Societies* (New Haven, CT: Yale University Press, 1968), 7.

1. John Maynard Keynes, *The General Theory of Employment, Interest and Money* (Cambridge: Macmillan / Cambridge University Press, 1973), 383.

2. Note the testimony of Douglas Feith, undersecretary of defense, to the Senate Foreign Relations Committee, which began with the presumption that problems would be temporary and administrative. "If U.S. and other coalition forces take military action in Iraq, they will, after victory, have contributions to make to the country's temporary administration and to the welfare of the Iraqi people. It will be necessary to provide humanitarian relief, organize basic services and work to establish security for the liberated Iraqis." Hearing of the Senate Foreign Relations Committee, *The Future of Iraq,* February 11, 2003, http://www.iraqwatch.org/government/US/HearingsPre paredstatements/sfrc-021103.htm.

3. "New State Department Releases on the 'Future of Iraq' Project," *The National Security Archive,* September 1, 2006, http://www2.gwu .edu/~nsarchiv/NSAEBB/NSAEBB198/.

4. James Fallows, "Blind into Baghdad," *Atlantic,* January/February 2004, http://www.theatlantic.com/magazine/archive/2004/01/blind -into-baghdad/302860/.

5. *The Future of Iraq Project,* The Working Group on Economy and Infrastructure: Economic Policy Subgroup, offered this advice. "Let others have endless discussions on why 'capitalism triumphs' in some countries and fails in most of the rest of the world. *We would rather roll up our sleeves and move heaven and earth to make a workable system of cooperative free enterprise triumph in Iraq in its hour of tremendous need.*" It thought the point warranted italicizing. June 22, 2005, 2, http://www2.gwu.edu/~nsarchiv /NSAEBB/NSAEBB198/FOI%20Economy%20and%20Infrastruc ture.pdf.

6. US Department of State, *The Future of Iraq Project,* Economy and Infrastructure (Public Finance) Workgroup, "New Currency, Fiscal and Monetary Policy, Tax System," December 20, 2002, 8, http://www2.gwu.edu/~nsarchiv/NSAEBB/NSAEBB198/FOI%20Economy%20and%20Infrastructure.pdf.

7. Ibid., Democratic Principles and Procedures Working Group, June 22, 2005, 53–57, http://www2.gwu.edu/~nsarchiv/NSAEBB/NSAEBB198/FOI%20Democratic%20Principles.pdf.

8. Some careful readers of Locke—Leo Strauss and John Dunn, most prominently—note that the law of nature is not always legible and that fear is abundant in Locke's state of nature. They contrast, for instance, sections 12 and 19 of Locke's *Second Treatise,* which stress the intelligibility of the law of nature and the great difference between a state of nature and a state of war, with sections 123–127, which stress the impotence of the law of nature and the way the state of nature—in the absence of artificially created order—collapses immediately and inevitably into a state of war. For this point, see Strauss, *Natural Right and History.* For this and other reasons, Strauss argues that differences between the states of nature in Hobbes and Locke are exaggerated. While the argument advanced here resembles the more common interpretation of Locke in emphasizing the differences, what matters most to the argument is that the common reading of Locke invites Americans to think of order as spontaneous and natural. When Americans read Locke, they understand him to confirm the self-understanding of American liberals as reported by Louis Hartz and as discussed in Chapter 7. Even if the differences between Hobbes and Locke are mainly rhetorical, then, they matter because Locke's rhetoric continues to orient and articulate the unconscious assumptions of American liberals. See also John Dunn, *Locke: A Very Short Introduction* (Oxford: Oxford University Press, 2003), 52–58.

9. Thomas Hobbes, *Leviathan,* ed. Edwin Curry (Indianapolis: Hackett, 1994), 76 (chap. 13, sec. 8).

10. John Locke, "An Essay Concerning the True Original, Extent and End of Civil Government," in *Social Contract,* ed. Ernest Baker (London: Oxford University Press, 1960), 5 (sec. 6).

11. Locke, "Essay," 7 (sec. 8).
12. Ibid., 73 (sec. 124).
13. Ibid., 100 (sec. 168).
14. Hobbes, *Leviathan*, 80 (chap. 14, sec. 4).
15. Ibid., 78 (chap. 13, sec. 13).
16. Ibid., 79 (chap. 14, sec. 1).
17. Ibid., 75 (chap. 13, sec. 4).
18. Ibid., 74 (chap. 13, sec. 1).
19. Ibid., 76 (chap. 13, sec. 8).
20. Ibid., sec. 9.
21. Locke, "Essay," 33 (sec. 57).
22. Max Weber, "Politics as a Vocation," in *From Max Weber: Essays in Sociology*, ed. H. H. Gerth and C. Wright Mills (New York: Oxford University Press, 1969), 78. Italics in original.
23. Ibid., 78.
24. Thomas J. Knock, *To End All Wars: Woodrow Wilson and the Quest for a New World Order* (Princeton, NJ: Princeton University Press, 1992), 201–202.
25. The Covenant of the League of Nations, art. 22, Yale Law School, Avalon Project, http://avalon.law.yale.edu/20th_century/leagcov .asp.
26. Toby Dodge, *Inventing Iraq: The Failure of Nation Building and a History Denied* (New York: Columbia University Press, 2003), 35.
27. Adeed Dawisha, *Iraq: A Political History from Independence to Occupation* (Princeton, NJ: Princeton University Press, 2009), 13.
28. Peter Sluglett, *Britain in Iraq: Contriving King and Country, 1914–1932* (New York: Columbia University Press, 2007), 4.
29. The parallels between the League of Nation's idea of trusteeship and notions of racial segregation are striking. Jan Smuts was the dominant white politician in South Africa for the first half of the twentieth century, an eminent figure in British politics, having served in the British cabinet during World Wars I and II, and a respected intellectual too. He gave a famous lecture at Oxford University in 1929 defending segregation as good for blacks. Expecting the African to integrate with whites would "turn him either into a beast of the field or into a pseudo-European." Whites must "evolve a policy which [would] preserve [African] unity with her own past, conserve what is

precious in her past, and build her future progress and civilization on specifically African foundations." J. C. Smuts, *Africa and Some World Problems* (Oxford: Clarendon Press, 1930), 76, 78. What segregation meant in practice in South Africa was white supremacy, much as trusteeship meant European supremacy. Both segregation and trusteeship presented supremacy as self-sacrifice that must be borne disinterestedly by more advanced civilizations for the benefit of the less advanced. See Michael MacDonald, *Why Race Matters in South Africa* (Cambridge, MA: Harvard University Press, 2006), 8–10.

30. Abbas Kadhim, *Reclaiming Iraq: The 1920 Revolution and the Founding of the Modern State* (Austin: University of Texas Press, 2012), 4–5.

31. Peter Sluglett, *Britain in Iraq,* 36–37.

32. Dawisha, *Iraq,* 14.

33. Judith S. Yaphe, "The View from Basra," in *The Creation of Iraq, 1914–1921,* ed. Reeva Spector Simon and Eleanor H. Tejirian (New York: Columbia University Press, 2004), 32–33. See also Marion Farouk-Sluglett and Peter Sluglett, *Iraq since 1958: From Revolution to Dictatorship* (London: I. B. Tauris, 2001), 11.

34. Dawisha, *Iraq,* 14.

35. Sluglett, *Britain in Iraq,* 40.

36. Dawisha, *Iraq,* 151.

37. Charles Tripp, *A History of Iraq,* 3rd ed. (Cambridge: Cambridge University Press, 2007), 51.

38. Eric Davis, *Memories of State, Politics, History, and Collective Identity in Modern Iraq* (Berkeley: University of California Press, 2005), 30.

39. Tripp, *A History of Iraq,* 38.

40. Dodge, *Inventing Iraq,* 84–85.

41. Max Weber, *Economy and Society: An Outline of Interpretive Sociology,* ed. Guenther Roth and Claus Wittich (Berkeley: University of California Press, 1978), 227–241.

42. Peter Sluglett, *Britain in Iraq,* 169–173.

43. Dawisha, *Iraq,* 151; Tripp, *A History of Iraq,* 74.

44. Tripp, *A History of Iraq,* 38.

45. Dodge, *Inventing Iraq,* 87.

46. Ibid., 128.
47. Davis, *Memories of State,* 58.
48. Farouk-Sluggett and Sluglett, *Iraq since 1958.*
49. Davis, *Memories of State,* 68, 77.
50. Ibid., 56–57.
51. Gordon and Trainor, *Cobra II,* 60–61, 118.
52. For several classic treatments of totalitarianism, see Franz Neumann, *Behemoth: The Structure and Practice of National Socialism, 1933–1944* (Chicago: Ivan R. Dee, 2009); Carl Friedrich and Zbigniew Brzezinski, *Totalitarian Dictatorship and Autocracy* (Cambridge, MA: Harvard University Press, 1965); and Juan J. Linz and Alfred Stepan, *Problems of Democratic Consolidation* (Baltimore: Johns Hopkins University Press), 1996.
53. Weber, *Economy and Society,* 231.
54. Clement Moore Henry and Robert Springboard, *Globalization and the Politics of Development in the Middle East,* 1st ed. (Cambridge: Cambridge University Press, 2001), 99–133; Patrick Cockburn, *Muqtada: Muqtada Al-Sadr, The Shia Revival, and the Struggle for Iraq* (New York: Scribner, 2008), 33.
55. Phebe Marr, *The Modern History of Iraq,* 3rd ed. (Boulder, CO: Westview Press, 2012), 138, 161.
56. Ibid., 138.
57. Robert Wade, *Governing the Market: Economic Theory and the Role of Government in East Asian Industrialization* (Princeton, NJ: Princeton University Press, 1990), 195–227; Chalmers Johnson, *MITI and the Japanese Miracle: The Growth of Industrial Policy, 1925–75* (Stanford, CA: Stanford University Press 1982), 35–82.
58. Davis, *Memories of State,* 156.
59. Rory Stewart, *The Prince of the Marshes and Other Occupational Hazards of a Year in Iraq* (Orlando, FL: Harcourt, 2006).
60. Davis, *Memories of State,* 192.
61. Ali A. Allawi, *The Occupation of Iraq: Winning the War, Losing the Peace* (New Haven, CT: Yale University Press, 2007), 45–50.
62. Patrick Cockburn, *Muqtada,* 72, 76.
63. Joy Gordon accepts the estimate of fatalities as "at least 500,000." Joy Gordon, *Invisible War: The United States and the Iraq Sanctions* (Cambridge, MA: Harvard University Press, 2010), 37.

64. Ibid., 21.

65. Allawi, *The Occupation of Iraq,* 122–123.

66. Ibid., 115.

67. Tripp, *A History of Iraq,* 48.

68. Miranda Sissons and Adulrazzaq Al-Saiedi, "A Bitter Legacy: Lessons of De-Baathifcation in Iraq," International Center for Transitional Justice, March 2013, http://ictj.org/sites/default/files/ICTJ-Report -Iraq-De-Baathification-2013-ENG.pdf. Sissons and Al-Saiedi estimate that the Iraqi state employed about 900,000 to more than 1,000,000 in civil service positions (22). Of the civil servants, about 150,000 are estimated to have been Ba'athists (6). If 50,000 is taken to be the number of Ba'athists to have been fired (and some who were fired were later rehired), that would suggest that about 95 percent of the civil service was not fired.

69. One publicized example provides the flavor of the corruption. James McCormick, a former British police officer, sold a device named ADE 651 to various governments in developing countries, including Iraq, that ostensibly could detect traces of TNT. Iraq spent $85 million, some of which was returned as bribes to state officials, to buy the contraption. The devices, which were made from detectors for novelty golf balls, were inserted with cards. The cards, although they detect only shoplifters and not car bombs, were installed at security checkpoints, including the justice and foreign affairs ministries that later were bombed. Although McCormick was convicted in a trial that was reported widely in Britain and the British government notified the Iraqi government that the devices are useless, they remained in use. Maliki noted that no detectors are perfect and insisted the ADE 651 devices work. http://www.bbc.co .uk/news/uk-22204076; http://www.bbc.co.uk/news/uk-22380368; http://www.bbc.co.uk/news/uk-england-somerset-22532249; http:// www.independent.co.uk/news/world/middle-east/exclusive-iraq-still -using-bogus-bomb-detectors--and-thousands-pay-the-price -8854567.html.

70. Eric Herring and Glen Rangwala, *Iraq in Fragments: The Occupation and Its Legacy* (Ithaca, NY: Cornell University Press, 2006), 3, 127–129.

71. See Farouk-Sluglett and Sluglett, *Iraq since 1958,* 47–106, for a good treatment of this period.

72. Davis, *Memories of State*, 2005, 43–48, 148.
73. Gordon and Trainor, *Cobra II*, 60.

7. The Semi-Sovereign Shi'i State

Epigraph: Alexis de Tocqueville, *Democracy in America* (New York: HarperPerennial, 1988), 509.

1. Charles Tilly, *Coercion, Capital, and European States, AD 990–1992* (Cambridge, MA: Blackwell Publishing, 1992).
2. John Locke, "An Essay Concerning the True Original, Extent and End of Civil Government," in *Social Contract*, ed. Ernest Barker (Oxford: Oxford University Press, 1960), 29, sec. 49.
3. Louis Hartz, *The Liberal Tradition in America* (Orlando, FL: Harcourt, 1991), 3.
4. Barrington Moore, *Social Origins of Dictatorship and Democracy: Lord and Peasant in the Making of the Modern World* (Boston: Beacon Press, 1967), establishes the role of revolution and civil war in eliminating the enemies of liberal order. Liberal politics becomes possible because interests and classes that are committed to blocking it are defeated, usually by illiberal means. See pages 111–155 for Moore's explanation for why the American Civil War was necessary and decisive in establishing liberal principles as sovereign in the United States.
5. The logic of neoconservative interpretations of regime change predicted a long transforming struggle in Iraq, but neoconservative policy-makers rarely apprehended the logic they were serving. Figures like Wolfowitz and Feith adopted neoconservative calls for war, but shared the expectation of pragmatists that the war would raise only transitional problems, not fundamental questions about what principles would organize the country.
6. Allawi, *The Occupation of Iraq*, 195.
7. Analysis and overview from Iraq Body Count (IBC), "Iraqi Deaths from Violence, 2003–2011," January 2, 2012, http://www.iraqbodycount.org/analysis/numbers/2011/.
8. Hans J. Morgenthau, *Politics among Nations: The Struggle for Power and Peace*, 5th ed., rev. (New York: Alfred A. Knopf, 1978), 173–204.
9. Iraq ranked 169th in transparency of the 174 countries ranked by Transparency International in 2012. http://cpi.transparency.org/cpi2012/results/.

10. According to the Brookings Institute, "As of late 2012, energy produced was enough to provide the typical Iraqi consumer 10–12 hours
   of power a day." "Iraq Index Tracking Variables of Reconstruction
   and Security in Iraq," July 11, 2013, http://www.brookings.edu/~/
   media/centers/saban/iraq%20index/index20130726.pdf.

11. Thomas E. Ricks, *The Gamble: General David Petraeus and the
   American Military Adventure in Iraq, 2006–2008* (New York: Penguin
   Press, 2009), 34. See also Allawi, *The Occupation of Iraq*, 179.

12. Ricks, *The Gamble*, 36.

13. Ibid., 37.

14. The Republican members were James Baker, Lawrence Eagleburger,
   Edwin Meese III, Sandra Day O'Connor, and Alan Simpson. The
   Democrats were Lee Hamilton, Vernon Jordan, Leon Panetta,
   William Perry, and Charles Robb. Rudy Giuliani and Robert Gates
   resigned.

15. Iraqi Study Group, "Report" (Washington DC: United States
   Institute of Peace, 2006), 36, http://media.usip.org/reports/iraq_study
   _group_report.pdf.

16. Brown, "Review Symposium," 354–357. The congruence between
   the Surge and the Elite Consensus might account for why Hillary
   Clinton, in spite of her public opposition to the war, is said by
   former secretary of defense Robert Gates to have supported the
   Surge privately. "Hillary told the president that her opposition to the
   [2007] surge in Iraq had been political because she was facing him in
   the Iowa primary." Bob Woodward, "Robert Gates, Former Defense
   Secretary, Offers Harsh Critique of Obama's Leadership in 'Duty,' "
   Washington Post, January 7, 2014, http://www.washingtonpost.com
   /world/national-security/robert-gates-former-defense-secretary-offers
   -harsh-critique-of-obamas-leadership-in-duty/2014/01/07/6a6915b2
   -77cb-11e3-b1c5-739e63e9c9a7_story.html.

17. "Iraq Looms Large in Nationalized Election," Pew Research Center,
   October 5, 2006, http://www.people-press.org/2006/10/05/iraq
   -looms-large-in-nationalized-election/. Andrew Kohut, "The Real
   Message of the Midterms," Pew Research Center, November 14,
   2006, http://www.pewresearch.org/2006/11/14/the-real-message-of
   -the-midterms/.

18. The U.S. Army/Marine Corps, *Counterinsurgency Field Manual*
   (Chicago: University of Chicago Press, 2007), 4.

19. Ibid., 2.
20. Ibid., 3.
21. Ibid., 6.
22. Ibid., 16.
23. Ibid., 174.
24. Charles Tilly, "Reflections on the History of European State-Making," *The Formation of National States in Western Europe* (Princeton, NJ: Princeton University Press, 1975), 42.
25. *Counterinsurgency Field Manual,* 56.
26. Iraq Coalition Causality Count, "Operation Iraqi Freedom," *icasualties.org,* http://icasualties.org/Iraq/index.aspx for totals by month; Iraq Body Count, "Documented Civilian Deaths from Violence," http://www.iraqbodycount.org/database/ for civilian totals from 2003.
27. See James Mann, *The Obamians: The Struggle inside the White House to Redefine American Power* (New York: Viking, 2012), 119–123; Woodward, *Obama's Wars;* Michael R. Gordon and General Bernard E. Trainor, *The Endgame: The Inside Story of the Struggle for Iraq, from George W. Bush to Barack Obama* (New York: Random House, 2012), 308.
28. Joe Biden, *Promises to Keep: On Life and Politics* (New York: Random House, 2007), 342.
29. Colonel Gian P. Gentile, *Wrong Turn: America's Deadly Embrace of Counterinsurgency* (New York: New Press, 2013), 1–9.
30. Gordon and Trainor, *The Endgame,* 343–350.
31. Hashim, *Insurgency and Counter-Insurgency*, 104–108.
32. David Kilcullen, *The Accidental Guerrilla: Fighting Small Wars in the Midst of a Big One* (Oxford: Oxford University Press, 2009), 158–166.
33. Stephen Biddle, Jeffrey A. Friedman, and Jacob N. Shapiro, "Testing the Surge: Why Did Violence Decline in Iraq in 2007?," *International Security* 37, no. 1 (Summer 2012): 7–40, http://muse.jhu.edu/journals/international_security/v037/37.1.biddle.html.
34. Ibid., 10–11.
35. Ibid., 14.
36. Ibid., 15.
37. Ibid.
38. Charles Tilly, "War Making as Organized Crime," in *Bringing the State Back In,* ed. Peter B. Evans, Dietrich Rueschemeyer, and Theda Skocpol (New York: Cambridge University Press, 1985), 169–191.

39. Sarah Sewall, introduction to *Counterinsurgency Field Manual,* xxiv.

40. Robert Thompson, *Revolutionary War in World Strategy, 1945–1969* (New York: Taplinger, 1970), 128–130.

41. Richard Stubbs, *Hearts and Minds in Guerrilla Warfare: The Malayan Emergency, 1948–1960* (Oxford: Oxford University Press, Oxford, 1989), 254.

42. Cockburn, *Muqtada,* 20.

43. Stephen M. Walt, *The Origins of Alliances* (Ithaca, NY: Cornell University Press, 1987), 17, distinguishes between power and threat.

44. Morgenthau, *Politics among Nations,* 197.

45. Ibid., 201.

46. Ibid., 215.

47. Thomas Hobbes, *Leviathan,* Edwin Curry, ed. (Indianapolis and Cambridge: Hackett Publishing, 1994), chap. 13, sec. 9, 76.

48. James Fallows, *Blind into Baghdad*, provides roundabout support for this point. His book deals with the difficulty of instituting regime change and addresses the problems that should have been expected to confront the United States a day, a week, a month, and a year after the invasion. Fallows does note the need to change Iraqi values, although only in passing (perhaps because most of his American and Iraqi sources were liberals). That is, even a skeptic who investigated the problems of implementing regime change focused on issues of humanitarian crises, infrastructure reconstruction, and costs, not on the risks of fundamental disagreement about the principles that were to govern Iraq. The problem, therefore, was in the execution of the war and the implementation of regime change. "What went wrong in Iraq . . . can be traced back to the way the administration made decisions" (212). Specifically, the Bush administration ignored experts who understood the difficulty of the project.

49. Donald L. Horowitz, *Ethnic Groups in Conflict* (Berkeley: University of California Press, 1985), 83–89, 291–332, discusses the role of given identities in determining voting.

50. Juan Cole, "Iraq's al-Maliki Seeks Arrest of Sunni VP as Terrorist, Parliament in Uproar," *Informed Comment,* December 18, 2011, http://www.juancole.com/2011/12/iraqs-al-maliki-seeks-arrest-of -sunni-vp-as-terrorist-parliament-in-uproar.html.

51. Tim Arango and Kareem Fahim, "Iraq Again Uses Sunni Tribesmen in Militant War," *New York Times,* January 19, 2014, http://www

.nytimes.com/2014/01/20/world/middleeast/iraq-again-uses-sunni
-tribesmen-in-militant-war.html?hp.
52. MacDonald, *Why Race Matters,* 172–176, makes a similar point
about racial identities in postapartheid South Africa.

Conclusion

Epigraph: Madeleine Albright, "Conversations at the Carter Center," February 22,
2007, http://www.reuters.com/article/2007/02/23/us-usa-iraq-albright
-idUSN2220804120070223.

1. Plato, *Republic,* Book I.
2. Sasha Polakow-Suransky, *The Unspoken Alliance: Israel's Secret
Relationship with Apartheid South Africa* (New York: Pantheon
Books, 2010), 140–153, 222–232; Helen E. Purkitt and Stephen F.
Burgess, *South Africa's Weapons of Mass Destruction* (Bloomington:
Indiana University Press, 2005), 50–52, 75–76.
3. The US Department of State, *The Future of Iraq Project,* "Democratic Principles and Procedures Working Group."
4. Carr, *The Twenty Years' Crisis;* Kissinger, *A World Restored.*
5. George W. Bush, "Remarks by President George W. Bush at the 20th
Anniversary of the National Endowment for Democracy," November
6, 2003, http://www.ned.org/george-w-bush/remarks-by-president
-george-w-bush-at-the-20th-anniversary; Condoleezza Rice, "Remarks
at American University in Cairo," June 20, 2005, http://2001-2009
.state.gov/secretary/rm/2005/48328.htm.
6. Kevin M. Woods, David D. Palkki, and Mark E. Stout, eds., *The
Saddam Tapes: The Inner Workings of a Tyrant's Regime, 1978–2001*
(Cambridge: Cambridge University Press, 2011), 256; Gordon and
Trainor, *Cobra II,* 65.

Acknowledgments

I owe thanks to many people for helping me with this book. Williams College has provided research assistance, leaves of absence, talented faculty and students, and, most of all, the freedom to teach, think, and write. One advantage of teaching at a liberal arts college is that faculty are not confined to working within the boundaries of a discipline, subfield or, increasingly, specialties within subfields. My understanding of the war in Iraq was enriched by addressing the war from different perspectives in courses that transgress the boundaries of subfields and even disciplines.

My research assistants—Noah Bonsey, Anne Peckham, Aroop Mukharji, Will Pierson, Rodrigo de las Casas, and Alex Verschoor-Kris—have helped immeasurably. The Stanley Kaplan Program in American Foreign Policy funded several of them. I owe Lizzy Kildahl special thanks for drawing together and checking the notes.

This book takes seriously Thomas Hobbes and John Locke for the insights they offer into what American policy-makers were, and were not, thinking. Russ Muirhead and Melissa Matthes read these portions of the manuscript graciously and charitably, gently directing me away from some of my more embarrassing points and formulations. Robyn Marasco kicked around ideas with me when they were forming, and Nicole Mellow always shared her insights into American politics. Peter Dombrowski, Robert Horwitz, Paul MacDonald, James McAllister, and Josh Rovner offered suggestions, criticisms, and careful reading during various stages of the manuscript. José

Martinez progressed from student to incisive reader and critic. Dave Lister also took the time to identify some holes that needed filling. I am grateful to all of them. I also owe debts of gratitude to two anonymous reviewers for Harvard University Press.

Two colleagues—Magnus Bernhardsson and Bill Darrow—were generous in reducing the faults in this book and in steering me in more fruitful directions. Magnus was a source of particular insight into Iraqi history, and Bill, a friend for many years, shared his wisdom about the Middle East, Iraqi history, and Islam. Bill and I taught several courses together on the religion, culture, history, and geopolitics of Iraq and the Middle East at the time I was beginning this book. I benefited inestimably from his deep learning.

My colleagues in the Political Science Department at Williams, Ngoni Munemo and Darel Paul, shared conversations and ideas with me. Both treat important issues seriously, intelligently, and originally. Ngoni showed me the relevance of Max Weber to understanding Saddam Hussein's regime. Darel talked about global political economy, neoliberalism, and finance capital with me daily as I was writing this book. He and Bill Darrow also deserve particular thanks for conveying, tactfully but clearly, that what I thought was the final draft of this book really was the penultimate draft.

In writing a book about a destructive and irrational war, I benefited in ways too deep to describe from two long-ago teachers. Mike Rogin taught me about the rational character of irrationality and the genius of destruction in experiencing itself as constructive. Hanna Pitkin taught me how to read, think, and write about books, and, most of all, the value of using works of classical political theory to understand contemporary politics.

Mike Aronson, my editor, recruited, supervised, and improved this book. He was enthusiastic from the beginning, perhaps more than the early drafts warranted, and he knew what the project needed and how to get it. The book would be much worse without his talents, and it is a pleasure to honor his contribution.

Jim Shepard has read key chapters several times and was astute in his suggestions, generous in sharing his knowledge of writing, and unstinting in his time. He grasped implications immediately and, most remarkably, both understood what I was saying and yet maintained his sense of outrage about the war.

My daughter, Marichal, asked me what I was doing when she knew I was writing, slipped in deceptively intriguing questions, read the manuscript, and smiled all the while. My son, Colin, asked me question after question about Iraq during the years I was figuring out how to understand the war and prodded me for better answers. My wife, Mary, bore the brunt of my gift for disorganizing our household as I work. She had every right to expect better from me. Instead, Mary took my work on this book as a contribution to our marriage. I dedicate it to her.

Index